FIRST
BOOK OF
KNOWLEDGE

This is a Parragon Book
This edition published in 2000

Parragon
Queen Street House
4 Queen Street
Bath BA1 1HE, UK

Copyright © Parragon 2000

Produced by Miles Kelly Publishing Ltd
Bardfield Centre, Great Bardfield, Essex CM7 4SL

Cover design by David West Children's Books

British Library Cataloguing-in-Publication Data

A catalogue record for this book is available from the British Library.

ISBN 0-75253-664-8

Printed in Italy

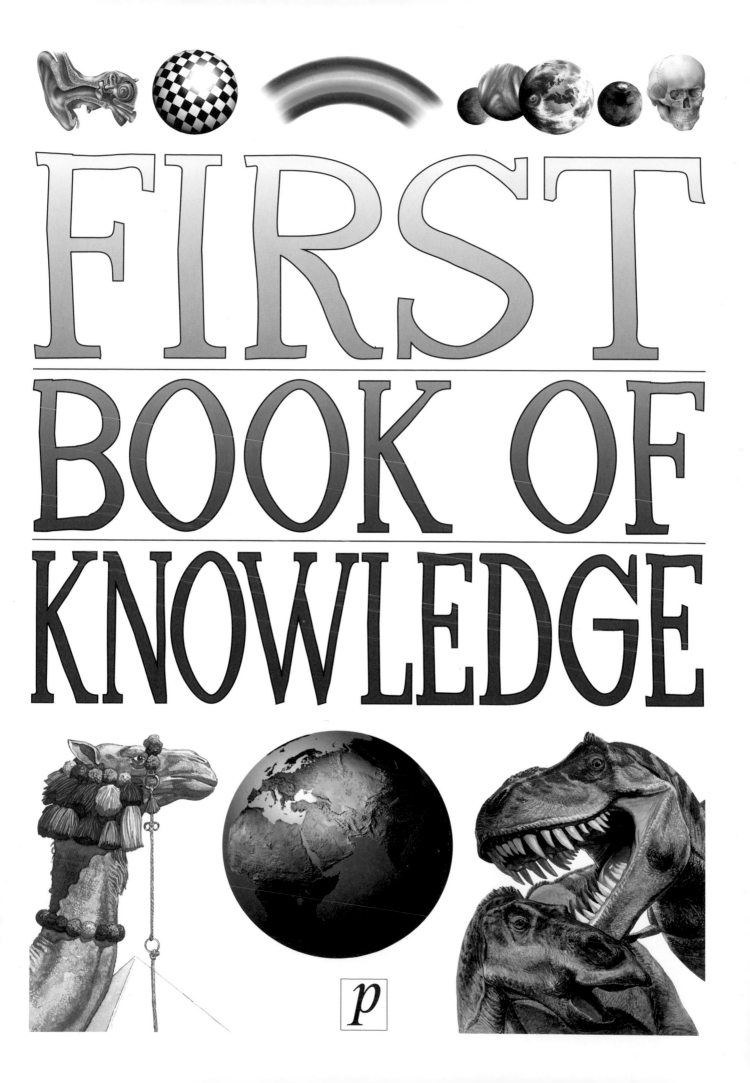

FIRST
BOOK OF
KNOWLEDGE

p

CONTENTS

FIRST ENCYCLOPEDIA

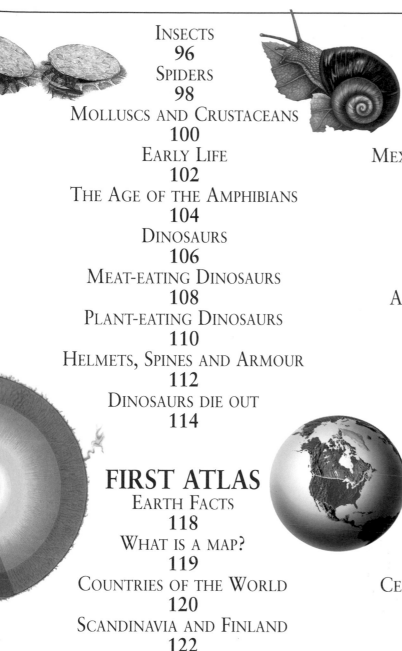

FIRST ATLAS

FIRST DICTIONARY

INDEX

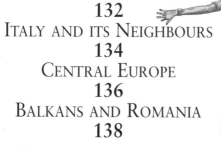

F I R

ENCYCL

S T

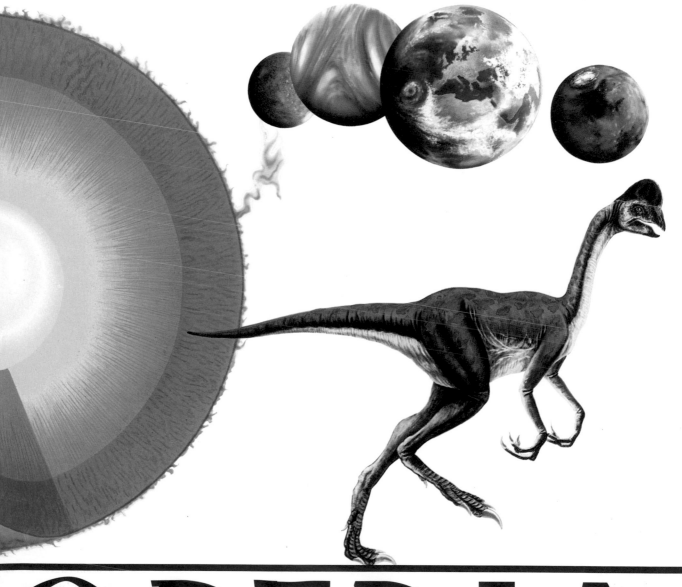

OPEDIA

Our Planet

We live on the planet Earth. On our planet there are high mountains and hot deserts, huge oceans and freezing cold regions. A blanket of air is wrapped around the Earth. This air allows us to breathe and live. Beyond the air, our planet is surrounded by space. A long way away in space, there are other planets and stars. Most planets have satellites, or moons, which circle around them.

△ **From space, Earth** looks like a mainly blue and white planet. It looks blue because water covers most of its surface. The white swirling patterns are clouds, and the brown and green areas are land.

Earth has a diameter of over 12,700 kilometres, almost four times bigger than the Moon. The Moon is about 384,000 kilometres away from Earth.

The Moon circles the Earth once a month. On its journey, different amounts of its sunlit side can be seen from Earth. This makes the Moon seem to change shape during the month.

△ **The Moon spins** as it circles the Earth, so the same side always faces us. People had never seen the other side of the Moon until a spacecraft travelled around it.

New Words

asteroid A miniature planet.

crater A round dent in a planet's surface.

diameter The width of a circle or ball.

satellite A planet that travels around another planet or a star. Earth is a satellite of the Sun.

△ **The Moon** was probably formed when a huge asteroid crashed into the Earth billions of years ago. The crash threw rock fragments into space, and these came together to form the Moon.

▷ **The Moon's surface** is full of craters. These were formed by chunks of space rock crashing into it. There is no air or water on the Moon, so it is odd that we call the Moon's vast, dry plains "seas".

The Solar System

Nine planets, including Earth, travel around the Sun. Along with moons, comets and lumps of rock, they make up the Solar System.

This system is Earth's local neighbourhood in space. Everything in it is connected to the Sun by a force that we cannot see. This force is called gravity.

The largest planet, Jupiter, is big enough to hold over 1,300 Earths. The smallest planet, Pluto, is smaller even than our Moon.

▽ **Among the planets** there are four giants – Jupiter, Saturn, Uranus and Neptune. Each has a small rocky core, surrounded by a thick layer of ice or liquid, with gas on the outside. Along with Pluto, these giants are called the outer planets.

Mercury

Venus

Earth

Mars

Jupiter

PLASTICINE PLANETS
Mould plasticine around beads, marbles and ping-pong balls to make planets. Earth can be blue and white, Mars red and Jupiter orange. Mould a big yellow Sun around a tennis ball. Use black card for a space background and arrange the nine planets in the right order. You could put a label next to each one.

Pluto

Neptune

Uranus

Saturn

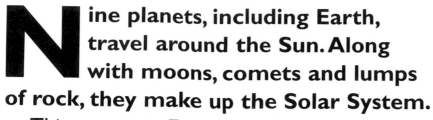

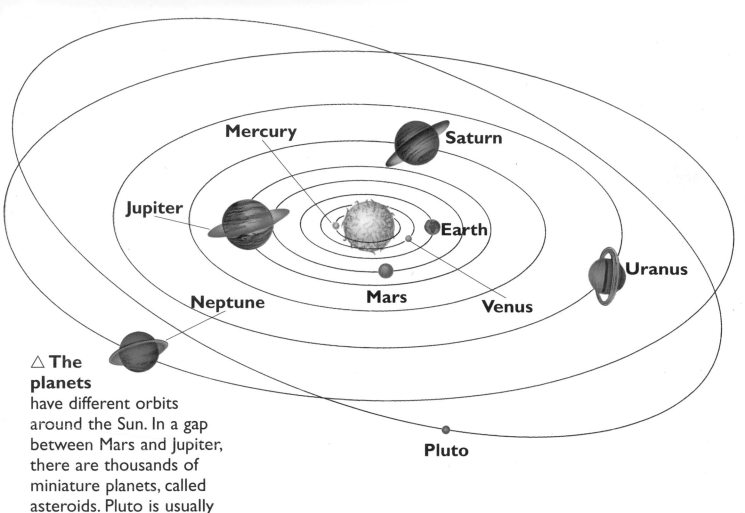

Mercury

Saturn

Jupiter

Earth

Neptune

Mars

Venus

Uranus

Pluto

△ **The planets** have different orbits around the Sun. In a gap between Mars and Jupiter, there are thousands of miniature planets, called asteroids. Pluto is usually the furthest planet from the Sun, but sometimes its path crosses Neptune's.

Mercury is a small, rocky planet. It is closest to the Sun and travels around it six times in one of our Earth years.

NEW WORDS

comet A snowball of ice and dust that travels around the Sun.

gravity A force that pulls everything towards it.

orbit To travel around something.

solar To do with the Sun.

PLANETS NAMED AFTER GODS

Mercury, messenger of the gods

Venus, goddess of love

Mars, god of war

Jupiter, king of the gods

Saturn, father of Jupiter

Uranus, god of the heavens

Neptune, god of the sea

Pluto, god of the underworld

Our Star

Aquarius,
the Water-carrier,
20 Jan-18 Feb

Pisces,
the Fish,
19 Feb-20 Mar

Aries,
the Ram,
21 Mar-19 Apr

Taurus,
the Bull,
20 Apr-20 May

Our Solar System has one star, which we call the Sun. Stars burn, and the sunlight that gives us life is the light of our burning star.

The Sun is a vast, fiery ball of gases. The hottest part of the Sun is its core, where energy is produced. The Sun burns steadily and its energy provides the Earth with heat and light. We could not live without the Sun's light, which takes just over eight minutes to travel through space and reach us.

You must never look directly at the Sun. Its light is so strong that this would harm your eyes.

photosphere

sunspot

Twinkle, twinkle, little star
Seen from Earth, stars seem to twinkle. This is because starlight passes through bands of hot and cold air around the Earth, and this makes the light flicker. In space, stars shine steadily.

▷ **Heat from the core** surges up to the Sun's surface, called the photosphere. Sunspots are dark, cooler patches. Prominences are jets of gas that erupt from the surface.

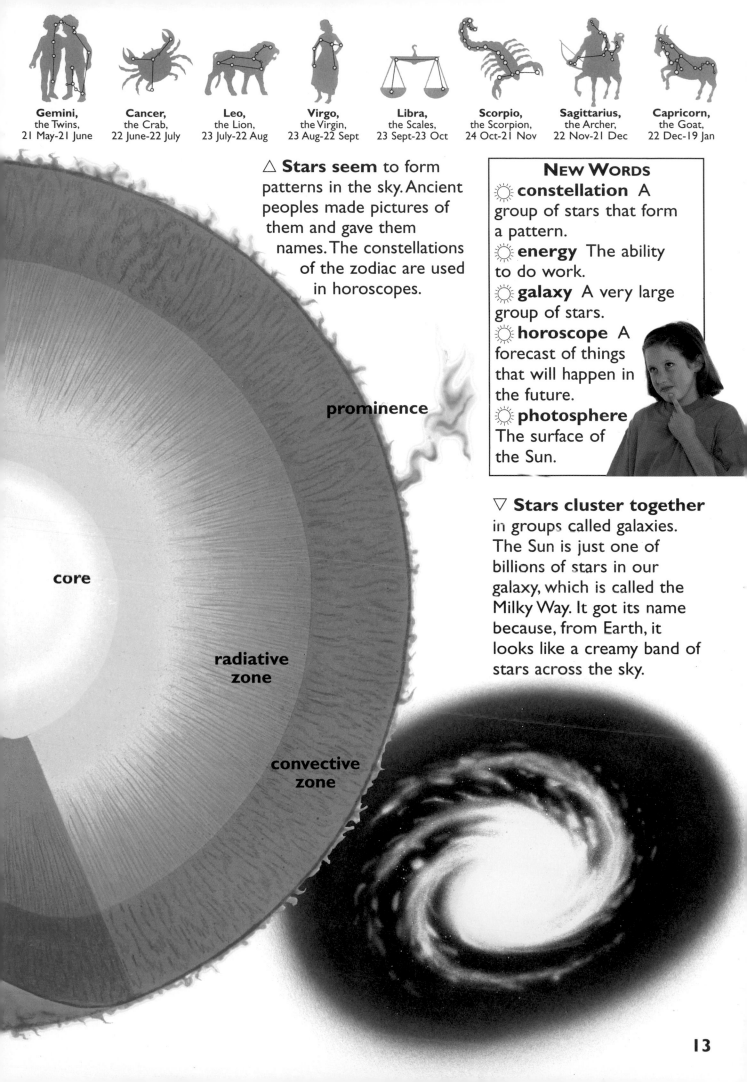

Gemini,
the Twins,
21 May-21 June

Cancer,
the Crab,
22 June-22 July

Leo,
the Lion,
23 July-22 Aug

Virgo,
the Virgin,
23 Aug-22 Sept

Libra,
the Scales,
23 Sept-23 Oct

Scorpio,
the Scorpion,
24 Oct-21 Nov

Sagittarius,
the Archer,
22 Nov-21 Dec

Capricorn,
the Goat,
22 Dec-19 Jan

△ **Stars seem** to form patterns in the sky. Ancient peoples made pictures of them and gave them names. The constellations of the zodiac are used in horoscopes.

NEW WORDS

☼ **constellation** A group of stars that form a pattern.

☼ **energy** The ability to do work.

☼ **galaxy** A very large group of stars.

☼ **horoscope** A forecast of things that will happen in the future.

☼ **photosphere** The surface of the Sun.

prominence

core

radiative zone

convective zone

▽ **Stars cluster together** in groups called galaxies. The Sun is just one of billions of stars in our galaxy, which is called the Milky Way. It got its name because, from Earth, it looks like a creamy band of stars across the sky.

13

▷ **Millions of years** after the Big Bang, gases clustered into clouds. These clouds clumped together to form galaxies.

The planets formed later from clouds of gas, dust and rocks. As the Universe expands, the galaxies are moving further apart.

galaxies form

△ **There are countless** billions of stars in the Universe. Sometimes a very old star explodes. We call this a supernova. New stars are being created all the time in different sizes.

▽ **The Sun** is an ordinary yellow star. It is much bigger than a red dwarf star, which is half as hot. A blue giant is at least four times hotter than the Sun. A red supergiant is five hundred times the Sun's width.

red dwarf

yellow star (like the Sun)

blue giant

red supergiant

NEW WORDS

expand To become larger.

scientist A person who studies the way things work.

supernova A very old star when it explodes.

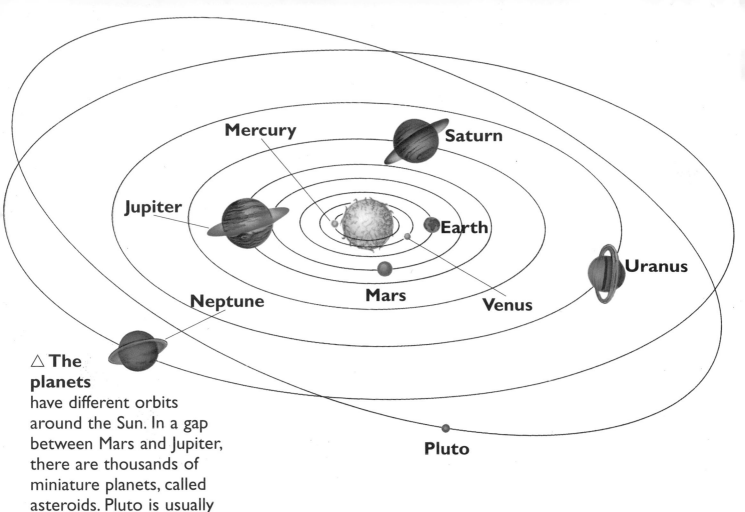

Mercury

Saturn

Jupiter

Earth

Uranus

Neptune

Mars

Venus

Pluto

△ **The planets** have different orbits around the Sun. In a gap between Mars and Jupiter, there are thousands of miniature planets, called asteroids. Pluto is usually the furthest planet from the Sun, but sometimes its path crosses Neptune's.

Mercury is a small, rocky planet. It is closest to the Sun and travels around it six times in one of our Earth years.

NEW WORDS

comet A snowball of ice and dust that travels around the Sun.

gravity A force that pulls everything towards it.

orbit To travel around something.

solar To do with the Sun.

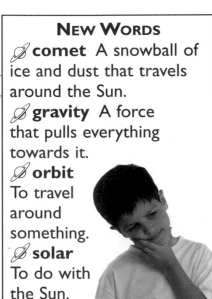

PLANETS NAMED AFTER GODS

Mercury, messenger of the gods

Venus, goddess of love

Mars, god of war

Jupiter, king of the gods

Saturn, father of Jupiter

Uranus, god of the heavens

Neptune, god of the sea

Pluto, god of the underworld

Our Star

Aquarius,
the Water-carrier,
20 Jan-18 Feb

Pisces,
the Fish,
19 Feb-20 Mar

Aries,
the Ram,
21 Mar-19 Apr

Taurus,
the Bull,
20 Apr-20 May

Our Solar System has one star, which we call the Sun. Stars burn, and the sunlight that gives us life is the light of our burning star.

The Sun is a vast, fiery ball of gases. The hottest part of the Sun is its core, where energy is produced. The Sun burns steadily and its energy provides the Earth with heat and light. We could not live without the Sun's light, which takes just over eight minutes to travel through space and reach us.

You must never look directly at the Sun. Its light is so strong that this would harm your eyes.

Twinkle, twinkle, little star
Seen from Earth, stars seem to twinkle. This is because starlight passes through bands of hot and cold air around the Earth, and this makes the light flicker. In space, stars shine steadily.

photosphere

sunspot

▷ **Heat from the core** surges up to the Sun's surface, called the photosphere. Sunspots are dark, cooler patches. Prominences are jets of gas that erupt from the surface.

12

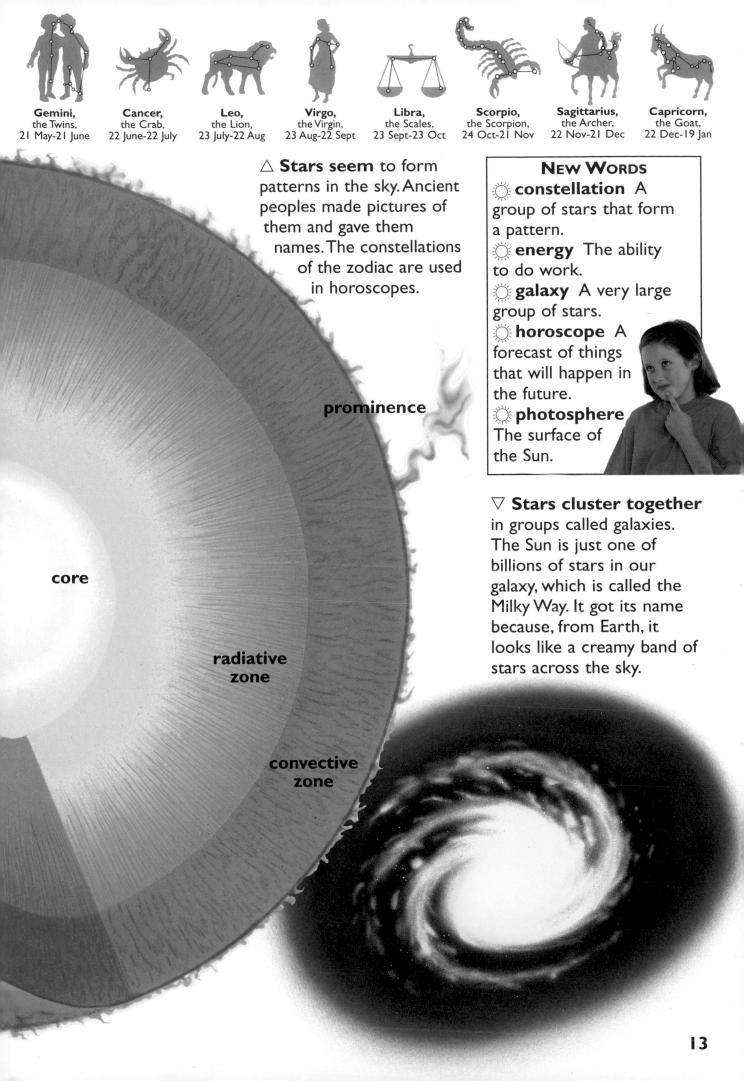

Gemini,
the Twins,
21 May-21 June

Cancer,
the Crab,
22 June-22 July

Leo,
the Lion,
23 July-22 Aug

Virgo,
the Virgin,
23 Aug-22 Sept

Libra,
the Scales,
23 Sept-23 Oct

Scorpio,
the Scorpion,
24 Oct-21 Nov

Sagittarius,
the Archer,
22 Nov-21 Dec

Capricorn,
the Goat,
22 Dec-19 Jan

△ **Stars seem** to form patterns in the sky. Ancient peoples made pictures of them and gave them names. The constellations of the zodiac are used in horoscopes.

prominence

core

radiative zone

convective zone

NEW WORDS

☼ **constellation** A group of stars that form a pattern.
☼ **energy** The ability to do work.
☼ **galaxy** A very large group of stars.
☼ **horoscope** A forecast of things that will happen in the future.
☼ **photosphere** The surface of the Sun.

▽ **Stars cluster together** in groups called galaxies. The Sun is just one of billions of stars in our galaxy, which is called the Milky Way. It got its name because, from Earth, it looks like a creamy band of stars across the sky.

▷ **Millions of years** after the Big Bang, gases clustered into clouds. These clouds clumped together to form galaxies.

The planets formed later from clouds of gas, dust and rocks. As the Universe expands, the galaxies are moving further apart.

galaxies form

△ **There are countless** billions of stars in the Universe. Sometimes a very old star explodes. We call this a supernova. New stars are being created all the time in different sizes.

▽ **The Sun** is an ordinary yellow star. It is much bigger than a red dwarf star, which is half as hot. A blue giant is at least four times hotter than the Sun. A red supergiant is five hundred times the Sun's width.

red dwarf

yellow star (like the Sun)

blue giant

red supergiant

NEW WORDS
expand To become larger.
scientist A person who studies the way things work.
supernova A very old star when it explodes.

The Universe

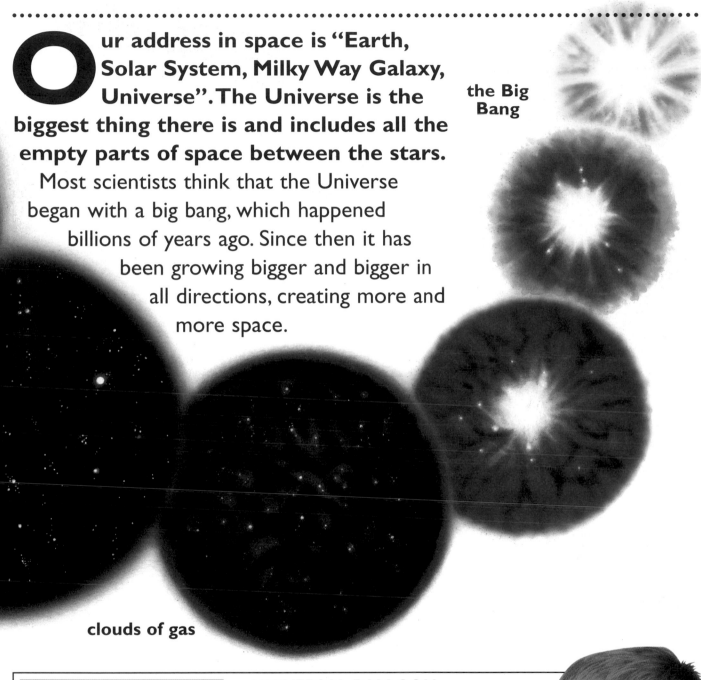

Our address in space is "Earth, Solar System, Milky Way Galaxy, Universe". The Universe is the biggest thing there is and includes all the empty parts of space between the stars. Most scientists think that the Universe began with a big bang, which happened billions of years ago. Since then it has been growing bigger and bigger in all directions, creating more and more space.

the Big Bang

clouds of gas

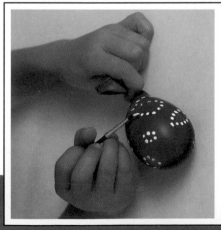

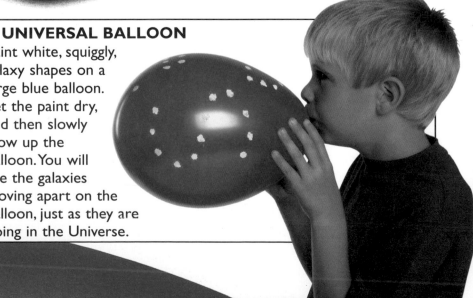

UNIVERSAL BALLOON
Paint white, squiggly, galaxy shapes on a large blue balloon. Let the paint dry, and then slowly blow up the balloon. You will see the galaxies moving apart on the balloon, just as they are doing in the Universe.

Days and Seasons

As the Earth travels around the Sun, it spins like a top. It turns right round once every 24 hours, and this gives us day and night.

The part of the Earth facing the Sun is in daylight. When that part turns away from the Sun, it gets dark and has night-time.

We have seasons because the Earth has a tilt, so that north and south are not straight up and down. When the northern half of the Earth is tilted towards the Sun, it is summer there. At that time it is winter in the southern half of the world, because it is tilted away from the Sun's warmth.

NEW WORDS
🌳 **equator**
An imaginary line around the middle of the Earth.
🌳 **landscape** The way the surface of the Earth looks.
🌳 **season**
One of the four main parts of the year – spring, summer, autumn and winter.

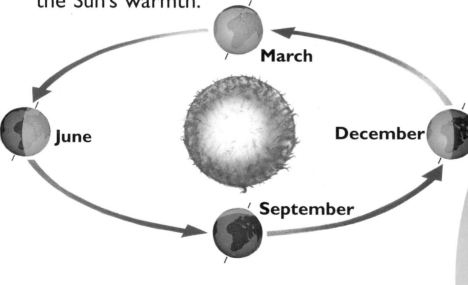

March

June

December

September

spring

△ **In June** the northern part of the Earth is tilted towards the Sun. It is summer there then, with long, light days and short, dark nights. In December it is the exact opposite. Then the Sun shines more directly on the southern part and makes it warmer.

🌳 **It takes a year** for the Earth to travel all the way around the Sun. During that time the Earth spins round 365 times, giving that number of days. At the same time the Moon travels around the Earth 12 times, giving that number of months.

In some places around the middle of the Earth, near the equator, there are only two seasons. One part of the year is hot and dry, and the other part is warm and wet.

▽ **The Earth's landscape** changes with the seasons. Many trees grow new leaves in spring. The leaves are green and fully grown in summer. They turn brown and start to fall in autumn. In winter, the trees' branches are bare.

winter

summer

autumn

Travelling in Space

Spacecraft are blasted into space by powerful rockets. Once the rocket has used up its fuel, the spacecraft carries on under its own power.

Astronauts are space travellers. They live and work in space, sometimes for months on end. Astronauts have to do special training, because there is so little gravity in space. This means that everything in a spacecraft floats about, including the astronauts.

▷ **The space shuttle** is a reusable spacecraft. It rides on a huge fuel tank to take off, uses its own power in space, and lands back on Earth like a plane. Shuttles are used to take astronauts up to space stations.

◁ **In 1969,** American astronauts visited the Moon for the first time. They landed in a lunar module and wore spacesuits to walk on the Moon's surface. The suits protected them, provided them with air to breathe and kept them at the right temperature.

The first living thing to travel in space was a dog named Laika, in 1957. On April 12, 1961, Russian Yuri Gagarin circled the Earth once to become the first person in space. Just a few weeks later, Alan Shepard became the first American astronaut. His space flight lasted just about 15 minutes.

▷ **Astronauts can travel** a short distance away from their spacecraft by putting a special jet-unit on their back. They can move or turn in any direction with this Manned Manoeuvring Unit attached to them.

NEW WORDS

astronaut A person who travels in space.

lunar module The part of a spaceship that lands on the Moon.

magnetic Able to stick to metal objects by the power of magnetism.

space station A spaceship in which astronauts can live and work.

What do astronauts eat?
Most space food is dried, to save weight. Water is added to the food packets before they are heated. Astronauts have to hold on to their food, otherwise it just floats around the spacecraft. All knives and forks are magnetic, so that they stick to the meal trays.

PLANET EARTH PUZZLE

Place a piece of tracing paper on the map at the bottom of this page. Trace the thick lines of the plates with a black felt pen, and add the outlines of the continents in pencil. Then stick the traced map onto card and colour it in. Cut the map up into separate pieces to make your jigsaw. Jumble up the pieces, then use the plate lines to help you fit your jigsaw together again.

The Earth's crust is cracked into huge pieces that fit together like a giant jigsaw puzzle. These pieces are called plates. The Earth's oceans and continents are split up by the plates, which float on the mantle.

NEW WORDS

continent A huge land mass.
core The central part of the Earth.
crust The Earth's outer shell.
mantle A thick layer of hot rock.
molten Melted, or turned into hot liquid.
plate A piece of the Earth's crust.

▽ **Earth** looks cool from space, because of its water. Inside, it is incredibly hot. It is over 6,000 km from Earth's surface to its centre.

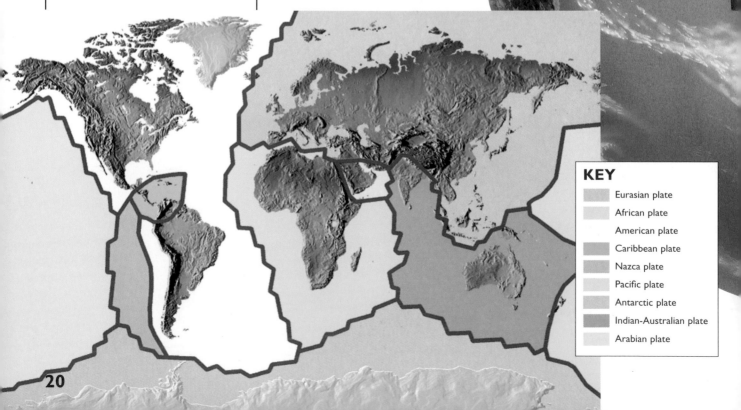

KEY

Eurasian plate
African plate
American plate
Caribbean plate
Nazca plate
Pacific plate
Antarctic plate
Indian-Australian plate
Arabian plate

Inside the Earth

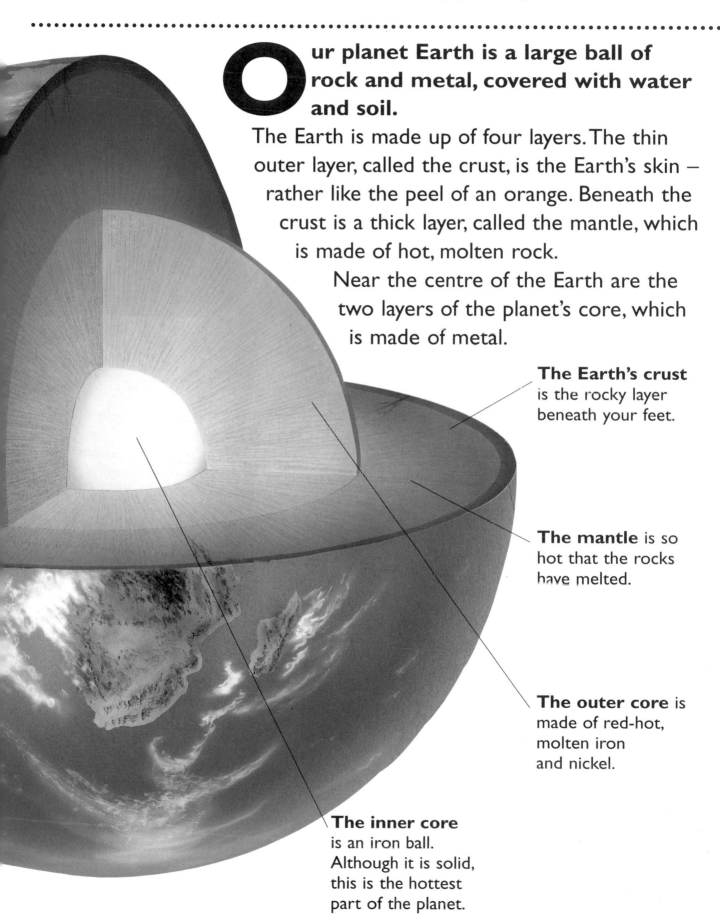

Our planet Earth is a large ball of rock and metal, covered with water and soil.

The Earth is made up of four layers. The thin outer layer, called the crust, is the Earth's skin – rather like the peel of an orange. Beneath the crust is a thick layer, called the mantle, which is made of hot, molten rock.

Near the centre of the Earth are the two layers of the planet's core, which is made of metal.

The Earth's crust is the rocky layer beneath your feet.

The mantle is so hot that the rocks have melted.

The outer core is made of red-hot, molten iron and nickel.

The inner core is an iron ball. Although it is solid, this is the hottest part of the planet.

21

Volcanoes and Earthquakes

△ **The San Andreas Fault**, in California, shows where two of the Earth's plates slide past each other. They move about 5 centimetres a year.

The plates that make up the Earth's crust slowly move and rub against each other. Though they only move a few centimetres each year, their buckling can cause volcanoes and earthquakes.

Volcanoes and earthquakes usually form near the edge of plates. Many of them happen in a region around the Pacific Ocean called the "Ring of Fire". They sometimes cause giant waves called tsunamis.

The strongest recorded earthquake happened in Ecuador in 1906. It measured 8.6 on the Richter scale, which is used to measure the strength of earthquakes. In 1995, an earthquake at Kobe, in Japan, killed 5,500 people and damaged 190,000 buildings.

◁ **Flyovers and bridges** are at great risk when they are shaken by an earthquake. The quake's waves move out from a point called the epicentre. Very often there are minor tremors before and after a big earthquake.

The world's largest active volcano is Mauna Loa, in Hawaii. It rises to 4,170 metres above sea level, and is over 9,000 metres high when measured from the ocean bed. It usually erupts about once every four years.

A volcano that has not erupted for a long time is called dormant, or "sleeping". If a volcano has done nothing at all for thousands of years, it is said to be extinct.

▽ **When a volcano** erupts, red-hot lava blasts up through an opening in the Earth's crust. The steep sides of a volcano mountain are made of layers of hardened lava and ash. These layers build up with each eruption.

NEW WORDS

epicentre The centre of an earthquake, where the shaking waves come from.

lava Melted rock that flows from a volcano.

tremor A shaking movement.

tsunami A giant wave that can cause great damage.

Water

Water falls from clouds in the sky in the form of rain, snow or hail.

When rainwater falls on the land, some of it seeps into the ground. In limestone areas, this water makes underground caves. Some water collects in lakes, but most forms rivers that finally find their way to the sea. On the way, the water picks up minerals that make it salty.

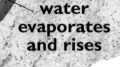

water vapour forms clouds

water droplets fall

water evaporates and rises

△ **Water goes round** in a never-ending cycle. First, it evaporates from the oceans. The water vapour rises and turns into clouds. When the droplets in the clouds get too heavy, they fall to land as rain. Some rain flows back to the oceans, and then the water cycle starts all over again.

MEASURING RAIN

To make your own rain gauge, use an empty jam jar. Pour in 200 ml of water, 10 ml at a time. Use a permanent marker to mark 10-ml levels on the jar. Empty the jar and put in a funnel. Then put your gauge outside to catch the rain.

NEW WORDS

cave An underground tunnel.

evaporate To turn into a vapour or gas.

gauge An instrument that measures something.

limestone A soft kind of rock.

mineral A hard substance that is usually found in the ground in rock form.

In caves, minerals in dripping water make stalactites. These hang down from the roof of the cave, while stalagmites grow up from the ground. Sometimes they meet up to form a column.

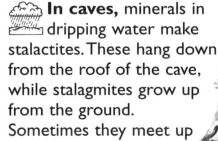

◁ **Most underground caves** are made by running water. Over many years, rainwater wears away at cracks in soft limestone rocks. The cracks grow wider, making holes and then wide passages. Constantly dripping water creates fantastic rock shapes inside caves.

▷ **Where a river** drops over the edge of a hard rockface, it becomes a waterfall. Victoria Falls plunges 108 metres on the Zambezi River in Africa.

▽ **This cross-section** shows how water wears away limestone rocks and hollows out caves. The stream on the surface drops into a sinkhole and forms a shaft.

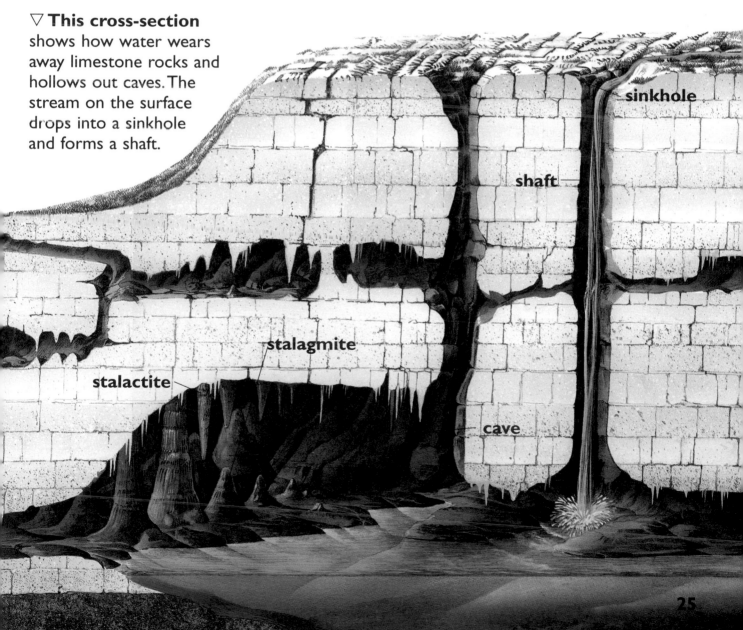

sinkhole

shaft

stalagmite

stalactite

cave

Mountains

There are high mountains all over the world. They took millions of years to form, as the plates that make up the Earth's crust squeezed and buckled.

Mountain ranges that lie near the edge of plates are still being pushed higher. They have steep, rocky peaks. Older ranges that lie further from the plate edges have been worn away over the years by rain, wind and ice.

It is cold on high mountains, and the peaks have no plants.

△ **The Earth's plates** are made up of layers of rock, called strata. As the plates move, the strata are bent into folds. In the mountains, you can often see how the layers have been folded into wavy lines.

▷ **The longest** mountain range on land is the Andes, which stretches for over 7,000 kilometres down the west coast of South America. The Transantarctic Mountains stretch right across the frozen continent of Antarctica.

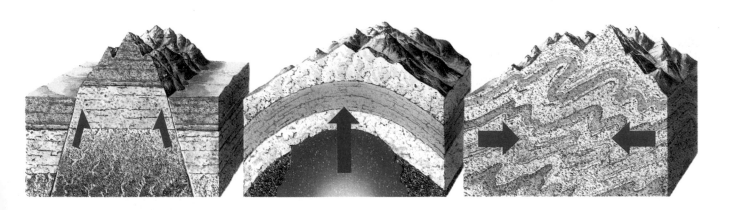

△ **Block mountains** are created when the Earth's crust develops cracks, called faults, and the chunk of land between them is pushed up.

△ **Dome mountains** form when the top layers of the Earth's crust are pushed up by molten rock underneath. This makes a big bulge.

△ **Fold mountains** are formed when one plate bumps and pushes against another. Rock is squeezed up into folds. The Andes were made this way.

Mountains are often joined together in a series, or range. The longest and highest ranges, such as the Andes and the Himalayas, form huge mountain systems. Few animals or people live on the highest mountains.

MOUNTAINS OF JUNK
Crumple newspaper into big balls and tape them onto a cardboard base. Make papier-mâché pulp by soaking newspaper pieces in a bucket of wallpaper paste. Cover the balls with the pulp to make mountains and valleys. When your landscape is dry, paint some snow-capped peaks with white paint. Sprinkle the base with sand and grit. You could add a mountain lake.

What is an ibex?
The ibex is a wild mountain goat that lives in the high mountains in some parts of the world. Ibexes are sure-footed and happy to climb along rocky crags. Male ibexes have long horns, which they sometimes use to fight each other.

The ten highest mountains on land are all in the Himalayas, to the north of India. The highest peak of all, Mount Everest, lies on the border between Nepal and Tibet. It is 8,863 metres high and is known to people of Tibet as Chomolongma, or "goddess mother of the world".

northern forest

temperate forest

▷ **The needle-leaved trees** of northern forests are called conifers. They bear their seeds in cones. Trees such as fir, pine, spruce and larch have to survive long, cold winters there.

▽ **Massive sequoia trees** grow in California, USA. Sequoias are evergreen conifers, and some are thousands of years old. The largest is over 83 metres tall, with a diameter of over 11 metres. Imagine trying to climb to the top!

▷ **Ash, beech, maple and oak trees** all grow in temperate forests. In the autumn, their leaves turn brown. Then they shed their leaves to save water and help them get through the winter.

Forests

Almost a third of the Earth's land surface is covered with forests. The trees that grow in forests vary according to the region's climate – how warm it is, how long the winter lasts and how much rain falls in that region.

Cool northern forests are full of evergreen trees. Temperate forests have deciduous trees that lose their leaves in winter. And tropical rainforests have an enormous variety of big, fast-growing trees.

NEW WORDS

climate The weather conditions of an area.

conifer A tree that makes its seeds in cones.

deciduous tree A tree that loses its leaves in the autumn.

evergreen tree A tree that keeps its leaves.

▽ **Rainforests** grow on warm, wet lowlands in regions near the equator. Most rainforest trees are evergreen. It rains almost every day in a rainforest.

The taiga is the world's largest forest, stretching 10,000 kilometres across northern Russia. The taiga is very cold during the long, dark winters, and summer in the forest is short and cool.

Millions of creatures live in rainforests, as there is plenty of warmth, water and food. There are parrots and toucans, monkeys and jaguars, frogs and snakes.

The Amazon rainforest is the biggest in the world. Parts are being cut down at an alarming rate.

rainforest

Deserts

scorpion

Most deserts are in hot parts of the world, where it is dry nearly all the time.

Some deserts are covered with huge, high sand dunes. But there are many other desert landscapes, including rocky hills and stony plains. In the world's largest desert, the Sahara in northern Africa, the temperature often reaches 50°C. Despite the heat and lack of water, these are not empty wastelands. Plants like the cactus and animals like the scorpion, and even some people, have become used to life in the desert.

🌵 **Most deserts** have small areas of water, where plants can grow and people can live. They are called oases. The Sahara has about 90 large oases.

▽ **In many desert regions**, rocks have been worn away over millions of years by the effects of heat and wind. The deserts of North America are full of strange-shaped, dramatic rock forms.

BAKING DESERT

Mix smooth dough from 6 cups of flour, 3 cups of salt, 6 tablespoons of cooking oil and water. Roll the dough and shape it into a desert landscape. Bake the desert at the bottom of the oven at a low temperature for 40 minutes. When it has cooled down, paint with PVA glue and sprinkle with sand. Paint a green oasis, and add tissue-paper palm trees and, perhaps, a plasticine camel for effect.

△ **Some of the Sahara's** sand dunes are up to 465 metres high. They are like seas of sand, and they change and drift with the action of the wind.

▷ **Cactus plants** store water in their fleshy stems. The giant saguaro cactus can grow over 17 metres tall. Other desert plants suddenly shoot up if it rains, flower quickly and scatter their seeds.

31

Polar Regions

▽ **There are icebergs** in the cold sea near both Poles. They are huge chunks of floating freshwater ice that break off from glaciers and ice shelves. Only about a seventh of an iceberg appears above the water, so they are much bigger than they look.

Near the North and South Poles, at the very top and bottom of the world, it is very cold.

The region around the North Pole is called the Arctic. This is a huge area of frozen sea. The Arctic Ocean is covered in thick ice, which spreads over a wider area in winter. Some Arctic people, such as the Inuit and the Lapps, live on frozen land in the north of Asia, Europe and North America.

The South Pole is on the frozen land of Antarctica, which is renowned as the coldest continent on Earth.

🏳 **The largest iceberg** ever seen was about 300 kilometres long and 100 kilometres wide. It was in the South Pacific Ocean.

◁ **Norwegian explorer Roald Amundsen** was first to reach the South Pole, in 1911. British explorer Robert Scott arrived a few weeks later, to find the Norwegian flag already flying there. At the South Pole, every way you look is north.

NEW WORDS
🏳 **crevasse** A deep crack in ice.
🏳 **glacier** A river of ice that moves very slowly.
🏳 **iceberg** A huge chunk of ice floating in the sea.
🏳 **treaty** A special, signed agreement between countries.

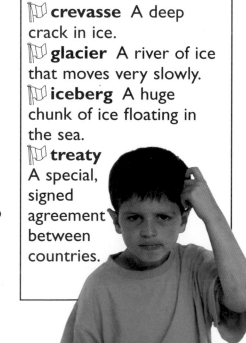

◁ **A glacier** is a mass of ice that moves slowly down a mountain like a river. As a glacier flows downhill, it often cracks into deep openings called crevasses.

In Antarctica, Lambert Glacier flows into an ice shelf, and altogether is over 700 kilometres long. Antarctica's Ross Ice Shelf is the world's largest sheet of floating ice. It is about as big as France!

▽ Working scientists are the only people who live in Antarctica. They try not to spoil the continent, which is protected by an international treaty. Greenpeace, shown here, keep a check on this. At a research station at the South Pole scientists learn about living in freezing conditions.

Time

When we are trying to find things out, time is very important. Scientists often need to measure how long it takes for things to happen.

The first clocks and calendars were invented thousands of years ago. They were based on the Earth's movements. We call one spin of the Earth a day. And we call the time it takes for the Earth to travel around the Sun a year. Our time is based on these movements.

▽ **The Earth** is divided into 24 time zones, one for each hour of the day. When it's 7 a.m. in New York City, USA, it's midday in London, UK, and already 9 p.m. in Tokyo, Japan.

△ **The sundial** is a type of shadow clock. The pointer's shadow moves around the dial as the Earth spins, pointing to the time. To us, it seems as if the Sun is moving across the sky.

●London

●New York City

●Tokyo

| 2.00 am | 4.00 am | 6.00 am | 8.00 am | 10.00 am | 12.00 midday | 2.00 pm | 4.00 pm | 6.00 pm | 8.00 pm | 10.00 pm | 12.00 midnight |

34

digital watch

candle clock

grandfather clock

pocket watch

▽ **The Earth** takes a year to travel around the Sun. We split this up into 12 calendar months of, usually, 30 or 31 days.

▽ **The Moon** makes 12 trips around the Earth during a year. These are called lunar months, but do not add up exactly to one year. Muslims keep to a lunar month.

WATER CLOCK

Make a small hole in the bottom of a yoghurt pot. Attach a length of string to the pot and hang it up. Put another yoghurt pot under it. Then pour water into the hanging pot. Use a watch to time a minute and mark the water level on the bottom pot with a permanent marker. Carry on timing and marking more minutes. Then empty the bottom pot and refill the hanging pot. The marks on your water clock will now show you the passing minutes.

NEW WORDS

◷ **calendar** A chart that shows us the days, weeks and months of the year.

◷ **Muslim** To do with the religion of Muslim people, called Islam.

◷ **candle clock** A candle marked to show the passing of hours.

Solids, Liquids and Gases

Everything in the Universe, from the tiniest speck of dust to the biggest giant star, is made up of matter. This matter can take one of three forms: solid, liquid or gas.

A solid is a piece of matter that has a definite shape. Wood is a hard solid, and rubber is a soft solid. A liquid, such as water or lemonade, does not have a definite shape, but takes the shape of its container. A gas, such as air, also has no shape, and spreads out to fill any container it is put in.

△ **When a candle burns,** its solid wax gets hot, melts and goes liquid. As it cools, the wax goes hard again.

▷ **Red-hot lava** comes shooting out of a volcano as a liquid. The lava cools and turns into solid rock. Whether the lava is liquid or solid depends on its temperature. This is the same with candle wax.

▽ **Concrete** is shaped when it is runny, and then it hardens. A solid concrete building cannot turn into a liquid again.

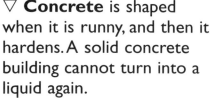

▽ **A cake is baked** from a runny mixture, but you can't change it back again.

▽ **You can fry** a runny raw egg until it goes solid, but you can't unfry it!

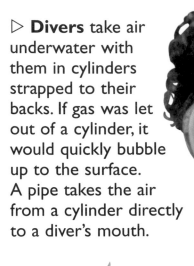

▷ **Divers** take air underwater with them in cylinders strapped to their backs. If gas was let out of a cylinder, it would quickly bubble up to the surface. A pipe takes the air from a cylinder directly to a diver's mouth.

SLOW FREEZER

Salty water does not freeze as easily as fresh water. To test this, dissolve as much salt as you can in a tin-foil container of cold tap water. Then put this in the freezer, along with another container of cold tap water. You will find that the fresh water turns to solid ice much quicker than the salty water. This is because the salty water freezes at a much lower temperature.

Can water flow uphill?
No, water always flows downhill. This is because it is pulled by the force of gravity, just like everything else. Water settles at the lowest point it can reach.

NEW WORDS

🕯️ **concrete** Cement mixed with sand and gravel, used in building.

🕯️ **dissolve** To mix a solid into a liquid so that it becomes part of the liquid.

🕯️ **steam** The very hot gas that boiling water turns into.

△ **If you pour water** into an ice tray and put it in the freezer, the liquid becomes solid ice. If you then heat the ice cubes, they become liquid again. When the water boils, it turns to a gas called steam. And when the steam cools on a mirror, it changes back to water!

37

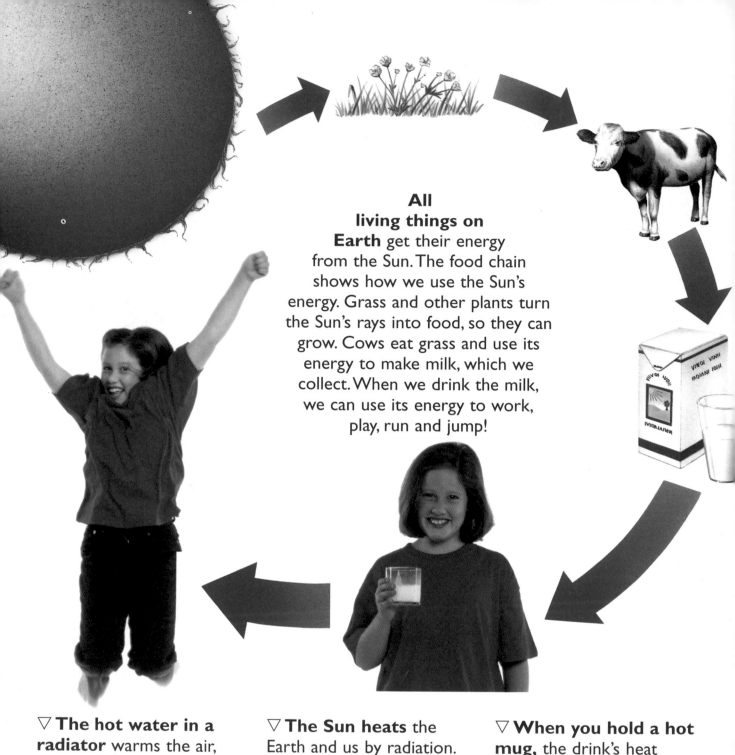

All **living things on Earth** get their energy from the Sun. The food chain shows how we use the Sun's energy. Grass and other plants turn the Sun's rays into food, so they can grow. Cows eat grass and use its energy to make milk, which we collect. When we drink the milk, we can use its energy to work, play, run and jump!

▽ **The hot water in a radiator** warms the air, which in turn warms us. This movement of heat energy is called convection.

▽ **The Sun heats** the Earth and us by radiation. On a summer's day, it is best to stay in the shade and drink a lot to stay cool.

▽ **When you hold a hot mug,** the drink's heat passes through the mug and warms your hands. The mug is said to conduct heat.

Energy

All the world's actions and movements are caused by energy. Light, heat and electricity are all forms of energy. Our human energy comes from food.

Energy exists in many forms, and it always changes from one form to another. A car's energy comes from petrol. When it is burned in a car, it gives out heat energy. This turns into movement energy to make the car go. Many machines are powered in this way by fuel.

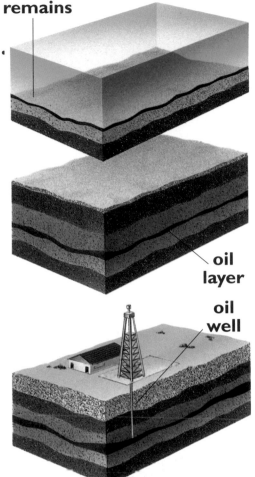

plant and animal remains

oil layer

oil well

NEW WORDS
fuel Stored energy used to power machines.

petrol A liquid made from crude oil, used to power cars and other machines.

radiator A device in the home that gives off heat. It is often part of a central heating system.

▷ **Millions of years ago**, the remains of dead sea plants and animals were covered by mud and sand. Heat and pressure turned these into oil, which was trapped between rocks. We drill down to the oil and bring it to the surface. We make petrol from the oil, which we put into our cars. Then stored energy is turned into movement.

What a shower!
We can save energy in the home by not wasting electricity or gas. Heating water takes up energy, and a shower uses less hot water than a bath. So when we shower, we save energy.

The Sun gives off light energy from 150 million kilometres away. This is known as solar power. It is the source of all the world's energy, and it can be collected directly by solar panels. These turn solar energy into electricity.

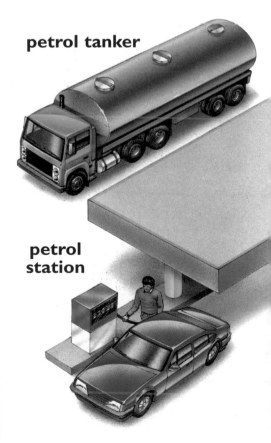

petrol tanker

petrol station

39

Electricity

Imagine what life would be like without the form of energy called electricity. You would not be able to make light or heat by flicking on a switch, and most of the machines in your home would not work!

The electricity we use at home flows through wires. We call this flow an electric current. When you turn on a light switch, a current flows to the bulb and makes it work.

Most electricity we use at home is made in power stations. There, fuel such as coal or oil is burned. The heat energy is used to turn a generator, which makes electricity.

◁ **Another form of electricity** does not flow through wires. It is usually still, or "static". Static electricity from a special generator can make your hair stand on end! You may have noticed this sometimes when your hair is combed quickly, especially on a cold, dry day.

Batteries make and store small amounts of electricity. They are useful because you can carry them around. A car battery is very big. A torch battery is smaller. The battery in a watch is tiny.

WARNING!
Never touch or play with plugs, sockets, wires or any other form of electricity. You will get an electric shock and this could kill you.

A flash of lightning makes a booming noise – thunder. We always hear this after we see the flash, because light travels much faster than sound.

An ancient Greek scientist called Thales discovered static electricity over 2,500 years ago, when he rubbed a piece of amber with a cloth.

△ **Lightning** is a form of static electricity. The electricity builds up inside storm clouds, and then jumps from cloud to cloud or from the cloud to the ground as brilliant flashes of lightning.

The American scientist and statesman, Benjamin Franklin, found out in 1752 that lightning is electricity. He did a famous and extremely dangerous experiment by flying a kite into a thunder cloud.

STATIC BALLOONS

Blow up a balloon and rub it up and down on a shirt. The rubbing makes static electricity on the plastic skin of the balloon. Hold the balloon against your clothes and let go. The static electricity will stick it there. You can also use the static to pick up small pieces of tissue paper. What happens when the static charge wears off?

SPINNING COLOURS

Here's a way to mix the colours of the rainbow back together. Divide a card disk into seven equal sections. Colour the sections with the seven colours of the rainbow. Push a sharpened pencil through the middle of the disc and spin it fast on the pencil point. The colours will all mix back to a greyish white.

◁ **Light bounces off** still water in the same way that it bounces back to you from a mirror. The image that we see in the water or in a mirror is called a reflection.

Shadows are dark shapes. They are made when something gets in the way of light and blocks it out. This happens because light travels in straight lines and cannot bend around corners.

NEW WORDS

lens A curved piece of glass or plastic that is used to change the direction of light.

prism A triangular piece of glass that breaks up the colours of light.

reflection The image of something that is seen in a mirror or another reflecting surface.

triangular Having three sides, like a triangle.

In this book, all the colours you see are made of a mixture of just four coloured printing inks – blue, red, yellow and black.

▷ **If you pass a beam of light** through a triangular piece of glass, called a prism, the light gets split up into its different colours, just like a rainbow. The band of rainbow colours is called the spectrum of light.

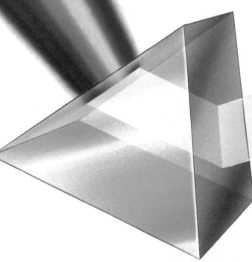

42

Light and Colour

Light is the fastest moving form of energy there is. Sunlight travels to Earth through space as light waves. We see things when light from them travels to our eyes.

Light seems to us to be colourless, but really it is a mixture of colours. These are soaked up differently by various objects. A banana lets yellow bounce off it and soaks up the other colours, so the banana looks yellow.

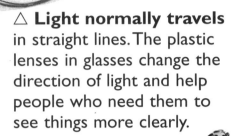

△ **Light normally travels** in straight lines. The plastic lenses in glasses change the direction of light and help people who need them to see things more clearly.

△ **The curved lens** in a magnifying glass also bends light, making things look bigger. You can move the position of the glass, to see things the size you want.

◁ **A rainbow** shows sunlight in seven different colours. This happens when sunlight passes through raindrops and gets split up. Starting with the outer circle, the colours of a rainbow are red, orange, yellow, green, blue, indigo and violet. The colours are always in the same order.

Sound

All sounds are made by things vibrating, or moving backwards and forwards very quickly. Sounds travel through the air in waves.

Our ears pick up sound waves travelling in the air around us. Sounds can move through other gases too, as well as through liquids and solids. So you can hear sounds when you swim underwater. Astronauts on the Moon, where there is no air, cannot speak to each other directly and have to use radio.

LOUD AND QUIET

Bigger vibrations make bigger sound waves and sound louder. We measure loudness in decibels. Leaves falling gently on the ground might make 10 decibels of noise. A jet plane taking off makes about 120 decibels.

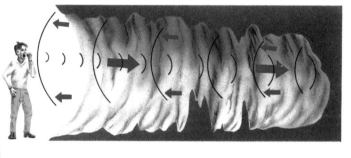

◁ **Sometimes sound waves** bounce back to you off a hard surface. When this happens, the sound makes an echo. A cave or a long corridor are good places to make an echo.

◁ **When you pluck a guitar string,** it vibrates very fast and makes sound waves. If you put your finger gently on a plucked string, you will be able to feel it vibrating. If you press down hard on the string and stop the vibration, you will also stop the sound.

Sound moves at a speed of about 1,225 kilometres an hour. That's 30 times quicker than the fastest human runner, but almost a million times slower than the speed of light! A Concorde supersonic jet can fly at twice the speed of sound.

HIGH AND LOW

A big horn makes lower sounds than a high-pitched whistle. A big cat makes a booming roar, while a mouse makes a high-pitched squeak. That's because they make different vibrations. The quicker something vibrates, the higher the sound it makes.

whistle

tiger

horn

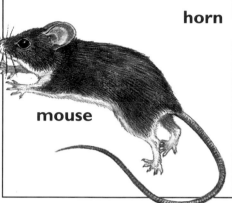
mouse

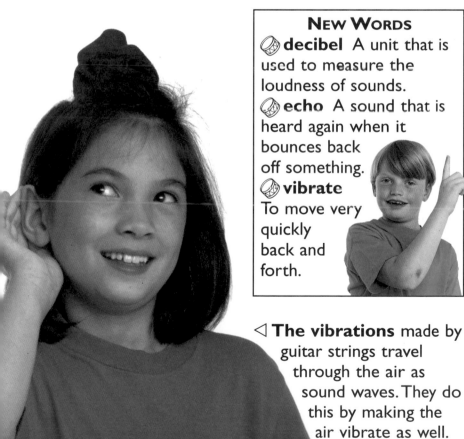

NEW WORDS

decibel A unit that is used to measure the loudness of sounds.

echo A sound that is heard again when it bounces back off something.

vibrate To move very quickly back and forth.

◁ **The vibrations** made by guitar strings travel through the air as sound waves. They do this by making the air vibrate as well. Sometimes people put a hand to their ear to try and collect more sounds.

Dogs can hear both lower and higher sounds than people can. Bats and dolphins can make and hear even higher-pitched sounds, and they use this ability to find their way around.

Why wear ear muffs?
People who work with loud machines wear muffs to protect their hearing. This is because loud noises are painful to the ears and can damage them, especially if the noise goes on for a long time.

Computers

Computers can do all sorts of different jobs for us, easily and very quickly. Many people use computers at home, as well as at work and at school.

We can use computers to write letters and reports; or to store lots of information, such as lists or addresses; or to do complicated sums; or to design things.

Most of the work you do on a computer can be seen on its screen. If you want to, you can also print work out on paper.

▽ **You can use a keyboard** and a mouse to put information into the computer. Then you can store your work on a disk, as well as inside the computer itself.

screen

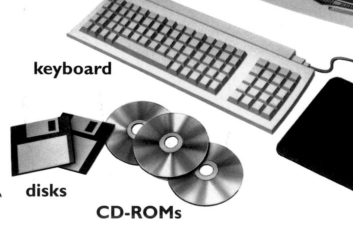

disk drive

keyboard

disks

CD-ROMs

mouse

What is E-mail?
It stands for electronic mail, a way of sending messages between computers all over the world. You write a letter on your computer, then send it down a telephone line to someone else's computer, instantly. In comparison, ordinary post is so slow that E-mailers call it "snail mail".

STRINGING ALONG
To create your own phone system, make a hole in the bottom of two plastic or paper cups, or yoghurt pots. Then thread a long piece of string through the holes and tie a knot at each end, inside the cup. Ask a friend to pull the string tight and put a cup to his ear. Now speak into your cup and he will hear you. It's as fast as E-mail!

▷ **There are lots** of exciting computer games. You play many of them by using a joystick.

NEW WORDS

🖥 **disk** A small piece of plastic that stores computer information.

🖥 **joystick** A device with a moving handle that is used to put information into a computer.

🖥 **keyboard** A set of keys used to type information.

🖥 **mouse** A control unit you can move and click to put information into a computer.

▽ **When you put on** a virtual-reality headset, you enter a pretend world created by a computer.

Inside the headset are two small screens, showing you pictures that look real. If you use a special glove to touch things, the computer reacts to every move you make. This picture shows how the system could be used to control planes. An air traffic controller could see the planes as if they were real and give commands to tell them what to do.

TV and Radio

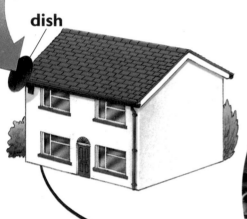

TV studio

satellite

transmitter

dish

pictures are seen in our home

Many people spend hours each day watching TV or listening to radio. Along with newspapers and magazines, TV and radio provide us with entertainment and information.

Television signals can be received by an aerial or by a satellite dish. Some people have TV signals brought straight into their homes through a cable. In most countries there are many different channels and programmes to choose from, day and night.

◁ **For satellite TV**, a programme is transmitted to a satellite in space. The signal is then beamed back to Earth by the satellite and is picked up by dishes on people's homes. Their television set changes the signal back into pictures.

△ **Working in a TV studio,** cameramen use video cameras to record programmes. These are bigger, more complicated versions of the camcorders that people use at home. Many different technicians work in TV and radio.

NEW WORDS

aerial A metal device that receives and sends TV and radio signals.

satellite dish A round aerial that receives TV signals bounced back from a satellite in space.

signal A series of radio waves that can make up pictures and sounds.

transmitter A device, usually a tall pole, that sends out radio and television signals.

△ **A TV set** receives electrical signals, which it changes into pictures. It fires streams of particles onto the back of the screen. They build up a picture, and this changes many times each second.

▽ **South Korea** makes more colour television sets than any other country: over 16 million every year!

▽ **A radio telescope** is used to send and receive radio waves. Both radio and TV signals travel as radio waves. Astronomers also use radio telescopes to pick up signals from parts of space that we can't see through other telescopes.

▽ **The largest radio telescope** in the world is at Arecibo, on the Caribbean island of Puerto Rico. The dish is 305 metres across and stands inside a circle of hills.

▽ **The world's first radio broadcast** was made in the USA in 1906. The first proper TV service began in 1936 in London. At that time there were just 100 television sets in the whole of the UK!

▽ **The leaves** and flowers of water lilies float on the surface of the water. We call these lily pads. The plants' stems are under the water, and their roots are in the mud and soil at the bottom of the pond.

▷ **Some bromeliads** live on other plants, in the rainforest. They grow in pockets of soil that form in the bark of trees. Their roots dangle freely and take in most of their moisture from the damp forest air.

The largest leaves of any plant grow on palm trees on islands in the Indian Ocean. The leaves are up to 20 metres long. The pads of some large water lilies grow over 2 metres across.

▽ **Leaves** take in carbon dioxide gas through tiny holes on their underside. They also give out oxygen, which is why plants are so important to all other living creatures, including us.

△ **Cacti** live in hot, dry regions, such as deserts. They store water in their fleshy stems. Their leaves are in the shape of sharp spines, which help protect them from desert animals.

NEW WORDS

carbon dioxide A gas used by plants to make their food; it is also the waste gas that we breathe out.

chlorophyll A green substance in plants, which they use to trap sunlight.

photosynthesis The process that plants use to make food, using sunlight and carbon dioxide and giving off oxygen.

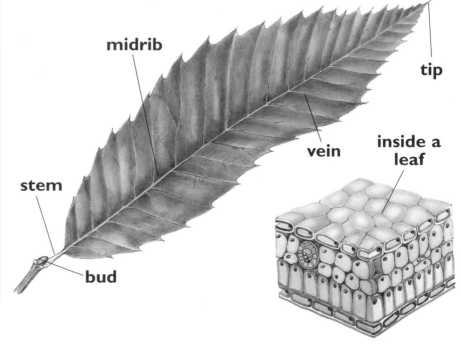

midrib

tip

stem

vein

inside a leaf

bud

Plants

flower

Living plants are found almost everywhere on Earth where there is sunlight, warmth and water. They use these to make their own food.

Plants have a special way of using the Sun's energy, with a green substance in their leaves called chlorophyll. They take in a gas called carbon dioxide from the air and mix it with water and minerals from the soil. In this way they make a form of sugar, which is their food. This whole process is called photosynthesis.

leaf

fruit

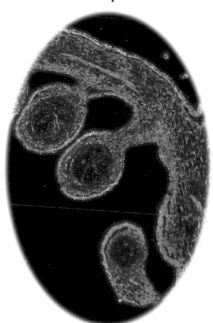

▷ **A plant's roots** grow down into the soil. They are covered in tiny hairs, which take in water and minerals. Water moves through the stem to the leaves, which make the plant's food.

stem

roots

◁ **Part of a fern** seen through a microscope. There are about 10,000 different kinds of ferns in the world. Most of these green plants are quite small.

SUN BLOCK

Cover a patch of green grass with an old tin or saucer – but not on someone's prize lawn! Lift the tin after a few days and you will see that the grass is losing its colour. After a week, it will be very pale.
This is because it couldn't make food in the dark. Take the tin away and the grass will soon recover.

Trees

Trees are not only among the largest living things on Earth, but also can live the longest.

A trunk is really just a hard, woody stem. Under the protective bark, water and food travel up through the outer layer of wood, called the sapwod, to the tree's crown of branches and leaves.

Fine roots take in the water, but trees have big, strong roots as well. These will help anchor the trees very firmly in the ground.

NEW WORDS

cone The cone-shaped fruit of conifer trees, containing the trees' seeds.

forester A person who works in and looks after a forest or wood.

heartwood The central core of hard wood in a tree trunk.

The oldest living trees on Earth are bristlecone pines in the USA. Some are over 5,000 years old.

Mangrove trees grow in swamps. They are the only trees that live in salty water.

▽ **The leaves of birch trees** are shaped like triangles, with toothed edges. In the autumn, they turn brown before falling from the tree. Native Americans used the bark of birch trees to make canoes.

▽ **Different leaves** do different jobs. Small leaves, like those on fir trees or cacti, lose less water than broad, flat leaves. Big leaves show a larger surface area to the Sun and so are able to make more food.

△ **The beautiful leaves** of the tamarind, an evergreen tree that grows in warm regions of the world. It can grow to a height of 24 metres.

◁ **As an oak tree grows** and the trunk widens, its bark breaks up into pieces like a jigsaw. In the middle of the trunk is a core of dark brown heartwood.

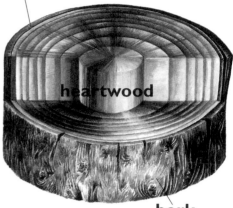

growth ring

heartwood

bark

△ **Trees grow** a new ring of wood every year. If there is lots of sunshine and rainfall, that year's ring is wide. Foresters count the rings of felled trees to see how old they are.

Many palm trees have no branches. Instead, they have large, fan-shaped leaves that grow straight out from the top of the trunk. Palms grow best in parts of the world where it is warm all year round.

BARK PATTERNS

Every tree has a unique pattern on its bark. You can see these wonderful patterns by transferring them to paper. Just attach or hold a sheet of paper firmly against a tree trunk. Then carefully rub over the paper with a crayon until the bark pattern shows up. Bark rubbings make beautiful pictures, and you can use different coloured crayons to make unusual effects.

Parts of the Body

head

hand

neck

arm

torso

leg

foot

Men and women, boys and girls are all human beings. Our bodies are all similar, though no two people look exactly the same.

The human body is made up of many parts, each having its own special job to do. These different parts are all controlled by the brain, which also enables us to think and move. Our senses of sight, hearing, touch, taste and smell help us in our daily lives. Our bodies need energy to make it work, which we get from our food.

Two thirds of your body's weight is made up of water. It also contains carbon, calcium and iron.

◁ **The largest part** of the body is called the torso, or trunk. The four limbs are joined to the torso. The hands at the ends of our arms help us touch and hold things. Our feet help us stand upright and walk. The head is on top of the neck, which can bend and twist. The brain is inside the head.

NEW WORDS

brain The control centre of the body, which also lets us think.
limb An arm or a leg.
nucleus The central part of a cell.
tissue Groups of similar cells that are joined together to form parts of the body.
torso The trunk of the human body, from below the neck to the top of the legs.

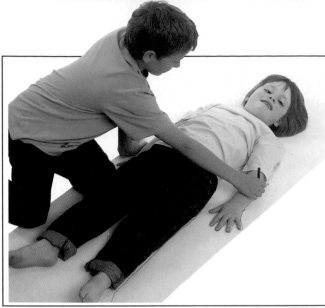

BODY SHAPES

To draw body shapes, you need some very big pieces of paper, such as lining paper or parcel wrap. Put the paper on the floor and ask a friend to lie on it. Draw around him or her with a pencil. Then take the paper away and cut out the outline shape. You can draw on a face and any other features you want, before pinning the picture up on the wall. Then you could ask a friend to draw your shape.

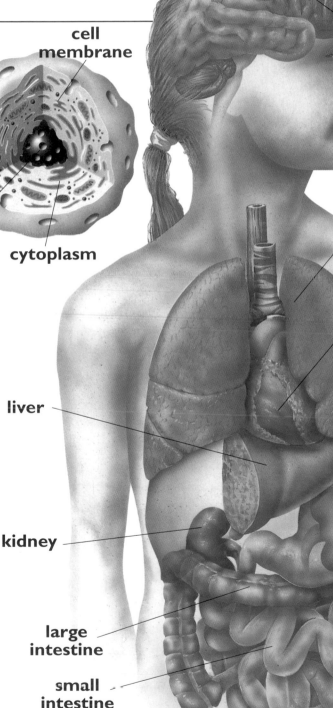

cell membrane

nucleus

cytoplasm

brain

lung

heart

liver

kidney

large intestine

small intestine

▷ **All parts of the body** are made up of tiny living units called cells. Every body contains billions of cells, so small that they can only be seen through a microscope. Most cells have three main parts. In the middle is a nucleus, the control centre that helps make new cells. This is surrounded by a soft fluid called cytoplasm. The outer surface of the cell is called its membrane.

We all begin life as one single cell. This divides into two, these cells also divide, and so on. Similar types of cells join together to make tissue.

▷ **We have many large organs** inside our bodies. These are parts that do special jobs for the rest of the body. Organs work together to make up different body systems.

55

Skeleton

skull

The skeleton is our framework of bones. Our bones provide a firm surface for muscles to attach to, helping us to move.

The skeleton also protects our body's organs. The skull protects the brain. Our heart and lungs are protected by the rib cage. The body's bones vary in shape and size. The places where they meet are called joints, which is where muscles move bones.

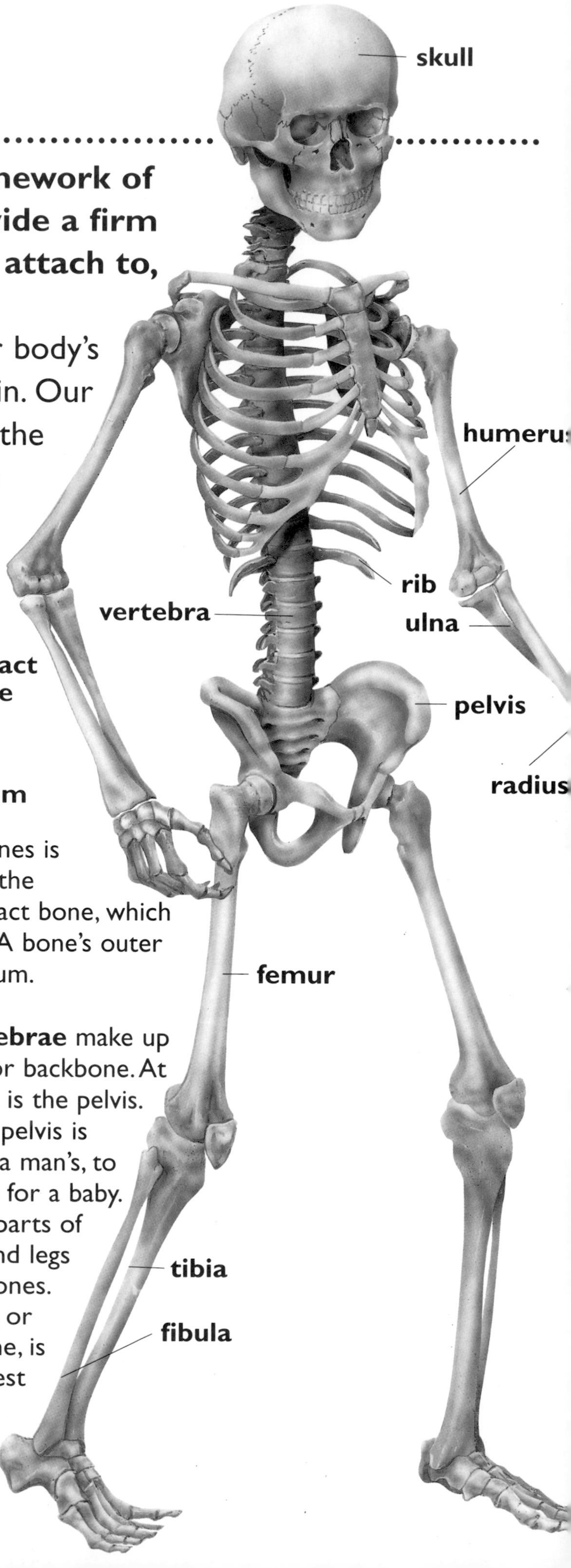

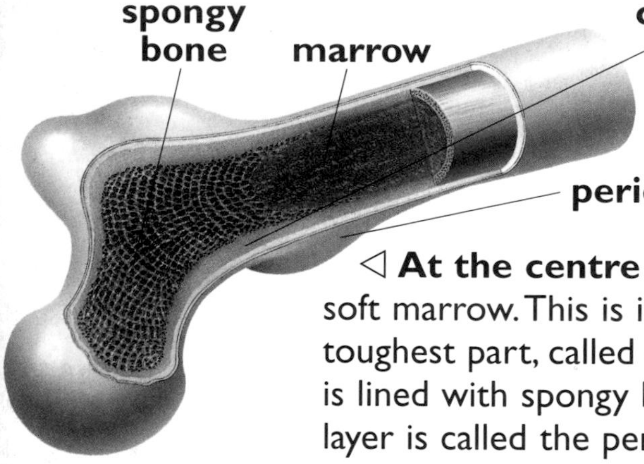

humeru

vertebra

rib
ulna

pelvis

radius

spongy bone   marrow   compact bone

periosteum

◁ **At the centre** of bones is soft marrow. This is inside the toughest part, called compact bone, which is lined with spongy bone. A bone's outer layer is called the periosteum.

femur

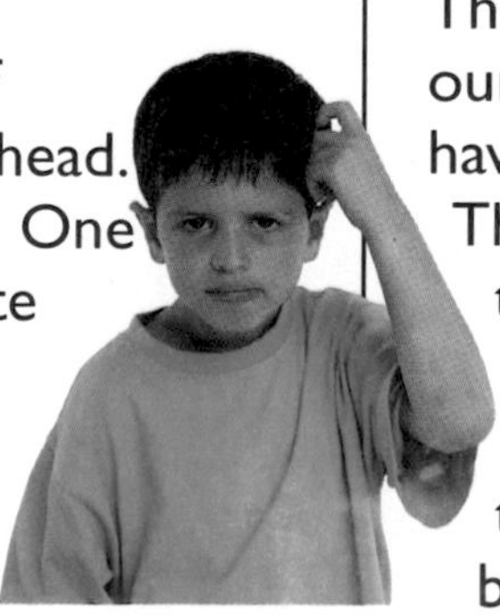

▷ **33 vertebrae** make up our spine, or backbone. At the bottom is the pelvis. A woman's pelvis is wider than a man's, to make room for a baby. The lower parts of our arms and legs have two bones. The femur, or thigh bone, is the largest bone in the body.

tibia

fibula

56

MOVING JOINTS

Joints let us move in different ways. The hip and shoulder are ball-and-socket joints. The knee and elbow are hinge joints. There is a pivot joint at the top of the spine, a saddle joint at the thumb's base.

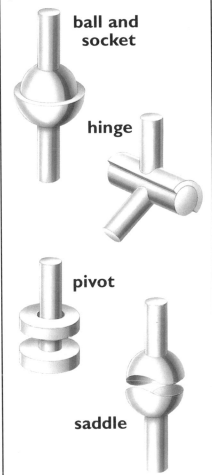

ball and socket

hinge

pivot

saddle

An adult has about 206 bones. Babies are born with as many as 270 small, soft bones. As a child grows, some of the bones join together.

You may be up to 1 cm shorter in the evening than when you wake up in the morning. The weight of your upper body squashes your spine slightly as you stand and walk during the day.

▽ **For broken bones** to heal properly, they have to be placed next to each other and kept still. That is why a doctor puts a broken arm or leg in a plaster cast. New bone tissue grows to join the broken bone ends together again.

△ **Insects,** such as this beetle, have their skeleton on the outside of their body. It acts like a shell, covering and protecting the soft parts underneath. It also protects the insect from its enemies.

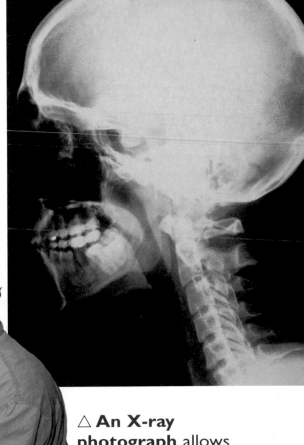

△ **An X-ray photograph** allows doctors to look at bones inside the body. They can then easily see if a bone has been broken or damaged.

Muscles

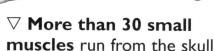

All our movements, from running and jumping, to blinking and smiling, are made by our muscles. The muscles do this by becoming shorter and pulling the bones to which they are attached.

The human body has about 620 muscles that it uses for movement. In addition there are many more that work automatically. These include the muscles that make the heart beat, the chest muscles that help us breathe and the stomach muscles that help us digest food.

chest muscles

biceps

abdominal muscles

sartorius

▷ **The body** is moved by several layers of muscles. There are large muscles near the surface under the skin, and others lie beneath them. Three layers of criss-crossing abdominal muscles connect the rib cage to the pelvis. The body's largest muscle is in the buttock.

▽ **More than 30 small muscles** run from the skull to the skin. These allow us to make facial expressions, which we use to show our feelings.

happy

shocked

sad

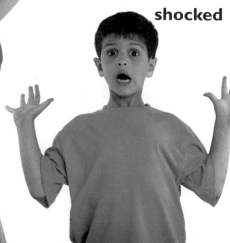

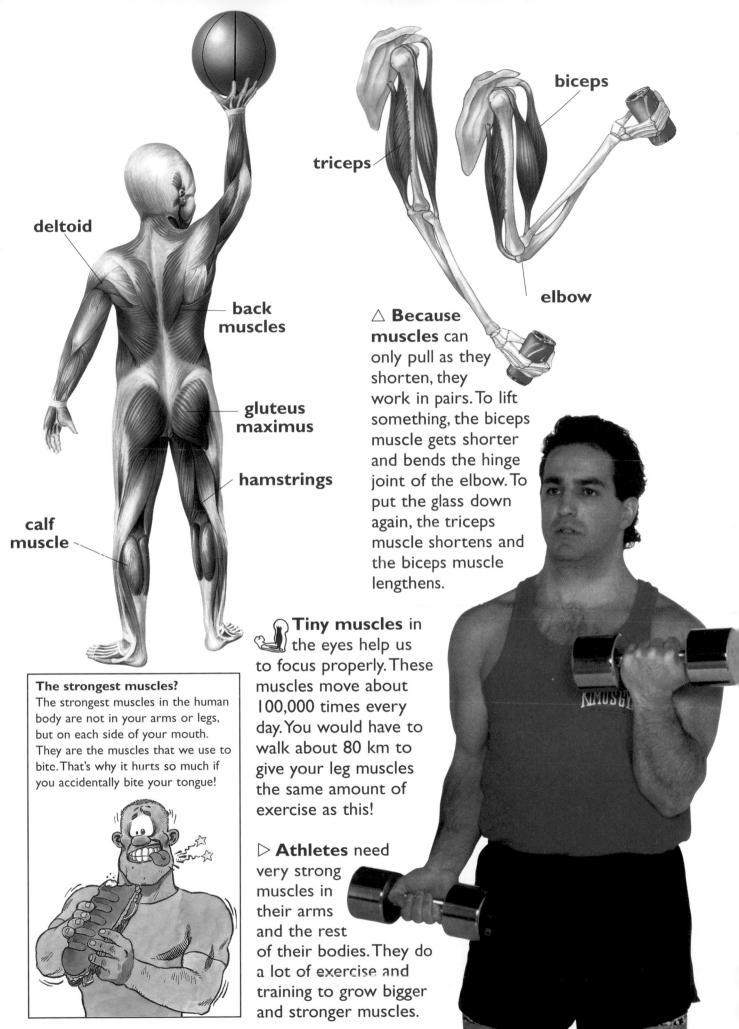

deltoid

back muscles

gluteus maximus

hamstrings

calf muscle

triceps

biceps

elbow

△ **Because muscles** can only pull as they shorten, they work in pairs. To lift something, the biceps muscle gets shorter and bends the hinge joint of the elbow. To put the glass down again, the triceps muscle shortens and the biceps muscle lengthens.

The strongest muscles?
The strongest muscles in the human body are not in your arms or legs, but on each side of your mouth. They are the muscles that we use to bite. That's why it hurts so much if you accidentally bite your tongue!

Tiny muscles in the eyes help us to focus properly. These muscles move about 100,000 times every day. You would have to walk about 80 km to give your leg muscles the same amount of exercise as this!

▷ **Athletes** need very strong muscles in their arms and the rest of their bodies. They do a lot of exercise and training to grow bigger and stronger muscles.

The Heart and Blood Circulation

The heart is a powerful muscle which pumps blood all around the body. The blood carries oxygen from the air we breathe and goodness from the food we eat.

The heart is pear-shaped and is about as big as your clenched fist. It lies in your chest, behind your ribs and just to the left of the bottom of your breastbone. If you put your hand on your chest near your heart, you can feel it beating. A child's heart rate is about 100 beats a minute. When you are running or if you are very active, your heart beats faster and your body's cells then need more oxygen and food.

heart

artery

vein

Hold one hand up and the other down for one minute.

△ **Blood** travels away from the heart in blood vessels called arteries. It travels back to the heart in veins. In the illustration, arteries are red and veins blue.

▷ **Your heart** has to work harder to pump blood upwards, because then it is working against gravity. If you hold one hand up for a minute, you'll see that it has less blood in it afterwards than the other hand.

60

▽ **The right side** of the heart pumps blood to the lungs to pick up oxygen. The left side pumps the blood around the body.

aorta

right ventricle

left ventricle

△ **A doctor** can use a special instrument to measure blood pressure. The instrument squeezes, but it isn't painful. Having high blood pressure can put an extra strain on a person's heart. because it has to work harder.

LISTEN TO THE BEAT

You can make your own stethoscope, so that you can easily listen to your own or a friend's heartbeat. Simply cut the top end off two plastic bottles. Then push the ends of some plastic tubing into these two cups. Put one cup over a friend's heart and the other cup over your ear.

An adult body contains about 5 litres of blood. So every day an adult's heart pumps over 7,000 litres of blood around the body.

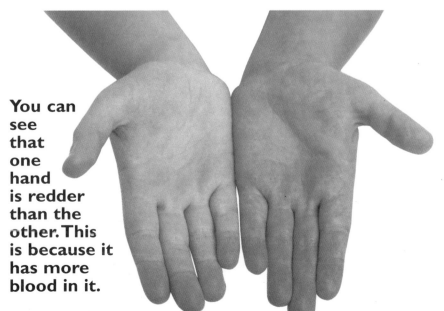

You can see that one hand is redder than the other. This is because it has more blood in it.

NEW WORDS

artery One of the tubes that carries blood away from the heart to all parts of the body.

stethoscope A doctor's instrument used for listening to sounds in a person's body.

vein One of the tubes that carries blood to the heart.

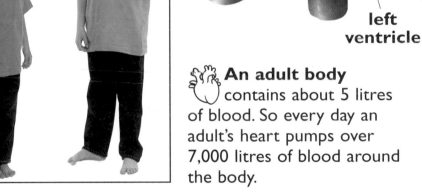

◁ **Runners** need to get a lot of oxygen to their muscles very quickly. To achieve this, they breathe hard and their hearts beat quicker. That's why you sometimes feel out of breath when you've been running.

An adult's lungs contain around 300 billion tiny blood vessels, called capillaries. If you could lay them end to end, they would stretch over 2,000 km.

We can't breathe underwater, so divers carry oxygen tanks on their backs. On the surface, they use snorkels. There is no air in space, so astronauts also carry backpacks of oxygen.

△ **This photo** of part of a lung was taken under a microscope, which magnifies it many times. The network of small passages inside the lung make it look and act rather like a sponge.

▷ **As you breathe in,** your rib cage expands and a large dome of muscle, called the diaphragm, flattens. When you breathe out, the diaphragm rises.

BREATH TEST

Fill a large plastic bottle and half-fill a large bowl with water. Cover the bottle top with your finger and turn it upside down in the bowl. You will find that the water will stay in the bottle. Take a plastic tube and carefully put one end of it into the neck of the bottle, under the water. Now everything is ready for the breath test. Blow hard into the free end of the tube. How much water can your breath push out of the bottle?

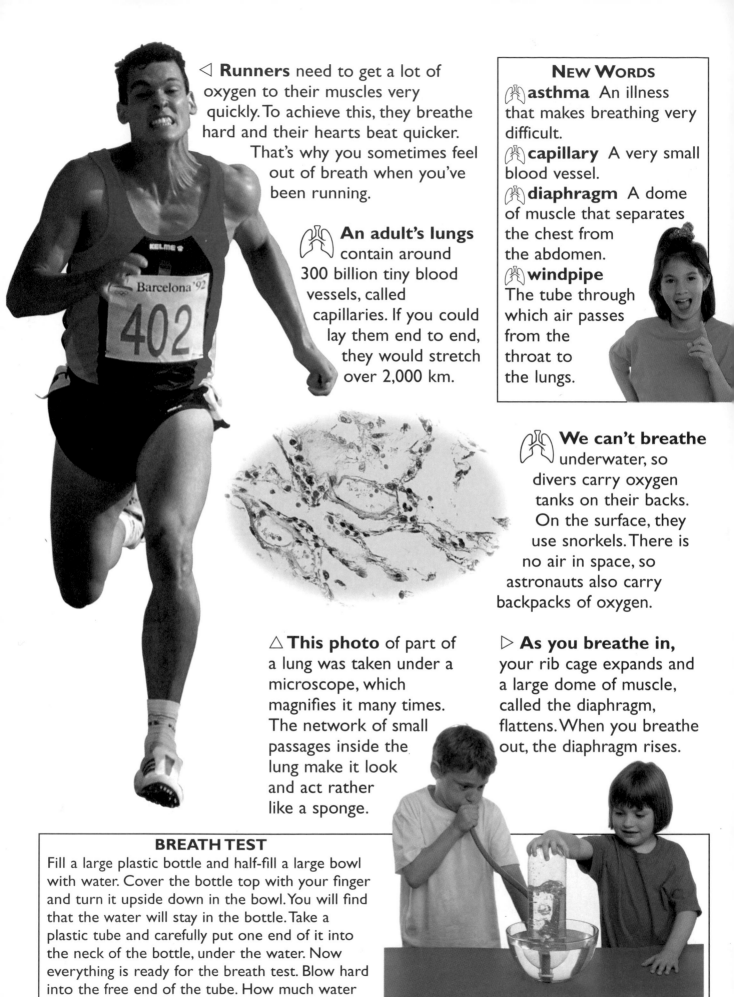

Breathing

Every time we breathe, we take in air containing a gas called oxygen. We need oxygen all the time to make our bodies work.

The air we breathe in passes into the two lungs, which are well protected inside the rib cage. The lungs take oxygen from the air and pass it into our bloodstream. Our blood takes oxygen all around the body.

When we breathe out, the lungs get rid of used air. Adults breathe about 18 times a minute, which is more than 25,000 times a day. Children usually breathe even faster.

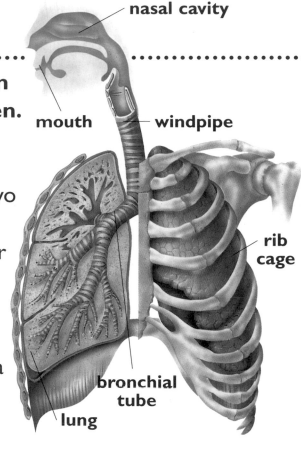

nasal cavity

mouth

windpipe

rib cage

bronchial tube

lung

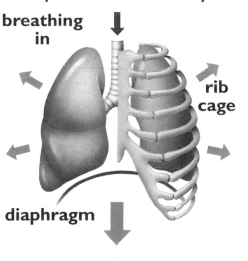

breathing in

rib cage

diaphragm

breathing out

▽ **People who suffer from asthma,** or other breathing difficulties, often use an inhaler to help them breathe. The inhaler puffs a drug down into the windpipe. This makes the air passages wider and they can breathe more easily.

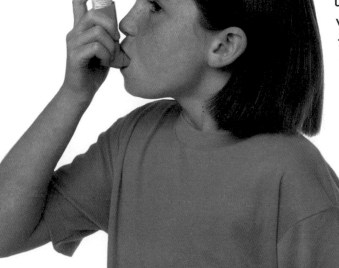

△ **The air we breathe** in through the nose and mouth goes down the windpipe. This branches into two bronchial tubes, one for each lung. Inside the lungs, the tubes divide and get smaller. Oxygen passes from the tiniest tubes to blood vessels and finally into the bloodstream.

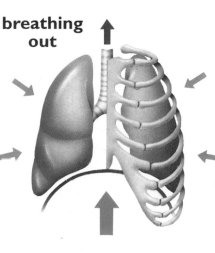

Central Nervous System

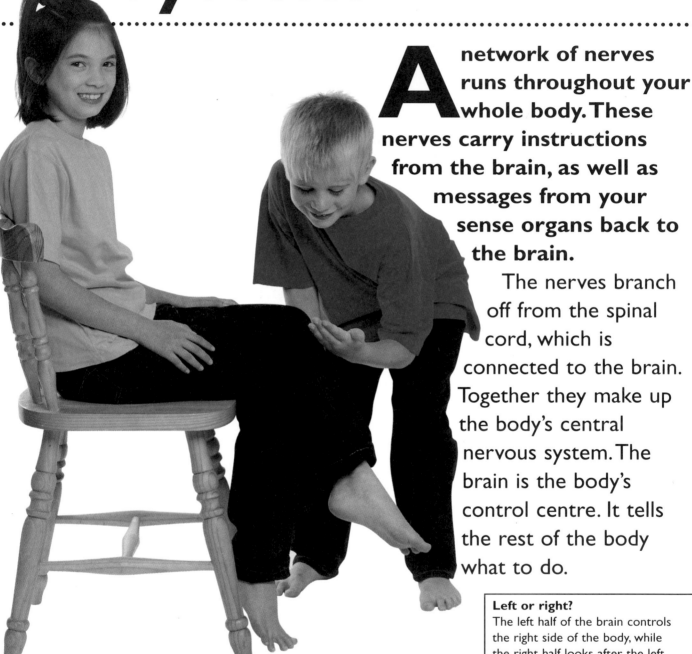

A network of nerves runs throughout your whole body. These nerves carry instructions from the brain, as well as messages from your sense organs back to the brain.

The nerves branch off from the spinal cord, which is connected to the brain. Together they make up the body's central nervous system. The brain is the body's control centre. It tells the rest of the body what to do.

△ **If you tap** the right point below someone's knee, their leg will jerk. This is called a reflex action. The spinal cord sends a signal back to the leg muscle before the original message has reached the brain.

Reflex actions help the body to protect itself quickly. So if you touch a sharp pin or something hot, you will pull your hand away before the message reaches your brain without thinking about it.

Left or right?
The left half of the brain controls the right side of the body, while the right half looks after the left side. Very few people can write or draw well with both hands. Try using your "wrong" hand, to see how hard it is.

64

NEW WORDS

central nervous system The brain and the spinal cord.

reflex action A response by the body that takes place without the brain being involved.

spinal cord The column of nerves running to and from the brain down the middle of the backbone.

△ **Memories** are stored in the brain. This couple will always remember their wedding day.

▷ **The brain** is connected to the spinal cord that runs down the body inside the backbone. Nerves run from the spine all over the body, even to your little toe.

Our brain uses an enormous amount of energy. It uses about a fifth of the oxygen we breathe, as well as a fifth of the energy in the food we eat. With this it produces its own electricity.

◁ **Our brain** helps us to see and hear, as well as to judge speed and distance. A racing driver needs to combine all of these abilities very quickly. His brain sends messages to his hands and feet to steer and control the car.

straight hair

wavy hair

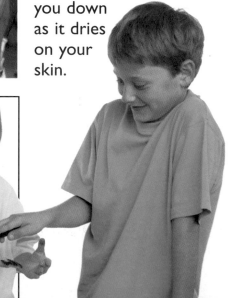
curly hair

△ **Hairs** grow from follicles, in the dermis. Different-shaped follicles make people's hair straight, wavy or curly.

No two fingerprints are the same. Every person in the world has their own special pattern. That's why fingerprints can be used to identify people.

◁ **People sweat** when they are hot, so athletes sweat more on a very hot day. Sweat takes heat from the body and helps cool you down as it dries on your skin.

COMPARE PRINTS

It's best to wear some old clothes and put down lots of newspaper for this activity. It can be a bit messy! Use a roller or a brush to cover your fingers or your whole hand in paint. Then press down firmly on a sheet of paper. This will leave fingerprints and perhaps a whole hand print. When you have finished, compare your prints with a friend's. Are the prints the same? You could try looking at them through a magnifying glass – you'll really see the difference.

The Skin, Hair and Nails

NEW WORDS
✋**cuticle** The skin at the base of a nail.
✋**dermis** The inner, deeper layer of the skin, beneath the epidermis.
✋**epidermis** The top layer of the skin, above the dermis.
✋**follicle** The hole in the skin where a hair starts to grow.

Skin protects the body and controls its temperature. It keeps out dirt, water and germs, shields us from the Sun's burning rays, and stops the body drying out.

nail
half-moon
cuticle
fat
bone
skin

△ **Nails** are made of a tough substance called keratin. New nail grows from the base, under the skin. The pale half-moon is nail that has just grown.

Our skin is full of nerve endings, so it can send messages to the brain about things such as heat, cold and pain. The skin produces nails to protect the tips of fingers and toes. It also makes hairs for extra warmth and protection.

▽ **The tough outer layer** of the skin is called the epidermis, which is waterproof and germproof. The inner layer, called the dermis, contains nerve endings. This is also where hairs grow and sweat is made.

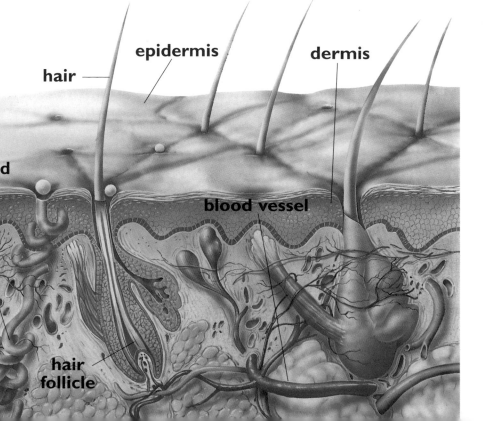

hair
epidermis
dermis
sweat gland
nerve ending
blood vessel
hair follicle

Food and Drink

We need energy to live, and we get that energy from what we eat and drink. Our bodies need important substances, called nutrients, that we get from food. They help us grow and repair damaged cells, as well as providing energy.

Different foods are useful to us in different ways. It is important that we don't miss out on any of the essential nutrients. To have a balanced diet, we must eat foods from various groups- carbohydrates, proteins, fats, and fibre, also vitamins and minerals.

△ **Cereals and vegetables** are good to eat because they contain a lot of fibre. This is very useful because it helps other foods pass more easily through the digestive system.

The body needs small amounts of minerals, such as calcium and sodium. Calcium is needed for healthy bones and teeth. Milk contains calcium, as well as water, fat, protein and vitamins.

◁ **Oranges** and other fruit contain a lot of Vitamin C, which keeps us healthy and helps us recover from illness. The body needs many other vitamins too.

▽ **Fats** such as cheese, butter and milk are full of energy, as well as important vitamins. Fats can be stored by the body to use later, but it is not good to eat too many fatty foods.

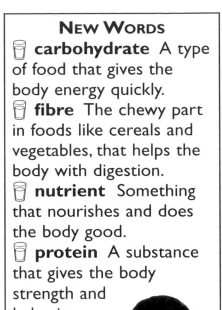
△ **Beans and meat** contain lots of proteins, which help us stay strong. They are also used to make body cells, so they help us grow and stay healthy.

▽ **Carbohydrates,** such as bread and pasta, give us a lot of the energy that we need for our daily lives. We can make use of this type of energy very quickly.

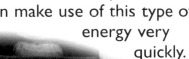

Why do we need water?
The body uses water in many ways. Water helps to make up our blood. It keeps us cool by making sweat. It carries wastes from the body in urine. We get water from other drinks too, as well as from many different kinds of food.

HOME-MADE MUESLI
Put 250 g oats, 150 g raisins and sultanas, and 100 g chopped nuts, along with some sunflower seeds, in a mixing bowl. Mix all the ingredients together. Then put your muesli in a screw-top jar. Label the jar, adding the date. You can eat your muesli with milk, yoghurt or fresh fruit juice, and have a healthy breakfast.

Smell and Taste

Smell and taste are important senses. Our sense of smell is much stronger than our sense of taste. When we taste food, we rely on its smell and texture to give us information about it as well.

We use our noses for smelling things. Tiny scent particles go into the nose with the air. The nose then sends messages through a nerve to the brain, which recognizes the smell.

The tongue also sends nerve signals to the brain about tastes. When we eat something, the tongue and the nose combine to let the brain know all about that particular food.

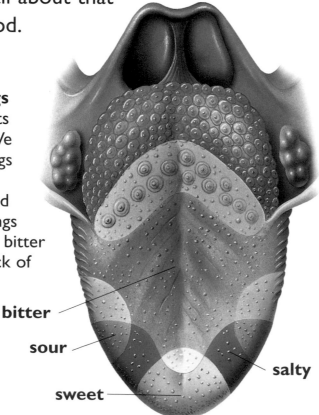

▷ **We taste different things** on different parts of the tongue. We taste sweet things at the tip, salty things just behind the tip, sour things at the sides, and bitter things at the back of the tongue.

bitter

sour

sweet

salty

△ **Flowers** give off a pleasant scent, to attract insects. A skunk can make a very nasty smell when it wants to put off enemies.

When you have a cold and your nose is blocked, you can't smell much and you can't taste your food properly either.

Why do we sneeze?
We sneeze to help clear our noses of unwanted particles, such as dust. When we sneeze, the explosive rush of air from the lungs can reach a speed of 160 kph in other words, as fast as a sports car!

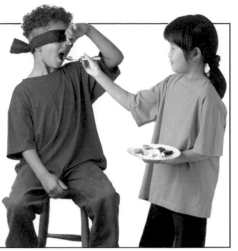

TASTE WITHOUT SMELL

See how much you can taste without the help of your nose. Cut an apple, a carrot, some cheese and other foods with a similar texture into cubes. Cover your eyes and nose and ask a friend to give you the pieces one by one. Can you taste the difference? Try the test on your friend too.

Most people can identify about 3,000 different smells.

▽ **This photo** of taste buds was taken through a microscope. Our tongue has about 10,000 taste buds, which pick up the four basic tastes and pass the information on.

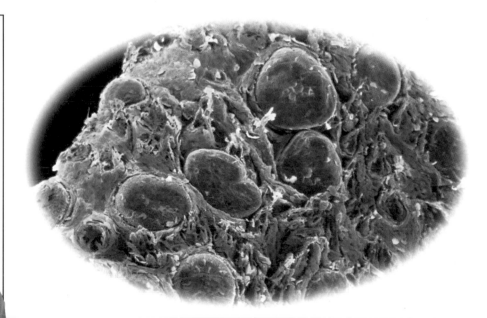

NEW WORDS

mucus A moist, sticky substance in the nose.

olfactory nerve A nerve that runs from the nose to the brain, taking messages about smells.

particle A very very small piece of something.

taste bud A sense organ on the tongue that helps us taste things.

Babies have taste buds all over the inside of their mouths. They are also very sensitive to smells. As we grow older, our sense of smell gets weaker.

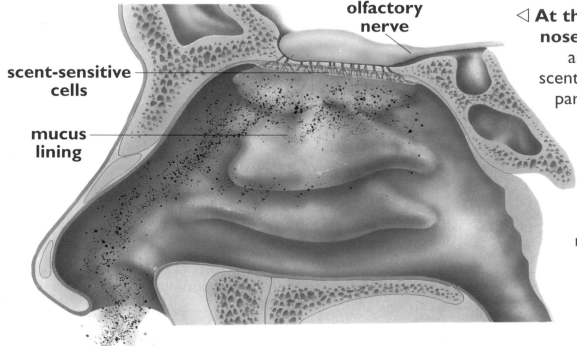

olfactory nerve

scent-sensitive cells

mucus lining

◁ **At the top of the nose** are cells that are sensitive to scent particles. The particles dissolve in a lining of mucus, and signals are sent along the olfactory nerve. This nerve leads to a special part of the brain, where smells are identified.

71

Hearing

hammer

anvil

stirrup

When we look at someone's ears, we see only a part of them. This part, called the outer ear, is shaped to collect sounds as they travel through the air.

All sounds are made by things vibrating. Sound waves make the eardrums and other parts vibrate. Information on vibrations is then sent to the brain, which lets us hear the sounds.

hammer

anvil

stirrup

outer ear

eardrum

cochlea

△ **A tiny bone** called the hammer is connected to the eardrum. The eardrum vibrates the hammer. The hammer then moves the anvil, which in turn moves the stirrup bone. Finally, the stirrup vibrates the cochlea.

△ **Sounds** pass into the ear and make the eardrum vibrate, which in turn vibrates tiny bones. The bones shake a spiral tube shaped like a snail shell, called the cochlea. Inside the cochlea is a fluid, which moves tiny hairs that send signals to the brain. Then we hear the sounds.

EARDRUM DRUM

To make a pretend eardrum, cut a large piece from a plastic bag. Stretch it over the top of a big tin and hold it in place with an elastic band. Sprinkle some sugar onto the plastic. Then hold a metal tray near to it and hit the tray with a wooden spoon. The grains of sugar will jump about as your drum vibrates with the sound.

▽ **An old-fashioned ear trumpet** worked by acting as a bigger outer ear and making sounds louder. Modern hearing aids have tiny microphones and speakers.

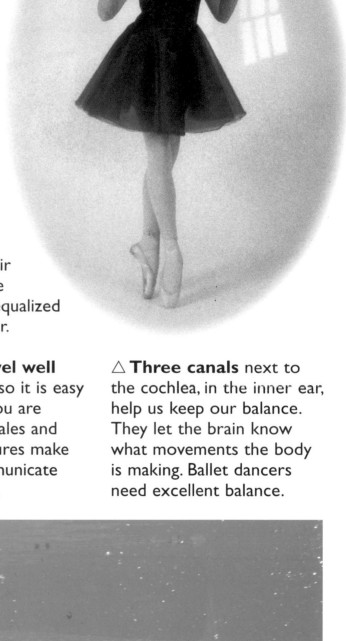

NEW WORDS

🔊 **auditory nerve** A nerve that carries messages from the ears to the brain.

🔊 **cochlea** A spiral tube in the inner ear, where vibrations are changed into nerve signals.

🔊 **eardrum** A fine sheet of skin inside the ear, which vibrates as sound waves hit it.

🔊 **Have you ever** felt your ears pop in a plane or a lift? This sometimes happens when air pressure outside changes and is equalized in the middle ear.

▽ **Sounds travel well** through liquids, so it is easy to hear when you are underwater. Whales and other sea creatures make sounds to communicate with each other.

△ **Three canals** next to the cochlea, in the inner ear, help us keep our balance. They let the brain know what movements the body is making. Ballet dancers need excellent balance.

Seeing

We use our eyes to see. Rays of light come into each eye through an opening called the pupil, which is in the middle.

A lens inside each eye then bends the light very precisely, so that it travels to an area at the back of the eye called the retina.

The light rays make an image on the retina, but the image is upside down. Nerves send information on the image to the brain, which lets us see it the right way up.

▽ **Our eyes** are about the size of table-tennis balls, but we only see a small part at the front when we look in the mirror. The pupil is surrounded by a coloured iris, which has a clear protective shield in front of it, called the cornea.

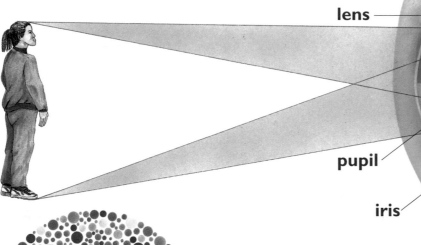

cornea

lens

pupil

iris

△ **Most people see** things in colour, but some are colour blind. This is a test card for colour blindness. Can you see the shape inside the circle?

▷ **The colour** of our eyes is really just the colour of the iris. We inherit this colour from our parents, and the most common colour is brown. If one parent has blue eyes and the other brown, their child will usually have brown eyes.

74

▷ **Many people** wear glasses or contact lenses to help them see better. These change the direction of light before it enters the eyes, so that it focuses better on the retina.

Why do we blink?
Our eyes make tears all the time. Tears are useful because they keep the cornea at the front of the eye damp. When we blink, it spreads the tears across the eyes. This keeps the eyes clean and stops them from drying out.

optic nerve

retina

day

night

NEW WORDS

cornea The clear protective layer that covers the pupil.

iris The coloured part of the eye surrounding the pupil.

pupil The opening at the front of the eye that lets in light.

retina The layer at the back of the eye that is sensitive to light.

You blink about 15 times each minute, without thinking about it. The brain controls many actions such as this automatically.

△ **When it is sunny or a bright day,** our eyes do not need to let in much light, and our pupils are small. But when there is less light, like at night-time, the pupils have to open more and they get bigger. Small muscles change the size of the iris around the pupil.

About one in every 12 men find it very difficult to tell the difference between some colours, especially red and green. Very few women are colour blind.

Mammals

There are many animals in the group we call mammals. Human beings are mammals, too. A mammal has hair or fur on its body, to help keep it warm. Baby mammals are fed with milk from their mother's body.

Mammals live all over the world, from the freezing polar regions to the hot tropics. Most mammals live on land, but whales live in the sea and bats can fly. They are known as warm-blooded animals.

△ **There are over 400** different breeds of sheep. We shear them so that we can use their furry coats to make wool.

◁ **A porcupine** has long spines, called quills. It can raise and rattle its quills to warn off any of its enemies.

△ **Some mammals,** such as this otter, have whiskers. These help them feel things and find their way about.

◁ **Bears** are large mammals with powerful legs and strong claws. They eat plants as well as meat. They live mainly on the ground but can stand on their back legs and can even climb trees.

The largest mammal is the blue whale. The largest on land is the African elephant. The tallest is the giraffe. The fastest is the cheetah. And the smallest is the tiny hog-nosed bat.

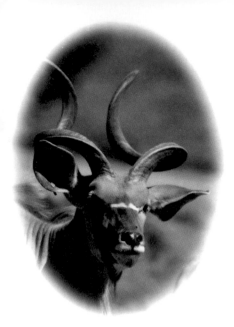

▷ **The white rhinoceros** is one of the world's five species of rhino. They all have horns and for this reason are under threat from hunters.

△ **Kudu antelopes** have beautifully curved horns. Males sometimes use these to fight each other. Kudus live in small groups in Africa, and their main enemies are leopards, lions and wild dogs.

NEW WORDS

✿ **breed** A variety of animal.

✿ **descendant** A person or animal that has come by birth from another person or animal.

✿ **tropics** The hottest part of the world, which is near the Equator.

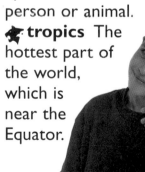

△ **Farmyard pigs** are descendants of wild boars. Farmers keep them for their meat, which we call pork, ham and bacon. The female pig, called a sow, lies down to feed milk to all her piglets at the same time.

SNOWED IN
Female polar bears dig a den in a snowdrift in the freezing Arctic region. There they give birth to their cubs in midwinter, protecting them from the severe cold and wind. The tiny cubs stay in the den for about three months. Their mother feeds them with her own milk, though she eats nothing herself. Mother and cubs come out onto the snow and ice in spring. Mother then spends most of her time looking for food, such as seals.

Apes and Monkeys

Apes are generally larger than monkeys, and they have no tails. There are four types of ape. Gorillas and chimpanzees live only in Africa, and orang-utans and gibbons live only in Southeast Asia.

Many different types of old-world monkeys are found in both Africa and Asia. The new-world monkeys of Central and South America have long tails, which they often use to hold on to branches as they swing through the trees.

Most apes and monkeys live in the world's rainforests, many of which are being destroyed.

△ **Male mandrills** have very colourful faces. Mandrills live in African forests, staying mainly on the ground in troops of up to 50 animals. They feed on fruit, nuts and small animals, and sleep in trees.

▷ **Many monkeys**, such as this macaque, live together in large troops. Each troop has a leader, usually an old, strong male. They spend most of their time in trees and have good eyesight, hearing and sense of smell.

NEW WORDS
grooming Cleaning the skin and fur.
timber Wood that is used for building or making things.
troop An organized group.

▷ **Orang-utans** live in the tropical rainforests of Borneo and Sumatra. In the Malay language, this ape's name means "man of the forest". In many places, its home is being cut down for timber. Reserves have been set up to protect it.

▽ **The gorilla** is the largest ape. Males are sometimes over 1.8 m tall, the same height as a tall man. They are powerful animals, but they are also peaceful and gentle. They rarely climb trees.

△ **Grooming** each other to get rid of irritating pests is an enjoyable group activity for these chimpanzees.

▷ **South American spider monkeys** have amazing tails which can wrap round and cling to branches.

Chimpanzees are good tool-makers. They use sticks to get honey and insects from nests, and they use stones to crack nuts.

MONKEY MOBILE
Trace this monkey (right) and cut out the shape. Draw round the shape on card and cut it out. Make two more monkeys and draw on faces. Make a small hole in each monkey and tie on pieces of thread. Roll some card into a rod and tie the monkeys to it. When the monkeys are balanced, fix the knots with a drop of glue.

79

Elephants

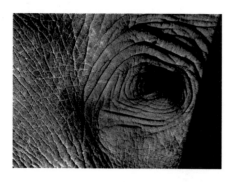

△ **Elephants** have thick, wrinkled skin. Their eyesight is not very good, but they have good hearing and an excellent sense of smell.

▷ **An elephant's tusks** are really two big teeth made of ivory. They are useful for digging and breaking off large branches. The trunk can be used to pick up food and guide it into an elephant's mouth.

▽ **Elephants love bathing.** They can give themselves a shower through their trunks and are good swimmers.

There are two species (or two different kinds), of elephant – African and Asian. The African elephant is the world's biggest land animal. Males can grow up to 4 m high at the shoulder, which is over twice as tall as a man. They can weigh up to 7 tonnes, which is as much as 90 people! Asian elephants are smaller and lighter, with smaller ears. They live in India, Sri Lanka and parts of Southeast Asia.

△ **A tree** is useful for scratching an annoying itch!

NEW WORDS
herd A large group of animals living together.
logging Cutting down trees to use the wood.
trunk An elephant's long, bendy nose.
tusk One of the two long pointed teeth sticking out of an elephant's mouth.

▷ **Asian elephants** are used in the logging industry, because they can move and carry very heavy loads. Riders sit behind the animal's neck. In some countries, elephants are still used as a means of getting about.

Elephants sometimes use their trunks as snorkels. When they swim, they can stick their trunks upwards so that they breathe in plenty of air.

Do elephants use skin care?
Yes! To prevent their skin from cracking, elephants wallow and cover themselves in cool mud. This dries on their bodies and helps protect them from the burning sun. It also gets rid of flies and ticks. An elephant's colour depends on the mud it wallows in.

◁ **Elephants** can reach food high up in trees. They are vegetarians, and their diet includes leaves, fruit, bark and roots.

Elephants live in family groups, which often join together to make large herds. Each group is led by a female elephant, who is usually the oldest. She decides which routes the herd should follow to find food and water, often travelling in single file.

81

Cats

△ **Cheetahs** are the fastest cats. In fact, they are the fastest runners in the world. They can reach a speed of 100 kph for a short distance.

Tigers are the biggest cats. From head to tail they are up to 3.7 m long. These powerful animals, however, make very good mothers to their baby cubs.

There are a number of species, or different kinds, of cats. Even the biggest wild cats are relatives of our pet cats at home!

Pet cats are used to living with people, and to being fed by their owners. But sometimes they hunt, chasing after birds and mice before pouncing. While lions and tigers roar, a pet cat just meows!

All cats are carnivores. They are built to hunt, and their bodies are powerful. To help them catch their prey, cats have sharp eyesight and a good sense of smell. They can run very fast too. Their size, colouring and coat patterns vary, but all cats have a similar shape.

▷ **Members of the cat family:** they look alike but live in different ways.

▷ **Male and female lions** look very different. The male has a big brown mane. Lions are the only cats that live together in groups, called prides. Lions like to sit around and let the lionesses do most of the hunting.

jaguar

puma

◁ **The top male** lion is challenged by other males in the pride from time to time. He has to fight them in order to keep his position as the dominant male in the group.

△ **Big cats** like flat, open country, where they can see a long way. They follow their prey until they are close enough to strike.

▷ **Pet cats** and many of the big cats don't like water. But tigers specially look out for it during the hottest part of the day. Then they are often found cooling off in a pool. They are excellent swimmers and can easily cross rivers.

Why do leopards have spots?
Because they make leopards difficult to see. From a distance, the black spots on the yellow fur look like light on the grass or in the trees. This is called camouflage. It helps the leopard to hide from the animals it is hunting, and from those hunting it.

leopard

black panther

lynx

cheetah

lions

WHALES TO SCALE

Draw whales and dolphins in scale with each other. You can use the scale 1:100. This means using a centimetre for every metre, so your blue whale will be 33 cm long. The whales' real lengths are: common dolphin 2 m, bottlenose dolphin 4 m, narwhal 6 m, pilot whale 8 m, killer whale 9 m and the huge blue whale 33 m.

△ **Pilot whales**, like the one at the top of the photo, have a big, round head. They live in large groups, called schools, of hundreds or even thousands. The other dolphin is a bottlenose.

NEW WORDS
baleen The whalebone at the front of some whales' mouths.
blowhole The nostril on top of a whale's head, through which it breathes.
dolphinarium A pool for dolphins, where they give public displays.
school A group of fish whales or dolphins.

▽ **The blue whale** is the largest animal in the world. It can grow up to 33 m long and weigh over 150 tonnes. Blue whales swim in all the world's oceans, usually alone or in small groups.

△ **These common dolphins** are leaping out of the water at great speed. Most dolphins swim at about 30 kph. This is over three times faster than even the quickest human swimmers can manage.

Instead of teeth, blue whales have strips of whalebone, called baleen. When the whales take in water, the baleen traps tiny shrimps called krill.

Other whales, such as killer whales and sperm whales, have teeth. Dolphins are small-toothed whales.

Whales and Dolphins

△ **The narwhal** is a small Arctic whale with a long tusk.

Whales and dolphins are mammals, and they cannot breathe under water like fish. So they come to the surface often, to take in air.

Whales and dolphins breathe in and out through a blowhole on the top of the head. When they let out used air, they usually send out a spray of water at the same time.

△ **Some whales and dolphins** are kept in zoos and dolphinariums. Killer whales are very popular performers. They can jump up to 5 m out of the water.

▷ **Many whales and dolphins** live and hunt for their food in groups. They eat fish, squid and shrimps.

blue whale

Reptiles

Snakes, lizards and crocodiles are all reptiles. Unlike mammals, these scaly-skinned animals are all cold-blooded. This means that they always need lots of sunshine to warm them up.

Reptiles are found on land and in water. Most live in warm parts of the world, and some live in hot deserts. They move into a burrow if it is too hot above ground, or if it is ever too cold in winter.

Most reptiles have four legs, but snakes are long, legless reptiles. All snakes are meat-eaters, and some kill their prey with poison from hollow teeth called fangs.

△ **Marine iguanas** are the only lizards that swim in the sea. They live around the Galapagos Islands, in the Pacific Ocean. They go to sea to feed on seaweed and then warm up on the islands' volcanic rocks.

The world's largest lizard is the Komodo dragon of Indonesia. It grows up to 3 m long.

▽ **The horned lizard** has strong armour, to protect it from its enemies. It has pointed scales, as well as horns behind its head. It lives in dry areas and deserts of America, where it feeds mainly on ants. The female horned lizard lays her eggs in a hole in the ground.

A skink is a kind of lizard. It can make its tail fall off if when it is attacked by an enemy. This usually confuses the enemy, so that the lizard can quickly escape. It then grows a new tail.

NEW WORDS

chameleon A lizard with a long tongue and the ability to change colour.

fang A snake's long, pointed, hollow tooth, through which it can pass its poison.

marine Living in, or from, the sea.

▷ **Chameleons** are slow-moving, tree-living lizards. If they see an insect within range, they shoot out a long sticky tongue to catch it. They can also change colour to suit their surroundings or their mood. An angry chameleon may turn black.

△ **Most reptiles lay eggs**, which are soft and leathery. Snakes lay their eggs in shallow holes and cover them with a thin layer of soil. When the baby snakes hatch out, they have to look after themselves.

The longest snake is the reticulated python of South-East Asia, which grows up to 10 m long. The most poisonous snake is the small-scaled snake living in Australia.

▽ **Emerald tree boas** live in the rainforests of South America. They wrap themselves around branches and watch out for prey, often birds and bats. They move fast and also swim very well.

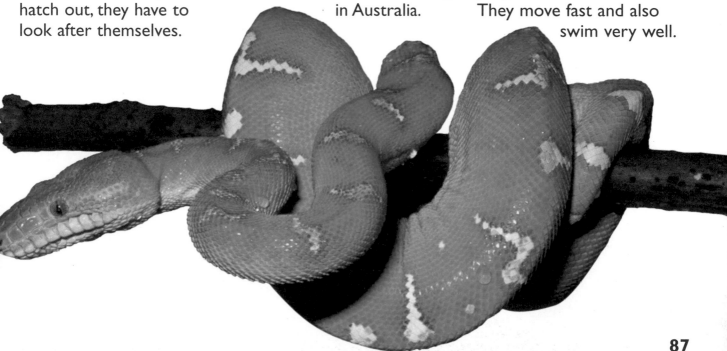

Birds

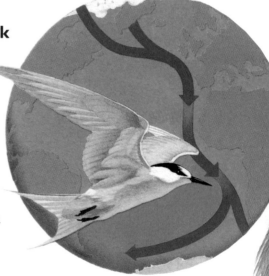

Birds are the only animals with feathers. They have wings, and most are expert fliers. There are more than 9,000 different kinds, living in all parts of the world.

Female birds lay eggs, and most build nests to protect them. When the eggs hatch out, the adults feed their young until the small birds can fly and leave the nest.

△ **Gulls** and other seabirds spend much of their time at sea. They glide over the water, waiting to swoop down to catch fish. Many seabirds nest on rocky cliffs.

▽ **Arctic terns** raise their young near the North Pole. Then they fly south to the Antarctic for the summer. In the autumn they fly north again, making a round trip of 36,000 km.

NEW WORDS
Arctic The very cold continent at the top of the world, also called The North Pole.
Antarctic The cold continent at the bottom of the world (or South Pole).
gull A large seabird.

◁ **The Indian peacock** spreads his tail feathers into a fan. He does this to attract the female peahen.

▽ **Birds** have various beaks. With its beak, a macaw can crack nuts, a pelican scoops fish, and an eagle can tear meat.

macaw

pelican

flamingo

DIFFERENT NESTS

osprey

horned grebe

barn swallow

weaver bird

willow flycatcher

ovenbird

bird of
paradise

BIRD OF PARADISE

Draw a bird of paradise on blue card with white crayon. Cut out pieces of sugar paper to fit the head and body, and stick feather shapes on the body. Add long strips of tissue paper for the tail, and don't forget feet, a beak and a button eye. You could make a rainforest background too, with real twigs and leaves.

toucan

bald eagle

△ **Rockhopper penguins** have long yellow or orange feathers above their eyes. They often nest on cliff-tops, using pebbles or grass. They reach their colony by hopping from rock to rock, as their name suggests.

△ **After a winter at sea,** Snares Island penguins arrive at the islands of the same name, south of New Zealand. They return to these islands every August to breed again.

▽ **These Adélie penguins** are waddling about on an iceberg, off the coast of Antarctica. To climb out of the sea, penguins first dive down and then shoot out of the water at great speed, landing on their feet. To get back into the sea, they simply jump in.

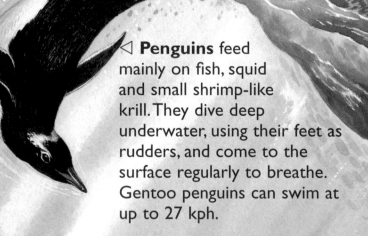

◁ **Penguins** feed mainly on fish, squid and small shrimp-like krill. They dive deep underwater, using their feet as rudders, and come to the surface regularly to breathe. Gentoo penguins can swim at up to 27 kph.

Penguins

Like all the world's birds, penguins are covered with feathers. But penguin feathers are short and thick. They are waterproof, and keep the animals warm in cold seas.

Penguins have a horny beak for catching food. They also have a small pair of wings, but nevertheless, can't fly. They use their wings as flippers. These birds spend most of their time at sea and are fast, skilful swimmers.

There are 18 different kinds of penguin, and they all live near the coasts of the cold southern oceans. Many live in the frozen region of Antarctica.

emperor penguin

little blue penguin

▷ **The smallest penguins** in the world are the little blues of Australia and New Zealand, standing 40 cm high. Emperor penguins are the biggest at 120 cm tall.

△ **Antarctic emperor penguins** keep their eggs and chicks on their feet, for warmth. It is the male bird who does this job, while the female feeds her young.

NEW WORDS

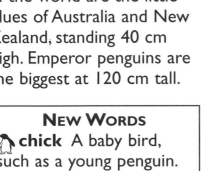

chick A baby bird, such as a young penguin.

krill Tiny shrimp-like creatures that are eaten by penguins and whales.

A PENGUIN PLAYMATE

Pour sand into an empty plastic bottle and tape a washball to the top. Tape a card beak to the head. Mix wallpaper paste and paste thin strips of newspaper over the whole penguin. Leave to dry. Then paint the penguin white. Leave to dry again before painting the head, back and flippers black, leaving white circles for the eyes. You could use your penguin as a bookend.

Amphibians

Frogs, toads, newts and salamanders belong to a group of animals called amphibians. They spend part of their lives on land and part in water, but amphibians don't live in the sea.

Amphibians go back to water when it is time to lay their eggs. Females may lay their eggs in or near a pond or stream. Most frogs and toads lay between 1,000 and 20,000 eggs. These large clusters of eggs are called spawn.

△ **Tree frogs** have round suckers at the end of their toes. These help them to grip trunks, branches and even shiny leaves.

▷ **Large North American bullfrogs** can grow up to 20 cm long. This bullfrog has caught an earthworm, but they eat much larger prey too. A big bullfrog might catch a mouse or even a small snake.

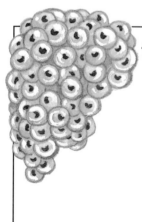

frogs eggs or spawn

froglet with legs

swimming tadpole

FROG LIFE CYCLE
A frog's eggs hatch into tadpoles in the water. The tadpoles grow legs and turn into froglets. Finally the young frogs can leave the water and hop out onto land.

young frog

◁ **This smooth-skinned giant salamander** lives in the rivers, lakes and cool, damp forests of western USA. It can grow to 30 cm long. Most salamanders are silent, but this one can make a low-pitched cry.

What are mouth-brooders?
A male mouth-brooding frog can gather up to 15 eggs with its tongue and put them in its mouth. But it doesn't eat the eggs. It keeps them in its vocal sac to turn into tadpoles. When the froglets are ready, they jump out.

▷ **Arrow-poison frogs** of South America are very poisonous. Females lay up to six eggs on land. When they hatch, the male carries the tadpoles on his back to a tree hole filled with water or to a water plant, so that they can begin life in water.

Toads usually have a rougher, bumpier skin than frogs which is often covered with warts. Toads usually live in drier places. They have wider bodies and shorter, less powerful legs, which means that they are not such good jumpers.

NEW WORDS
froglet A young frog that develops from a tadpole.
spawn The mass of eggs produced by amphibians.
tadpole The young frog or toad that develops from an egg and lives in water.
vocal sac Loose folds of skin in male frogs that can fill with air to make a noise.

△ **Frogs** have long back legs. These are good for swimming and we copy their action when we swim breaststroke. These powerful legs are also useful for jumping on land. Common frogs can leap about 60 cm, and South African sharp-nosed frogs can jump over 3 m!

Female surinam toads keep their eggs in holes in their skin. The young toads develop in these holes.

Fish

There are more than 20,000 different kinds of fish in the world's oceans, lakes and rivers. Like other animals, fish live in warm parts of the world, as well as in cold polar seas.

Many fish have streamlined bodies and fins, to help them swim. They have gills instead of lungs, so that they can breathe under water.

Fish have the same body temperature as the waters in which they live and swim.

△ **Some fish** have amazing defences. This porcupine fish has swollen up into a spiny ball. It must have sensed danger nearby.

▽ **Salmon** have to work very hard to make their way upriver from the ocean to breed. They swim against the current of the river and leap over the shallow, rocky parts.

◁ **The butterfly fish** has beautiful colours and strong contrasting markings.

▽ **The lionfish** has fins sticking out all over its body, and a row of poisonous spines. This odd fish grows up to 38 cm long.

NEW WORDS
breed To produce babies.
fin A thin flat part that sticks out of a fish's body and helps it to swim.
gill The parts of their bodies through which fishes breathe.
streamlined Shaped smoothly for moving faster.

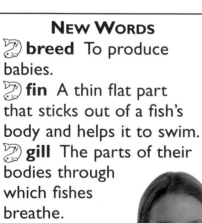

94

▽ **The ray** has a flat body, which helps it glide along the bottom of the sea. Rays feed mainly on shellfish, which they crack open with their strong teeth. Some kinds of rays can sting with their tails.

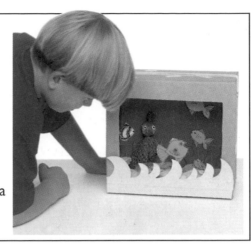

HOW FISH BREATHE
1. A fish takes in water through its mouth.

2. The water flows over its gills and oxygen passes into its bloodstream.

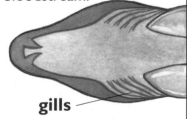

gills

3. The water is then pushed back out through the gill covers.

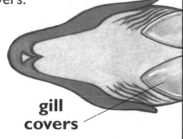

gill covers

▷ **Seahorses** look very strange. They swim in an upright position and live near seaweed, which they can hold on to with their tails. Seahorses are a fish which can change colour.

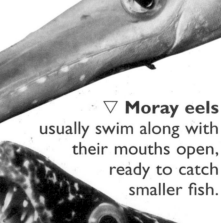

▷ **This trumpet fish** is long and thin, growing up to a metre long. Its eyes are set well back from its jaws. Compare its shape to the ray and the porcupine fish.

▽ **Moray eels** usually swim along with their mouths open, ready to catch smaller fish.

Electric eels kill fish and other sea animals with electric shocks from their tail. These big South American fish are up to 2 m long.

Insects

head

antennae

thorax

abdomen

△ **This wasp** shows the three basic body parts of an insect – a head, a thorax and an abdomen. Its legs and wings are attached to the thorax, and its antennae to the head.

▽ **This honey bee** is collecting nectar and pollen from a flower. The bee will take the food to its nest, where it will be stored as honey.

Insects are tiny animals that are found all over the world – from scorching deserts to steaming rainforests and icy lakes.

Insects have no backbone, and they are protected by a hard, outer skeleton or shell. Because they are so small, they can fit into tiny places and don't need much food to live on. They all have six legs, and most have wings and can fly. Many insects have two pairs of wings, but flies have just one pair.

termite mound

food stores

queen's chamber

tunnel

egg chambers

▷ **Termites** live in colonies and build huge mounds as nests. Each colony is ruled by a king and a queen. Soldier termites defend the nest, and most of the termites are workers.

◁ **Ladybirds** are a kind of beetle. They feed on much smaller insects, called aphids and scale insects, which they find on plants. The ladybird's hard, outer wings protect the flying wings underneath.

▷ **Female mosquitoes** are bloodsuckers. They insert a needle-like tube into birds and mammals, including humans, and suck up a tiny amount of blood.

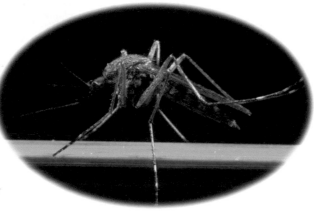

△ **Beetles** live just about everywhere on Earth. Some live in water, and many can fly. This horned beetle is found in Borneo, in Southeast Asia.

A single bee would have to visit more than 4,000 flowers to make one tablespoon of honey. A large beehive may contain 60,000 worker bees.

NEW WORDS
abdomen The lower or back part of an insect's body.
antennae An insect's very sensitive feelers, attached to its head.
aphid A tiny insect that feeds on plants.
termite Also called a white ant, this insect lives in a colony.
thorax The upper or front part of an insect's body, to which its wings and legs are attached.

◁ **Scorpions** have a poisonous sting in their tails, which they use to paralyse prey. They also have powerful claws.

▷ **A hunting spider** from Costa Rica in, Central America. But spiders also live in cold parts of the world.

△ **Trapdoor spiders** have a very clever system for catching insects. The spider digs a burrow, lines it with silk and covers the entrance with a trapdoor. Then it lies in wait. When an insect passes nearby, the spider feels the ground move. Then it jumps out and catches the insect, quickly dragging it into its burrow.

△ **Web-making spiders** feel the silk threads of the web move when an insect is caught. They tie their prey up in a band of silk.

◁ **Garden spiders** spin beautiful circular webs. These are easily damaged, and the spiders spend a lot of time repairing them. The webs show up well when the air outside is damp.

Spiders

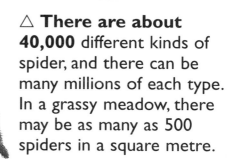

Spiders are similar in some ways to insects, but they belong to a different group of animals called arachnids. Scorpions, ticks and mites are arachnids too.

Spiders have eight legs, while insects have six. Many spiders spin silky webs to catch flies and other small insects. They have fangs for seizing their prey. Most spiders paralyse their prey with poison before they kill and eat them. But only a few spiders are poisonous to humans.

△ **There are about 40,000** different kinds of spider, and there can be many millions of each type. In a grassy meadow, there may be as many as 500 spiders in a square metre.

NEW WORDS
※ **arachnid** A group of animals that includes spiders, scorpions, ticks and mites.
※ **paralyse** To make something unable to move.
※ **spiderling** A young spider.

△ **Most spiders** and other arachnids have eight eyes. But spiders still do not see very well. They rely on touching things to know what is going on around them.

△ **A spider with its prey.** If spiders were not good hunters, the world would be overrun with insects.

◁ **Female spiders** lay up to 2,000 eggs, which they wrap in a bundle of silk threads. Spiderlings hatch from the eggs.

Molluscs and Crustaceans

Can squids shoot ink?
Squids and octopuses can shoot out a stream of inky fluid when they want to get away from enemies. The ink clouds the water and confuses the enemy, giving the mollusc time to escape.

Some molluscs, such as octopuses, have soft bodies. Others, such as snails, are protected by shells. Some molluscs live on land but many live in the sea.

Crustaceans get their name from their crusty covering. Most of them, such as crabs, lobsters and prawns, live in the sea. A few crustaceans, such as woodlice, live on land.

Molluscs and crustaceans all begin life as eggs, and most of them have a larva stage.

△ **Squids** are related to octopuses. They take in water and push it out again through a funnel behind their head. This acts like a jet engine and shoots them along backwards.

△ **Hermit crabs** use the shells of sea snails for protection. Some kill and eat the snail to get both a meal and a home. When it outgrows the shell, the crab looks for a new one.

The world's largest crustacean is the giant spider crab, with a leg-span of almost 4 m. The smallest are water fleas, less than 0.25 mm long.

△ **Sallylightfoot crabs** live on the rocky shores of the Galapagos Islands, off South America. As they grow, they shed their shell and grow a larger one. Their shell measures up to 15 cm across.

100

◁ **Octopuses** are eight-armed molluscs. Many are very small, but the largest have tentacles up to 3.5 m long. Octopuses can change colour according to their surroundings, so they can easily hide.

△ **Lobsters** are among the largest crustaceans. They walk across the seabed on four pairs of legs.

▷ Crabs' legs are made in such a way that they can walk sideways. The front pair of legs have strong pincers which they use for picking up food. They use the back pair of legs as paddles when they swim. Most crabs live in or near the sea.

△ **A garden snail's soft body** has a muscular foot, which it uses to creep along. The snail's whole body can be pulled safely into its shell if it is threatened by another animal.

NEW WORDS

🐌 **leg-span** The widest distance between the legs at full stretch.

🐌 **shed** To let something fall off.

🐌 **tentacle** A long bendy body part, like an arm, that is used for feeling, moving and grasping.

TREASURE CHEST
Collect some empty shells on holiday and wash them out. Paint a box and stick some shells on the lid with PVA glue. Paint the gaps with glue and sprinkle on some sand. Glue shells around the sides of the box in patterns. When the shells are firmly stuck, brush more glue on top to varnish them. Now you can lock away all your secrets – as well as any spare shells – in your treasure chest.

Early Life

Life on Earth has been developing and changing over billions of years. Scientists now believe that the simplest forms of life began in the world's oceans, probably over three billion years ago.

We can only guess what the very first plants and animals looked like. But we think that many early sea animals had soft bodies, without shells, bones or other hard parts. They included jellyfish, different kinds of worms and other creatures related to starfishes.

△ **This is blue-green algae,** one of the simplest forms of life, seen through a microscope. It is made up of a skin surrounding a watery "soup", and has no complicated parts.

◁ **These jellyfish,** sea pens and worms lived in the world's oceans about 650 million years ago. They were mainly on the seabed.

NEW WORDS
algae Plants that grow in the sea, without true stems, leaves or roots.
jellyfish A sea animal with an umbrella-shaped body like jelly.
sea pen A feather-shaped sea animal related to jellyfish.
starfish A sea animal that has the shape of a five-pointed star.

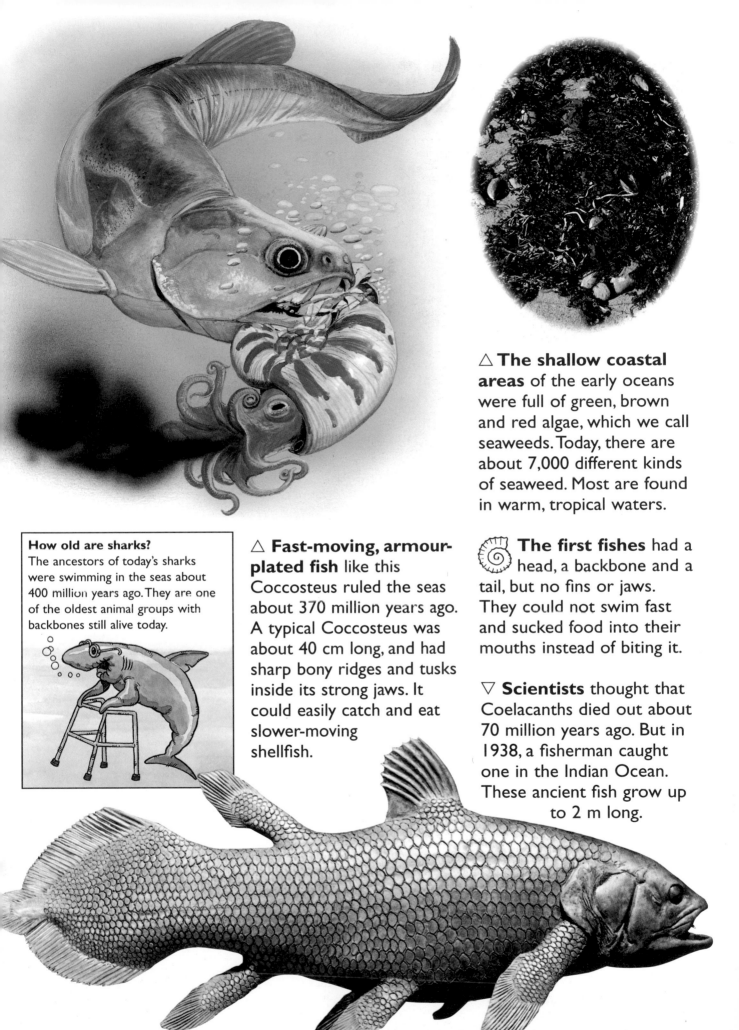

△ **The shallow coastal areas** of the early oceans were full of green, brown and red algae, which we call seaweeds. Today, there are about 7,000 different kinds of seaweed. Most are found in warm, tropical waters.

How old are sharks?
The ancestors of today's sharks were swimming in the seas about 400 million years ago. They are one of the oldest animal groups with backbones still alive today.

△ **Fast-moving, armour-plated fish** like this Coccosteus ruled the seas about 370 million years ago. A typical Coccosteus was about 40 cm long, and had sharp bony ridges and tusks inside its strong jaws. It could easily catch and eat slower-moving shellfish.

The first fishes had a head, a backbone and a tail, but no fins or jaws. They could not swim fast and sucked food into their mouths instead of biting it.

▽ **Scientists** thought that Coelacanths died out about 70 million years ago. But in 1938, a fisherman caught one in the Indian Ocean. These ancient fish grow up to 2 m long.

103

The Age of Amphibians

About 360 million years ago, some sea creatures left the water and crawled out onto land. Already there were many different fish in the sea, as well as plants and insects on land.

By now some animals could live on land and in water. We call these animals amphibians, which means "having a double life". Steamy swamps and forests were an ideal place for them to live. Amphibians laid their eggs in water. The eggs hatched into swimming tadpoles, and when they became adults, they moved onto the land. This is exactly how amphibians such as frogs and toads live today.

swampy forest

peat bog

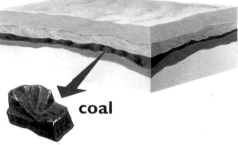

coal

△ **Dead leaves** and branches formed layers of plant material in the swampy forests of the early amphibians. This made peat, and when this was covered by rocks, the pressure turned it into coal.

▷ **Ichthyostega** was one of the first amphibians. It was about 1 m long. Giant dragonflies and many other insects lived among the tall, treelike ferns.

◁ **Ancient coal** has provided us with knowledge about the past, as well as fuel. Some leaves survived intact as the coal was formed and made fossils like this one.

▷ **This North American bullfrog** is a good example of a modern amphibian. Bullfrogs spend most of their time near water. All frogs breathe through lungs, as well as through their skin. Today there are about 4,000 different kinds of amphibians round the world, including frogs, toads, newts and salamanders.

Early amphibians were much bigger than they are today. The early giants died out about 200 million years ago. But there is one exception, a giant salamander, which lives in China and can grow to a length of 1.8 m.

PREHISTORIC LANDSCAPE

Use a large cereal box as a base, with the lid as a background. Cut and tape the box, line it with blue paper, cut out a volcano and stick it on. Use tissue paper for giant ferns, and put cellophane over some blue paper for a lake. Colour some sand green with food colouring and sprinkle it on the base. Build rocks with stones and cones, and add a plasticine dinosaur.

NEW WORDS

amphibian An animal that lives on land but lays its eggs in water.

dragonfly An insect with a long body and two pairs of thin wings.

peat Rotted plant material in the ground.

swamp An area of wet, low and marshy ground.

LIZARD HIPS AND BIRD HIPS

Scientists have divided dinosaurs into two main groups, according to the shapes of their hips. One group, including Tyrannosaurus (above right), had hips shaped like those of a modern lizard. The other group, which included Stegosaurus (below), had hips like a bird.

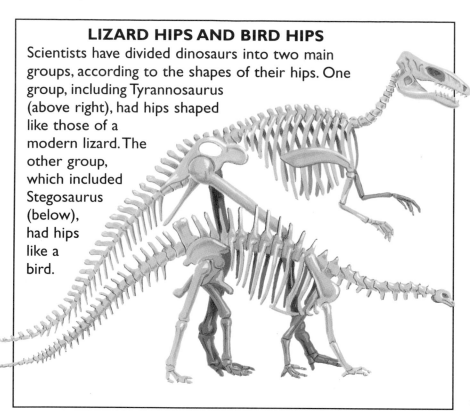

All the meat-eating dinosaurs and big four-legged plant-eaters were lizard-hipped. The later bird-hipped dinosaurs were all plant-eaters.

◁ **This scientist** is working at Dinosaur National Monument, in Utah, USA. More than 5,000 dinosaur fossils have been found there. The most common remains have been those of Stegosaurus.

▷ **This barrel-bodied plant-eater** used to be called Brontosaurus. But then it was found to be the same as earlier fossils called Apatosaurus, so the first name was chosen for this creature.

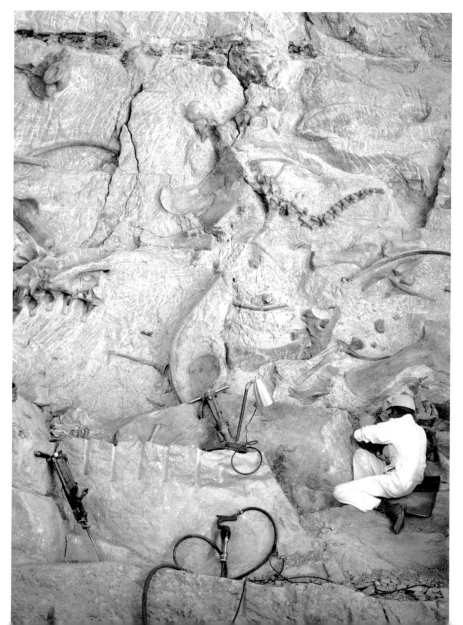

Dinosaurs

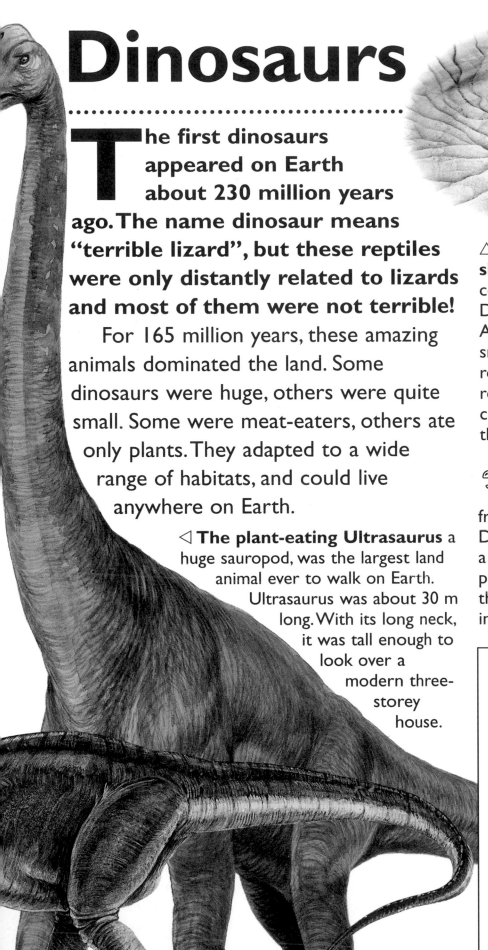

The first dinosaurs appeared on Earth about 230 million years ago. The name dinosaur means "terrible lizard", but these reptiles were only distantly related to lizards and most of them were not terrible!

For 165 million years, these amazing animals dominated the land. Some dinosaurs were huge, others were quite small. Some were meat-eaters, others ate only plants. They adapted to a wide range of habitats, and could live anywhere on Earth.

◁ **The plant-eating Ultrasaurus** a huge sauropod, was the largest land animal ever to walk on Earth. Ultrasaurus was about 30 m long. With its long neck, it was tall enough to look over a modern three-storey house.

△ **Hundreds of dinosaur skeletons** have been collected in the badlands of Dinosaur Provincial Park, in Alberta, Canada. Rain and snow have worn away the rocks, uncovering the reptile remains. Dinosaur collectors first rushed to the area in the early 1900s.

Today's scientists move large bones from regions such as Dinosaur Provincial Park by a helicopter or truck. They put the pieces together, and the skeletons are displayed in a nearby museum.

SIZES
Dinosaurs came in all sizes. Compsognathus was a small, fast-moving, meat-eater with very sharp teeth. It was 70 cm to 1.4 m long, including its long tail. It probably ate large insects, lizards and mouse-like mammals.

Meat-eating Dinosaurs

The dinosaur carnivores, or meat-eaters, were powerfully built animals. They walked upright on their two back legs, and their shorter arms ended in hands with clawed fingers.

The big meat-eaters, such as Tyrannosaurus, had a huge head on a short neck. They had very strong, sharp teeth. Nearly all meat-eaters had a long, muscular tail, which they carried straight out behind them. This helped them to balance their heavy weight. Their strong back legs made meat-eaters the fastest of all the dinosaurs.

△ **Oviraptor** had a tall crest on the top of its head. This bird-like creature fed on other dinosaurs' eggs, which it scooped up in its three-fingered hands and cracked open with its strong jaws. Oviraptors were about 2 m long.

Which was fastest?
We don't know how fast dinosaurs could run, but scientists think Struthiomimus was one of the fastest. It was 4 m long, looked like an ostrich and may have reached speeds of 50 kph.

◁ **Allosaurus** was one of the biggest meat-eaters before Tyrannosaurus. It was 11 m long. We don't know what colour dinosaurs were, but some might have been brightly coloured.

Ostrich-like Struthiomimus was an omnivore: it ate animals and plants. Its long claws could hook leaves and fruit from low trees. It also fed on insects and lizards.

MAKE A MEAT-EATER'S TOOTH

Model a big ball of self-hardening clay into the shape of a meat-eating dinosaur's tooth. Texture the surface and mark it so that it looks ancient and fossilized. It may take up to two days for the tooth to harden. When it is hard, paint your ferocious tooth.

Baryonyx claw

Tyrannosaurus tooth

△ **Baryonyx** had long, curved thumb-claws. Tyrannosaurus had enormous teeth. They were up to 18 cm long, with sharp edges like steak knives. Tooth finds have helped to tell us what different dinosaurs fed on.

🦖 **The Age of the Dinosaurs** is divided into three periods: the Triassic (240-205 million years ago), the Jurassic (205-138 million years ago) and the Cretaceous period (138-65 million years ago).

▷ **Tyrannosaurus** was about 12 m long and weighed over 6 tonnes. Its forward-facing eyes helped it to judge distance well as it moved in to attack smaller dinosaurs. Its tiny arms look feeble but held sharp claws.

Plant-eating Dinosaurs

Which had the longest neck?
Mamenchisaurus, a huge plant-eater found in China, had the longest neck of any animal ever known. Its neck was 15 m long - longer than eight tall men lying head to toe!

The dinosaur herbivores, or plant-eaters, fed on the vegetation they could reach. Small herbivores ate roots and plants on the ground, and others may have reared up on their back legs to reach higher leaves.

The long-necked sauropods, such as Diplodocus, were tall enough to reach the treetops. These huge animals must have spent nearly all their time eating.

NEW WORDS

herbivore A vegetarian animal that eats only plants.

rear up To raise itself on its back legs.

stud A curved lump or knob.

vegetation Living plants, including twigs and the leaves of trees.

Scutellosaurus was a tiny plant-eater, about the size of a modern cat. It had rows of bony studs along its back and tail, to protect it from attack by any larger meat-eaters. It could walk or run on its back legs, as well as on all fours.

IGUANODON
This large, heavy dinosaur was a peaceful plant-eater that could stand and walk either on its back legs or on all fours. It had spiked thumbs, which it may have used to defend itself if it was attacked by a hungry meat-eater.

◁ **Long-necked plant-eaters** may also have reared up to reach even higher treetops. Diplodocus picked leaves off with its front teeth, but had no back teeth for chewing.

The huge shoulder bones of Ultrasaurus were 2.7 m long, much longer than the tallest human. Its hip bones were also bigger than a man. Ultrasaurus was about 30 m long.

DIG UP A DIPLODOCUS
Cut up straws for bones and make them into a complete skeleton on a cardboard base. Brush each straw with PVA glue and fix them firmly into position. Leave the straws to dry, and then brush more glue between the bones and around the whole skeleton. Sprinkle all over with sand. After a few minutes, tip the surplus sand onto newspaper. Then you'll have your very own fossilized Diplodocus!

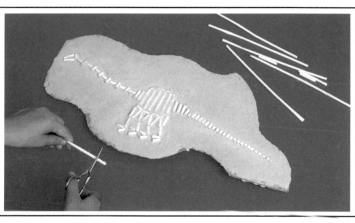

▽ **Diplodocus** was about 27 m long and weighed 12 tonnes. Its bones have been found in the western USA, and the first skeleton was discovered in Wyoming in 1899. Its whiplash tail was even longer than its neck and was made up of over 80 bones.

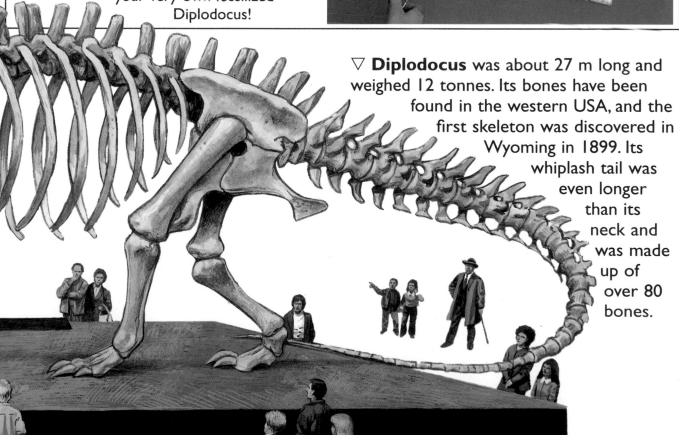

Helmets, Spines and Armour

Big, slow-moving animals need to protect themselves against fast, fierce meat-eaters. Many plant-eating dinosaurs had some form of armour-plating to offer this protection.

Some dinosaurs had plates and spines running down their back and tail. Others had spikes that grew in their skin. They even had a bony club at the end of their tail, which was a powerful weapon against attackers. One group of dinosaurs had thick, bony skulls, which they used to head-butt each other during fights.

△ **The largest** bone-headed dinosaur, Pachycephalosaurus, had a thick, dome-shaped skull. This head-butting creature was 4.6 m long.

Styracosaurus lived on Earth about 75 million years ago, and fossils have been found in the USA and Canada.

Triceratops' teeth were hard on one side. The other, softer side wore down faster, leaving a sharp cutting edge.

Stegosaurus was about 9 m long, but it had a small head and its brain was little bigger than a walnut. Dinosaurs' skulls were filled mainly with muscle and bone.

△ **Styracosaurus** had long spikes sticking out of a bony frill. It also had a large nose horn, like a modern rhinoceros.

CARD STEGOSAURUS

Cut the sides off some large cardboard boxes and tape them together. Draw the long dinosaur body shape of a Stegosaurus (see the photograph, right) and cut it out. Make plates and tail spikes from card, and use eggcups for scales. Paint the eggcups green and stick them on the body. Fasten the plates with tape. Screw up lots of pieces of tissue paper and glue them all over your dinosaur's body. You could use a bottle top for a beady, prehistoric eye!

◁ **Triceratops** means "three-horned face". Although the horns were for self-defence, scientists think that these dinosaurs may also have fought one another.

△ **Euoplocephalus** had slabs of bony armour, spikes on its back and a clubbed tail. It used its powerful muscles to swing its tail at any enemies.

NEW WORDS
armour A protective covering for the body.
club Something heavy, like a tail, that can be used as a weapon.
frill A fold of skin and bone for protection around the neck.
head-butt To use its head to hit another dinosaur on the head.

113

▷ **This is Meteor Crater,** in Arizona, USA. It is over a kilometre across and was made about 50,000 years ago when a meteorite hit Earth. Some scientists think a much bigger asteroid might have struck Earth 65 million years ago.

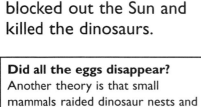 **A huge crashing meteorite** could have caused the dust that blocked out the Sun and killed the dinosaurs.

Did all the eggs disappear?
Another theory is that small mammals raided dinosaur nests and ate so many eggs all at once that there were no more dinosaur babies. This seems an unlikely story.

NEW WORDS
asteroid A tiny or minor planet.
erupt To throw out rocks, gases and other material.
meteorite A rock-like object from space that hits the Earth.

▷ **If we had not found fossilized bones,** we would not even know that dinosaurs ever existed.

▽ **It could be that many vast volcanoes** erupted over a period of a few years or even longer. This might have made the Earth too hot, poisoned the air and blotted out the Sun.

Dinosaurs Die Out

Dinosaurs became extinct, or died out, about 65 million years ago. The great reptiles of the sea and air disappeared at the same time. We are not sure why this happened.

It could be that at that time the Earth became covered in dust and smoke, blocking out sunlight for months or even years. Plants and many animals, including dinosaurs, could not have survived this catastrophe.

▽ **Plant-eaters** such as Saltasaurus (below) and meat-eaters like Tyrannosaurus, were among the last known dinosaurs. The meat-eaters ran out of food once the plant-eaters had died out!

FIR

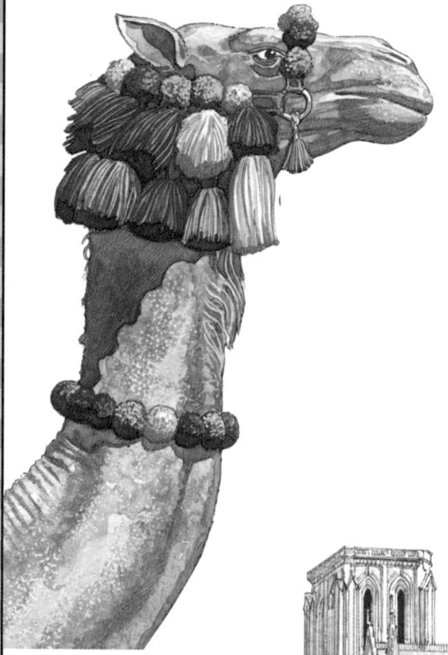

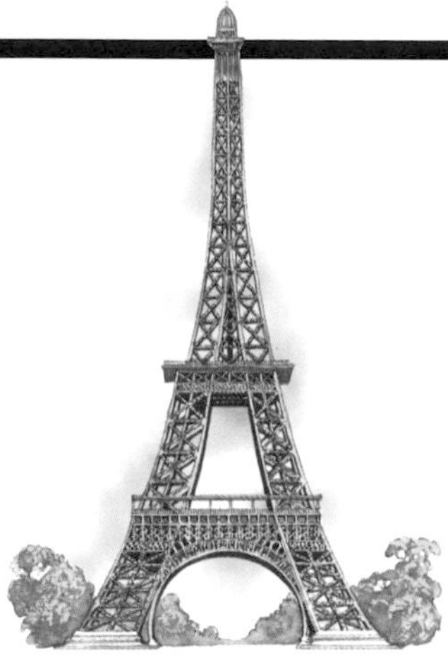

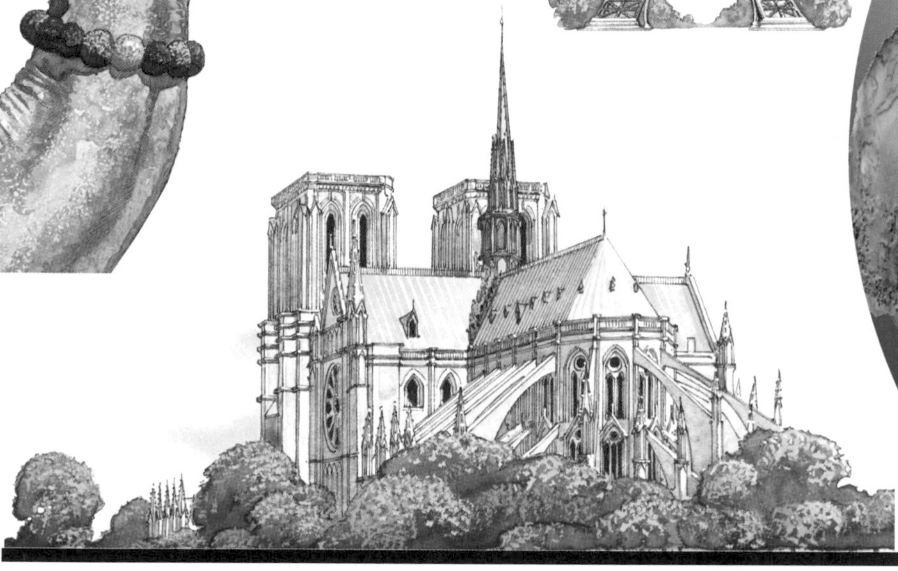

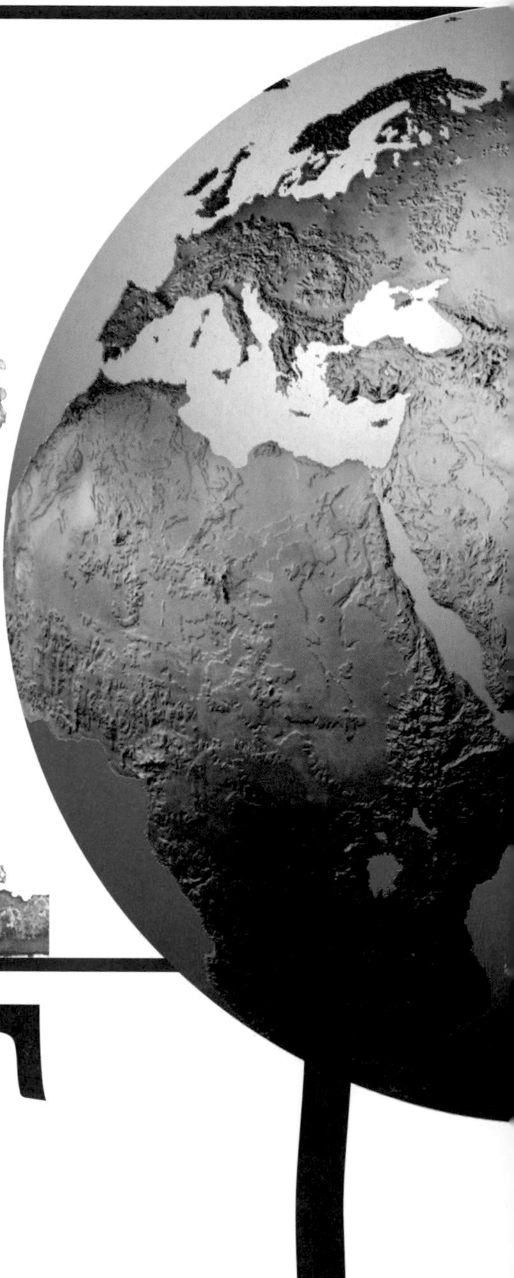

ATL

Introduction

Earth Facts

The world we live in is a planet, a huge ball of rock which flies through space. It is called Earth. The Earth travels around our local star, which is called the Sun. As it travels, it spins round and round. It stays on course because it is pulled towards the Sun by a force called gravity. The Earth is one of nine planets which circle the Sun. It is also the only planet on which living things are known to exist.

When we see pictures of Earth taken from out in space, it looks beautiful. We can see the bright blue of the oceans. We can see the brown of the rocks and soil that make up big areas of land. These are called continents. We can see swirling white patterns, too. These are clouds, made up of tiny drops of water. They float in the air which surrounds the planet. Air and water make it possible for us to live on Earth.

Deserts are very dry areas of rock, stones or sand. This desert is part of **Death Valley**, in the USA.

High mountain ranges are covered by snow and ice. These are the **Andes** mountains, in South America.

The giant clam is one of the fascinating and varied sorts of sea life found on the **Great Barrier Reef**, off the coast of Queensland in Australia.

118

What is a map?

A map is a plan showing the planet's surface. The Earth's surface is curved, so it can only be shown properly on a round globe. Maps are normally on paper, and so the surface has to be shown as if it were flat.

Many maps show the lie of the land. You can see which areas are low and which are high. You can pick out mountain peaks, coasts and rivers, lakes and seas. These are called natural features. Some maps just show the borders of countries, states and provinces. Some show cities, roads and railway lines. The maps in this atlas show the land and coastlines as well as national borders and cities.

Spot the mountain
Maps use little badges called symbols. A small black triangle means 'mountain'. Look for the name of the peak and its height in metres above sea level. Other symbols are shown below.

HOKKAIDO

Kuril Is. (Russia)

Asahi Mt. 2,290 m

Sapporo

Kitakami

Sendai

JAPAN

Read the map
This map is of Japan. What are the names of the four main islands? Is the land mostly flat or mountainous?

Mito

HONSHU

Tokyo

Yokohama

Mt. Fuji 3,776 m

Kyoto   Nagoya

Kobe

Hiroshima   Osaka

PACIFIC OCEAN

Kitakyushu

Fukuoka

SHIKOKU

Kii Channel

KYUSHU

Towns and cities
Towns and cities are shown by round dots. Each country's chief city, or capital, is shown by a square.

Where in the world?
Look for the little round maps to see just where each map fits on to the globe as a whole

Key to symbols
capital city	■
city or town	●
mountain	▲
national border	—
coastline	
river	—
lake	■
highlands	
plains	■

Introduction

Countries of the World

Bolivian women come into market, high in the Andes mountains of South America.

There are 192 countries in the world that are called independent. That means that they rule themselves. Many other lands are called dependencies or colonies, which means that they are ruled by other countries. The number of countries changes all the time, as some split up or else join together to make new nations. The world's biggest country is the Russian Federation, and the world's smallest is Vatican City, which fits inside Rome, the capital of Italy. The country with the most people is China. Nobody at all lives in Antarctica, apart from a few visiting scientists, but several countries claim parts of this land.

The ancestors of the **Araucanian peoples** lived in Chile long before their land was invaded by Europeans.

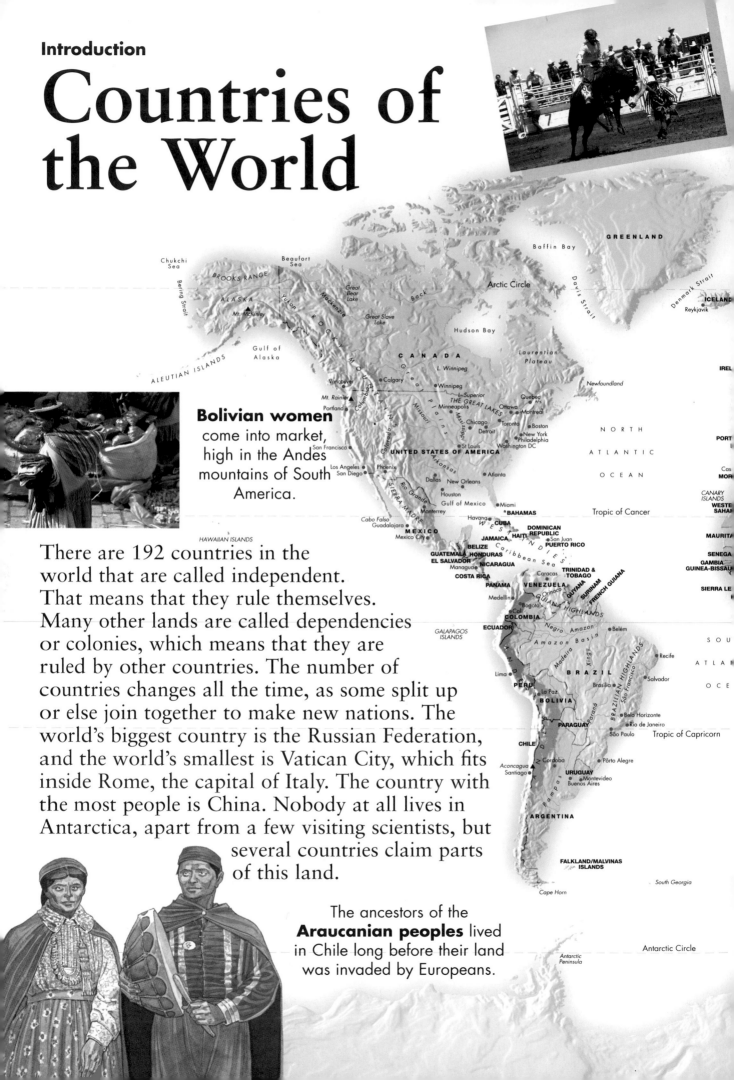

GREENLAND

Chukchi Sea
Beaufort Sea
Baffin Bay
Arctic Circle
ICELAND
Reykjavik
Denmark Strait
Davis Strait

BROOKS RANGE
ALASKA
Mt. McKinley
Yukon
Mackenzie
Great Bear Lake
Back
Great Slave Lake
Hudson Bay
Laurentian Plateau
Newfoundland
IREL

Bering Strait
Gulf of Alaska
ALEUTIAN ISLANDS
ROCKY MOUNTAINS
CANADA
Great Plains
L. Winnipeg
L. Superior
THE GREAT LAKES
Ottawa
Quebec
Montreal

Vancouver
Calgary
Winnipeg
Missouri
Mississippi
Chicago
Detroit
Toronto
Boston
New York
Philadelphia
Washington DC
NORTH
ATLANTIC
OCEAN
PORT

Mt. Rainier
Portland
Columbia
Minneapolis
St Louis
Cas
MOR

San Francisco
UNITED STATES OF AMERICA
Arkansas
Atlanta
CANARY ISLANDS
WESTE
SAHA

Los Angeles
San Diego
Phoenix
Dallas
New Orleans
SIERRA MADRE
Rio Grande
Houston
Gulf of Mexico
Miami
Tropic of Cancer
MAURITA

HAWAIIAN ISLANDS
Cabo Falso
Guadalajara
MEXICO
Mexico City
Monterrey
Havana
BAHAMAS
CUBA
WEST INDIES
DOMINICAN REPUBLIC
HAITI
San Juan
PUERTO RICO
SENEGA
GAMBIA
GUINEA-BISSAU

BELIZE
JAMAICA
GUATEMALA
HONDURAS
EL SALVADOR
NICARAGUA
Managua
Caribbean Sea
SIERRA LE

COSTA RICA
Caracas
TRINIDAD & TOBAGO
PANAMA
VENEZUELA
Medellin
Orinoco
GUYANA
SURINAM
FRENCH GUIANA

GALAPAGOS ISLANDS
ECUADOR
COLOMBIA
Bogota
Cali
GUIANA HIGHLANDS
Negro
Amazon
Belém
SOU
ATLA
OCE

Lima
PERU
La Paz
BOLIVIA
Amazon Basin
Madeira
Xingu
Tapajós
BRAZIL
Brasília
São Francisco
Recife
Salvador
BRAZILIAN HIGHLANDS

ANDES
PARAGUAY
Paraná
Belo Horizonte
Rio de Janeiro
São Paulo
Tropic of Capricorn

CHILE
Aconcagua
Santiago
Cordoba
Pampas
URUGUAY
Montevideo
Buenos Aires
Pôrto Alegre

ARGENTINA

FALKLAND/MALVINAS ISLANDS
South Georgia
Cape Horn

Antarctic Peninsula
Antarctic Circle

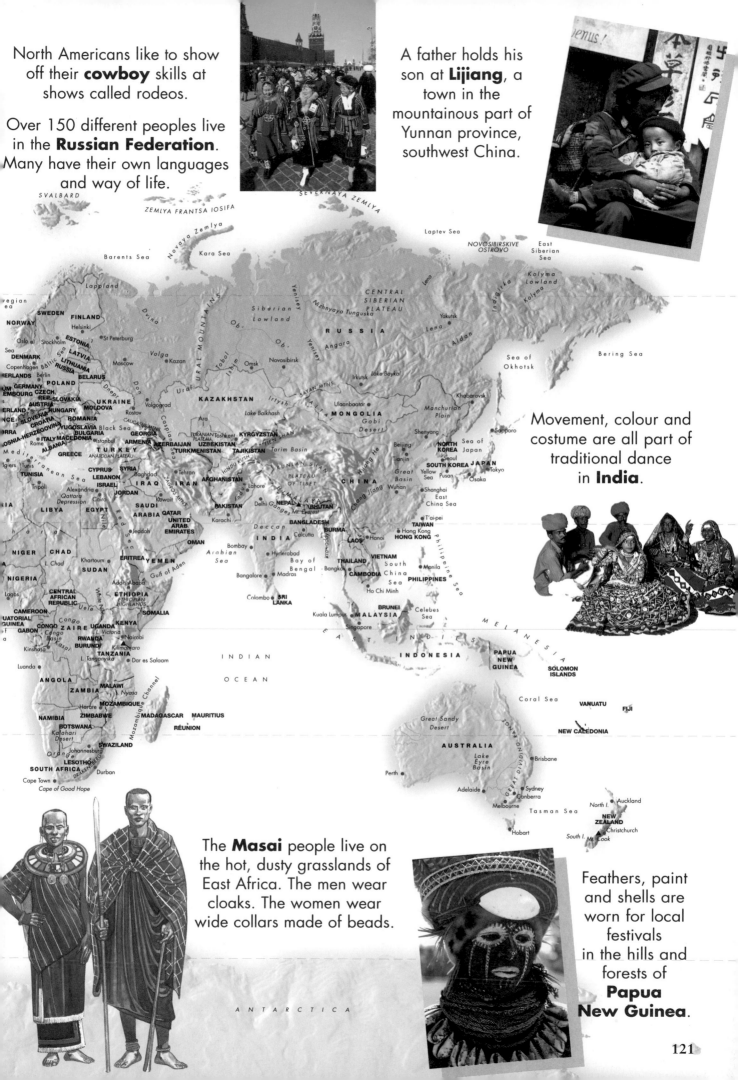

North Americans like to show off their **cowboy** skills at shows called rodeos.

Over 150 different peoples live in the **Russian Federation**. Many have their own languages and way of life.

A father holds his son at **Lijiang**, a town in the mountainous part of Yunnan province, southwest China.

Movement, colour and costume are all part of traditional dance in **India**.

The **Masai** people live on the hot, dusty grasslands of East Africa. The men wear cloaks. The women wear wide collars made of beads.

Feathers, paint and shells are worn for local festivals in the hills and forests of **Papua New Guinea**.

121

Europe

Scandinavia and Finland

The Baltic and the North Sea are divided by two long arms of the European mainland, which together are known as Scandinavia. The southern arm is called Jutland. Along with several large islands it makes up a country called Denmark. This land is flat and green. Its farms produce butter and bacon.

The other long arm of land stretches down from the Arctic. Its coastline is ragged, with deep sea inlets called fiords in the west. Mountains run down from north to south. There are big forests and thousands of lakes, sparkling blue in summer, but frozen over during the harsh northern winter. The western lands belong to Norway and the eastern lands to Sweden. Oil is taken from beneath the North Sea, metals from the land and timber from the forests. The eastern shores of the Baltic Sea are taken up by Finland, a land of forests and lakes stretching to the borders of Russia.

These soldiers are on duty outside **Amalienborg Castle** in **Denmark**. Their job is to guard the life of the Danish queen.

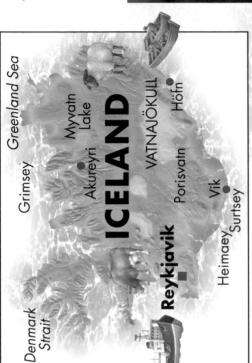

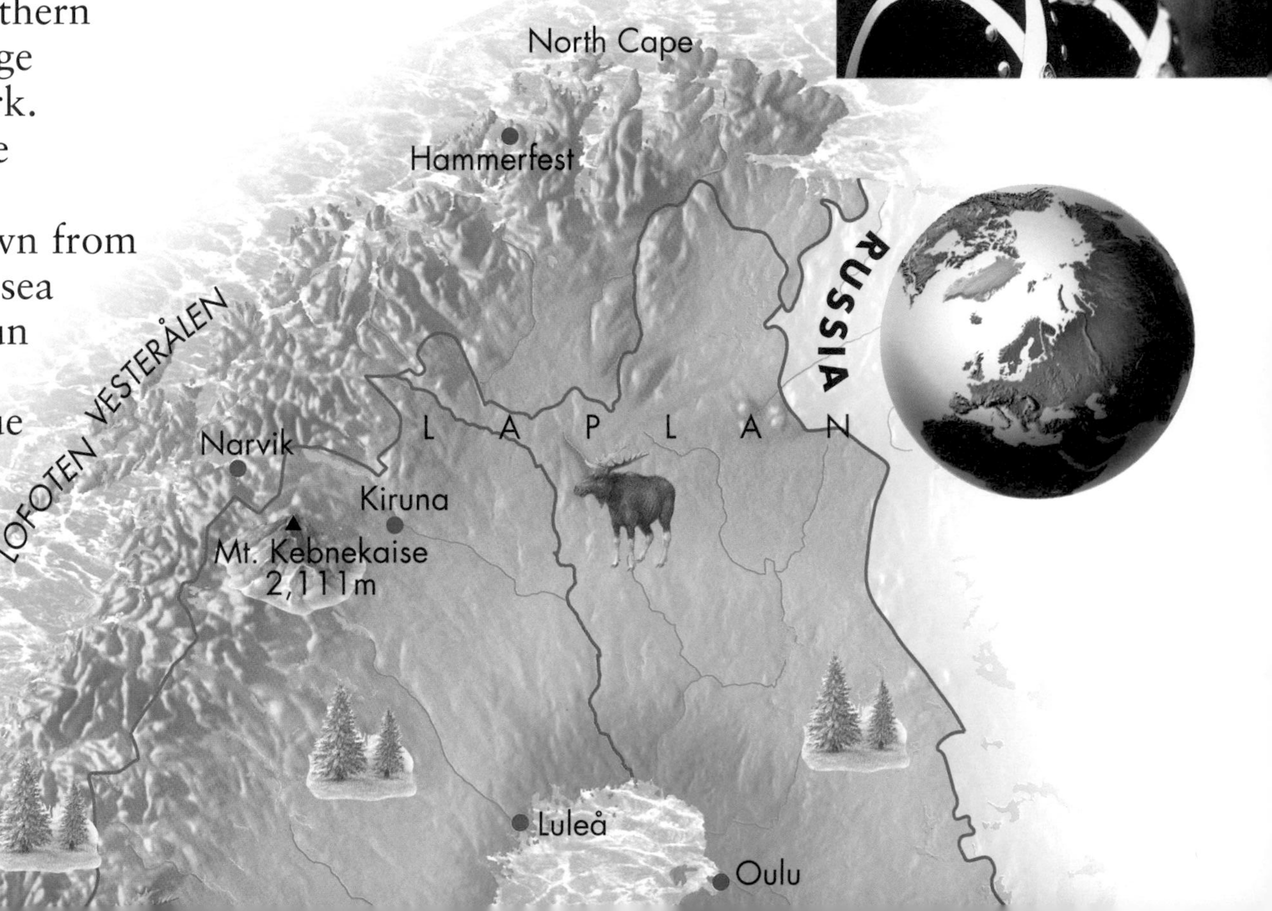

Iceland map:

Greenland Sea

Grimsey

Myvatn Lake

Akureyri

ICELAND

VATNAJÖKULL

Höfn

Porisvatn

Vik

Heimaey

Surtsey

Reykjavik

Denmark Strait

Main map labels:

RUSSIA

North Cape

Hammerfest

L A P L A N D

Oulu

Luleå

Kiruna

Mt. Kebnekaise 2,111m

Narvik

LOFOTEN VESTERÅLEN

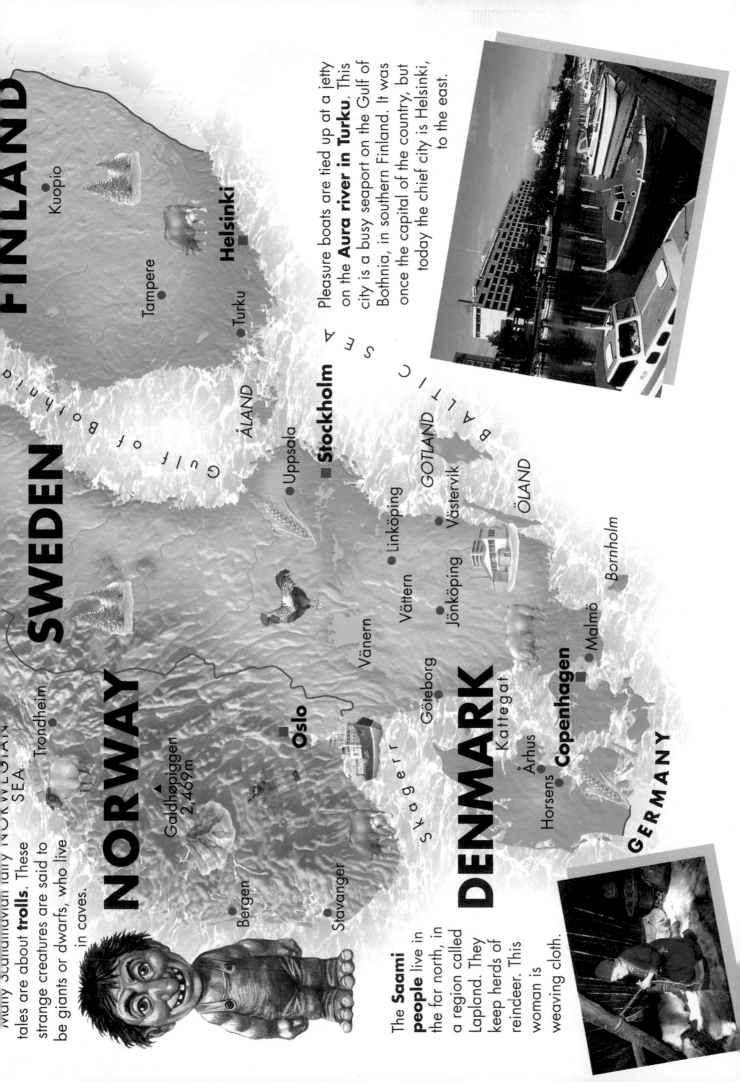

FINLAND

Kuopio

Tampere

Helsinki

Turku

ÅLAND

Pleasure boats are tied up at a jetty on the **Aura river in Turku**. This city is a busy seaport on the Gulf of Bothnia, in southern Finland. It was once the capital of the country, but today the chief city is Helsinki, to the east.

Gulf of Bothnia

SWEDEN

Uppsala

Stockholm

Linköping

GOTLAND

Västervik

ÖLAND

Vättern

Jönköping

Vänern

Bornholm

Göteborg

Malmö

BALTIC SEA

NORWAY

Trondheim

Galdhøpiggen
2,469m

Oslo

Bergen

Stavanger

S k a g e r r

Kattegat

DENMARK

Århus

Copenhagen

Horsens

GERMANY

Many Scandinavian fairy tales are about **trolls**. These strange creatures are said to be giants or dwarfs, who live in caves.

The **Saami people** live in the far north, in a region called Lapland. They keep herds of reindeer. This woman is weaving cloth.

NORWEGIAN SEA

Low Countries

The Netherlands and Belgium border the North Sea and are very low lying. For hundreds of years the people there have fought against floods and storms. They have learned to fill in coastal areas to make new farmland, called polder.

The lands near the coast are flat and green, drained by canals and by great rivers such as the Rhine, the Schelde and the Meuse. Windmills were once used to pump out the wet fields, and may still be seen today. In southern Belgium the land rises to a chain of wooded hills called the Ardennes. These stretch southwards into Luxembourg, a tiny country with rich farmland.

The Netherlands is famous for its cheeses, its vegetables, cut flowers and electrical goods. Belgium produces steel and machinery. Luxembourg produces wine and is a centre of business.

The lowlands region is home to several peoples including Frisians, Dutch, Flemings and Walloons.

Amsterdam, the capital of the Netherlands, is built around a network of canals. The Prinsengracht runs through the old part of the city, which was built in the 1600s.

Alkmaar is a town in the North Holland region of the Netherlands. Tourists like to visit its famous **cheese market**, and watch the big, round cheeses being carried out and weighed.

NETHERLANDS

Groningen

Enschede

IJsselmeer

West Frisian Islands

Waddenzee

Haarlem ■ **Amsterdam**

This is the **Atomium**, a strange-looking landmark in Brussels, the capital of Belgium. It was built forty years ago for a big international fair.

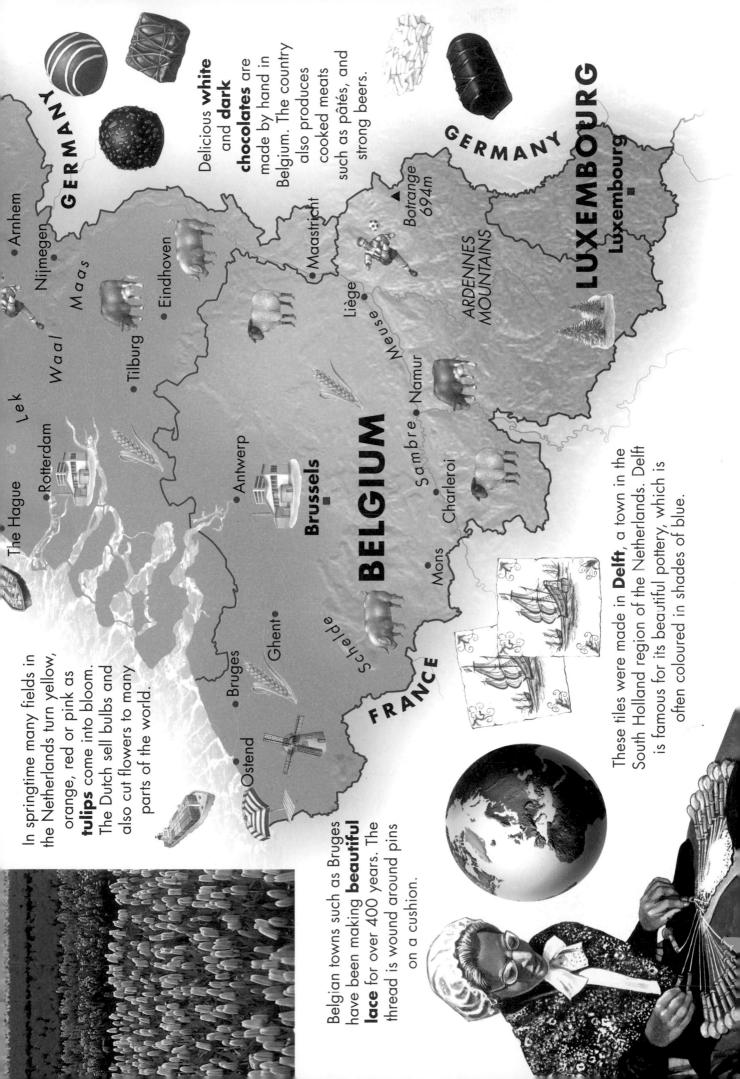

GERMANY

Delicious **white** and **dark** **chocolates** are made by hand in Belgium. The country also produces cooked meats such as pâtés, and strong beers.

GERMANY

LUXEMBOURG
Luxembourg

Arnhem

Nijmegen

Maas

Eindhoven

Maastricht

Botrange
694m

Liège

Meuse

ARDENNES
MOUNTAINS

Tilburg

Waal

Lek

Rotterdam

The Hague

Namur

Sambre

Charleroi

Mons

Antwerp

Brussels

BELGIUM

Schelde

Ghent

Bruges

Ostend

In springtime many fields in the Netherlands turn yellow, orange, red or pink as **tulips** come into bloom. The Dutch sell bulbs and also cut flowers to many parts of the world.

Belgian towns such as Bruges have been making **beautiful lace** for over 400 years. The thread is wound around pins on a cushion.

FRANCE

These tiles were made in **Delft**, a town in the South Holland region of the Netherlands. Delft is famous for its beautiful pottery, which is often coloured in shades of blue.

British Isles

The British Isles lie off the mainland of Europe. Ocean currents and winds keep the weather mild and moist. The largest island is Great Britain, which is made up of three countries joined together in a United Kingdom. These are England, Scotland and Wales. The second biggest island is called Ireland. The northern part of this is governed as part of the United Kingdom, but most of it is a separate country called the Republic of Ireland.

England has rich farmland in the south and bleak moors in the north. Both Scotland and Wales include highlands where sheep or cattle are raised. Many islands lie to the west and to the north of Scotland. There are many large cities in Great Britain. The biggest of all is London, on the River Thames. The Irish capital is called Dublin. Ireland is a land of green fields, peat bogs, mountains and rivers.

Bagpipes are played in the highlands of Scotland. Pipe music can be sad or stirring. Bagpipes are sometimes used by pop bands as well as by traditional pipers.

This brightly painted **longboat** is on the River Wey, in the southeast of England. Longboats like these were once used to transport pottery and other factory goods. Today they are mostly used for holiday cruises.

SHETLAND ISLANDS

ORKNEY ISLANDS

John o'Groats

NORTH SEA

Peterhead

Aberdeen

Inverness

Dundee

Loch Ness

NORTH WEST HIGHLANDS

Perth

Forth

Glasgow • Edinburgh

SCOTLAND

Ben Nevis 4,405 ft

Mallaig

Ayr

Skye

Islay

Lewis

OUTER HEBRIDES

INNER HEBRIDES

Newcastle

Londonderry

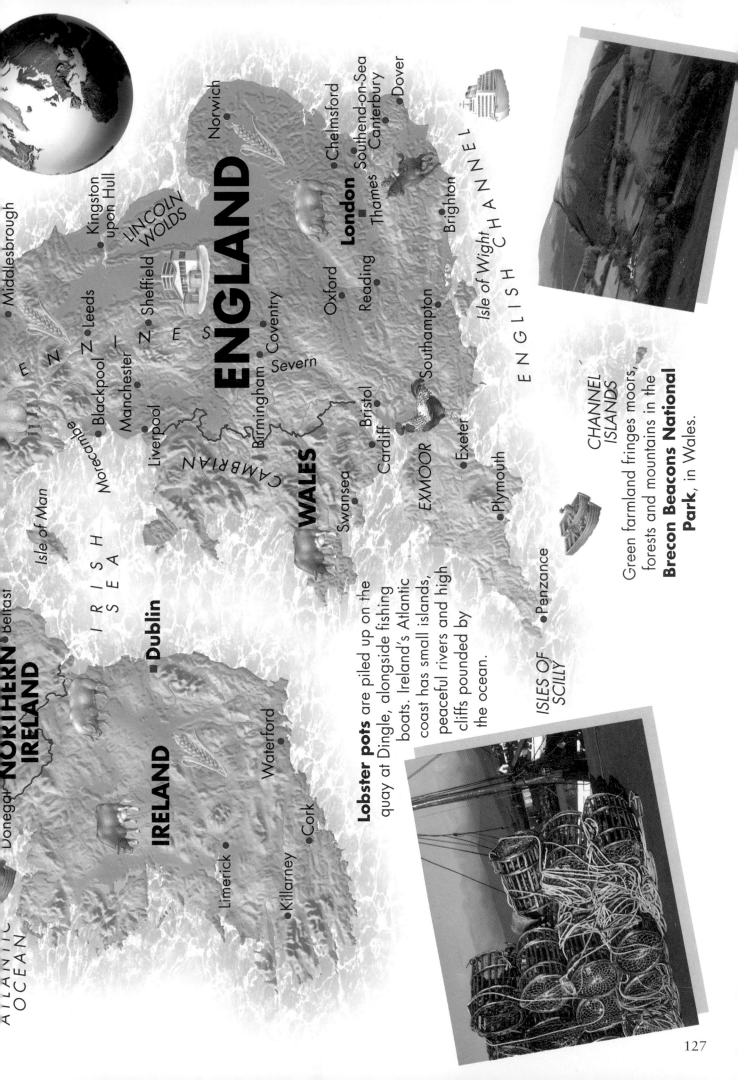

ATLANTIC
OCEAN

• Middlesbrough

• Donegal • Belfast

NORTHERN
IRELAND

Isle of Man

IRISH
SEA

■ Dublin

IRELAND

Limerick •

• Killarney

Waterford •

• Cork

Kingston
upon Hull

LINCOLN
WOLDS

• Leeds

Blackpool •

Morecambe

Manchester

• Liverpool

Sheffield •

CAMBRIAN

PENNINES

WALES

Swansea •

Cardiff •

Bristol •

Severn

Birmingham •

Coventry

ENGLAND

Norwich

Chelmsford •

Southend-on-Sea

Canterbury

• Dover

London

Thames

Oxford •

Reading •

Brighton •

Isle of Wight

ENGLISH CHANNEL

Southampton •

EXMOOR

• Exeter

• Plymouth

• Penzance

ISLES OF
SCILLY

CHANNEL
ISLANDS

Green farmland fringes moors,
forests and mountains in the
**Brecon Beacons National
Park**, in Wales.

Lobster pots are piled up on the
quay at Dingle, alongside fishing
boats. Ireland's Atlantic
coast has small islands,
peaceful rivers and high
cliffs pounded by
the ocean.

France and Monaco

France lies at the centre of western Europe. It is bordered by the Atlantic Ocean in the west and the Mediterranean Sea in the south. Two high mountain ranges, the Pyrenees and the Alps, divide France from Spain and Italy. In the north, a rail tunnel beneath the Channel links the country to England.

The north of the country is mostly flat farmland. The River Seine flows through the French capital, Paris. To the south are the highlands of the Massif Central and the broad valley of the River Rhône.

French farmers grow apples and pears and make all sorts of cheeses. French wines and French cooking too are famous around the world. France makes cars and trains and fashionable clothes.

Monaco is a tiny country on the Mediterranean coast, famous for its gambling and motor racing.

One of the best ways of seeing Paris is by taking a boat trip on the **River Seine**. The city has fine cathedrals and churches, art galleries and museums, bars and restaurants.

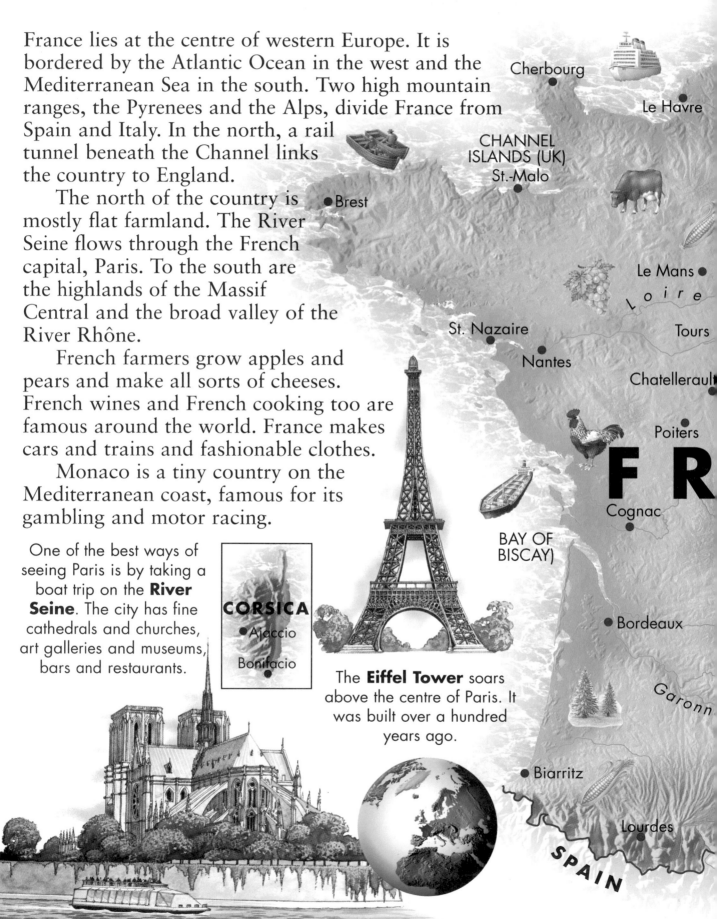

Cherbourg

Le Havre

CHANNEL ISLANDS (UK)

St.-Malo

Brest

Le Mans

Loire

St. Nazaire

Tours

Nantes

Chatelleraul

Poitiers

F R

Cognac

BAY OF BISCAY)

CORSICA
Ajaccio
Bonifacio

The **Eiffel Tower** soars above the centre of Paris. It was built over a hundred years ago.

Bordeaux

Garonn

Biarritz

Lourdes

SPAIN

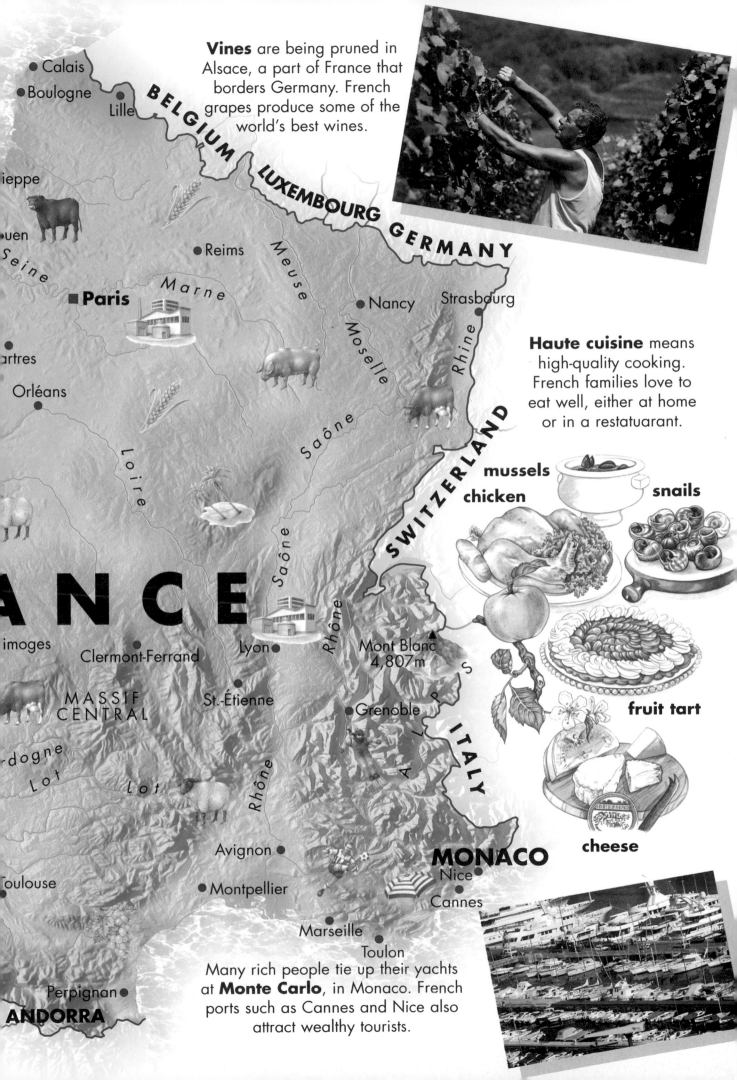

Vines are being pruned in Alsace, a part of France that borders Germany. French grapes produce some of the world's best wines.

Calais
Boulogne
Lille
ieppe
uen
Seine
Reims
Marne
Meuse
Paris
Nancy
Strasbourg
artres
Moselle
Rhine
Orléans
Saône
Loire

Haute cuisine means high-quality cooking. French families love to eat well, either at home or in a restatuarant.

mussels
chicken
snails

A N C E

imoges
Clermont-Ferrand
Lyon
Rhône
Mont Blanc
4,807m
fruit tart
MASSIF
CENTRAL
St.-Étienne
Grenoble
dogne
Lot
Lot
cheese
 A L P S
I T A L Y
S W I T Z E R L A N D
Saône

Avignon
MONACO
oulouse
Montpellier
Nice
Cannes
Marseille
Toulon

Many rich people tie up their yachts at **Monte Carlo**, in Monaco. French ports such as Cannes and Nice also attract wealthy tourists.

Perpignan
ANDORRA

Germany and the Alps

Three small countries take in most of western Europe's highest mountain range, the Alps. They are Switzerland, Liechtenstein and Austria. Here, snowy peaks and rivers of ice tower over green valleys, dark forests and deep lakes. Wooden houses stand in Alpine meadows. They are covered with snow in winter, but are bright with flowers in summer. Languages spoken in the Alps include German, French, Romansh and Italian.

The Alps stretch northwards into southern Germany. Germany is a large country which lies at the heart of Europe. It has forests and steep river valleys, rolling heath and flat plains. Sandy coasts border the North Sea and the Baltic Sea. Germany has many big cities, with factories producing cars, chemical and electrical goods, but it also has pretty villages dating back to the Middle Ages. The German language is spoken throughout, but with many different accents.

The **Matterhorn** is a great needle of rock and ice. It rises in the Swiss Alps, near the Italian border.

NORTH SEA

EAST FRISIAN

Hambu

Bremen

Weser

Hannover   Al

HARZ M

Rhine

Dortmund

Essen

Düsseldorf

Cologne (Köln)

Bonn

GERMA

Rhine

Frankfurt am Main

FRANCE

Rhine

BLACK FOREST

Stuttgart

Lake Constan
(Bodensee)

Zurich

LIECHTENSTE

Vaduz

Bern

SWITZERLAND

Lake Geneva

ALPS

Geneva

130

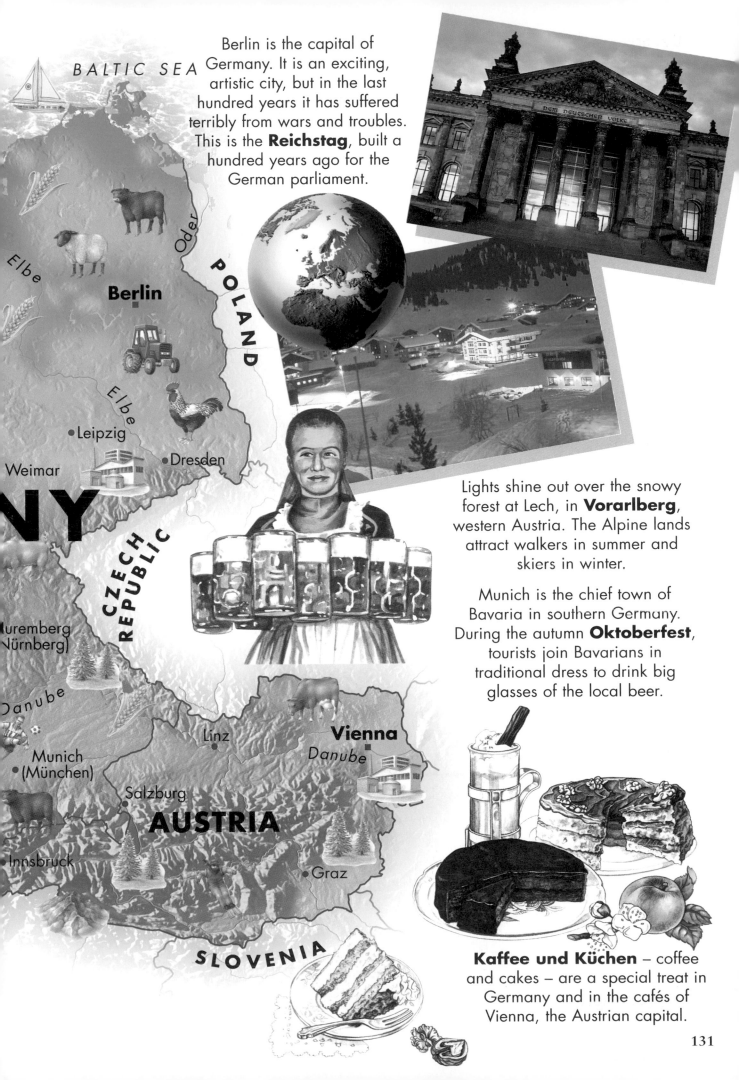

Berlin is the capital of Germany. It is an exciting, artistic city, but in the last hundred years it has suffered terribly from wars and troubles. This is the **Reichstag**, built a hundred years ago for the German parliament.

BALTIC SEA

Berlin

Elbe
Oder
POLAND

Leipzig
Elbe
Dresden
Weimar

NY

CZECH REPUBLIC

uremberg (Nürnberg)

Danube

Munich (München)

Linz
Vienna
Danube

Salzburg

AUSTRIA

Innsbruck

Graz

SLOVENIA

Lights shine out over the snowy forest at Lech, in **Vorarlberg**, western Austria. The Alpine lands attract walkers in summer and skiers in winter.

Munich is the chief town of Bavaria in southern Germany. During the autumn **Oktoberfest**, tourists join Bavarians in traditional dress to drink big glasses of the local beer.

Kaffee und Küchen – coffee and cakes – are a special treat in Germany and in the cafés of Vienna, the Austrian capital.

131

Spain and Portugal

The Iberian peninsula is a great block of land which juts out into the Atlantic Ocean. It is ringed by the snowy mountains of the Pyrenees, the Cantabrian ranges and the Sierra Nevada. Much of it is dry and hot in summer. Rivers cross the western plains and flow into the Atlantic.

The region grows grapes for wine, olives, oranges and cork. There are large fishing fleets. Factories produce cars and leather goods. Many tourists spend their holidays on the coasts.

There are three nations on the Iberian peninsula. The smallest is Andorra, high in the Pyrenees. Portugal, in the west, is a beautiful country with its own language. The largest country is Spain. Here, Spanish is spoken everywhere, but a number of other peoples have their own languages and way of life, including the Basques, Galicians and Catalans. A fourth piece of land, Gibraltar in the far south, is a British colony.

Bay of Biscay

La Coruña

Gijón

CANTABRIAN

CAPE FINISTERRE

Vigo

Valladolid

Porto

Douro

PORTUGAL

Coimbra

Tajo

Tagus

Lisbon

Guadiana

Córdoba

Seville · Guadalquivir

Gulf of Cadiz
A thousand years ago, Arab peoples from North Africa ruled most of Spain. They were Moslems and built beautiful **mosques** such as this one in Cordoba.

Cádiz

Gibraltar (U.K.

Strait of Gibralta

Ronda is a small town of white houses in Andalucía, in southern Spain. It is built on the edge of towering cliffs which are linked by high bridges.

FRANCE

PYRENEES

ANDORRA
Andorra la Vella

Bilbao

MOUNTAINS

Vitoria

Pamplona

Ebro

Duero

Saragossa

Barcelona

S P A I N

Menorca

Madrid

Mallorca

Palma

Valencia

Ibiza Spanish girls in traditional
Ibiza costume enjoy all the fun of
the fair. Spain has many
festivals called **fiestas**.
Many of these celebrate
Christian saints' days.

adiana

Alicante

La Carolina
Linares

Murcia

Granada

Portuguese food includes
delicious seafood dishes,
sardines, fruits and wines. The
drink port takes its name from the
town of Oporto.

MEDITERRANEAN SEA

133

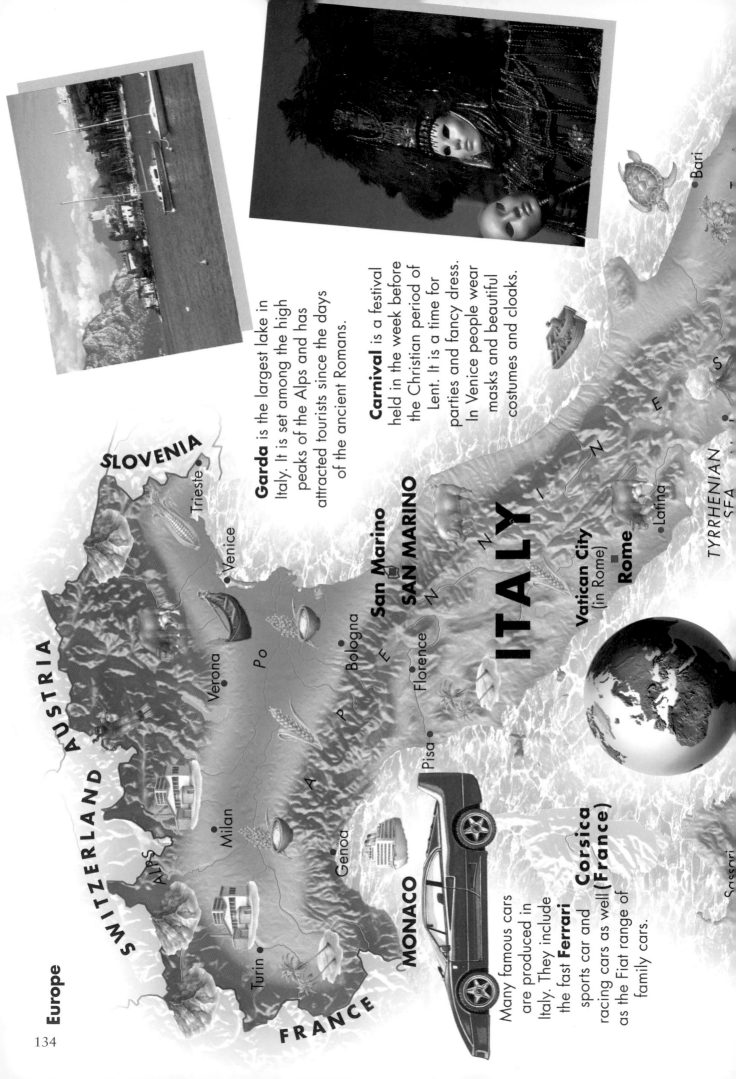

Garda is the largest lake in Italy. It is set among the high peaks of the Alps and has attracted tourists since the days of the ancient Romans.

Carnival is a festival held in the week before the Christian period of Lent. It is a time for parties and fancy dress. In Venice people wear masks and beautiful costumes and cloaks.

SLOVENIA

Trieste

Venice

San Marino

SAN MARINO

ITALY

Vatican City
(in Rome)

Rome

Latina

TYRRHENIAN SEA

Bari

Verona

Po

Bologna

Florence

AUSTRIA

SWITZERLAND

ALPS

Milan

Genoa

Turin

Pisa

MONACO

Corsica (France)

Many famous cars are produced in Italy. They include the fast **Ferrari** sports car and racing cars as well as the Fiat range of family cars.

FRANCE

Sassari

134

Italy and its Neighbours

Italy is a long strip of land stretching into the Mediterranean Sea. In the north are the Alps, a range of high mountains. Below these is a wide plain, crossed by the River Po.

The Appenine mountains run down the centre of the country. Southern Italy includes large areas of dry scrubland. Volcanoes and earthquakes are common. Italy also includes the islands of Sicily and Sardinia.

Italy is the world's biggest wine producer and also exports many foods, including pasta, sauces, olives and salami sausages. Factories in the north produce cars, clothes and leather goods.

Inside Italy there are two other countries, tiny San Marino and also Vatican City, headquarters of the Roman Catholic Church. Another small country, Malta, lies to the south of Sicily.

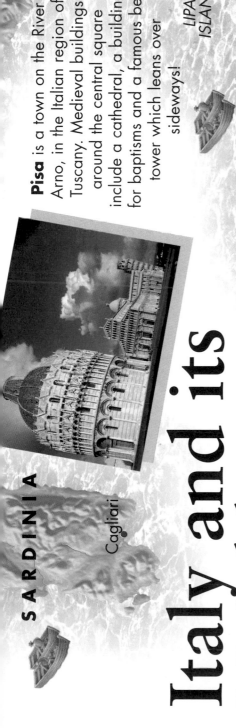

SARDINIA

Cagliari

Pisa is a town on the River Arno, in the Italian region of Tuscany. Medieval buildings around the central square include a cathedral, a building for baptisms and a famous bell tower which leans over sideways!

LIPARI ISLANDS

Palermo

SICILY

Catania

IONIAN SEA

Fishing boats are moored in the harbour of Valletta, the capital of **Malta**. This island nation lies to the south of Sicily.

MALTA

Italy is famous for making some of world's most delicious ice-creams. An ice-cream parlor is called a **gelateria.**

135

Central Europe

Three small countries border the Baltic Sea. Estonia, Latvia and Lithuania include large areas of forest, bog and open farmland. Until the 1990s these Baltic lands were a part of Russia, which was then called the Soviet Union. Poland, to the south, is a much larger country, lying on a wide open plain between Germany in the west and Belarus and Ukraine in the east. In the south are wooded hills and the high peaks of the Tatra mountains, on the Slovakian border. The Czech and the Slovak republics include rugged mountains and rich farmland. The River Danube flows along the Czech border and through the plains of central Hungary.

Central Europe has warm summers but cold, snowy winters. Industries include machinery, cars, mining, and the making of beers, wines and jams. More and more tourists come to visit beautiful old cities such as Krakow, Prague and Budapest.

Lithuania, like Poland, is a strongly Roman Catholic country. Latvia and Estonia are largely Protestant.

RUSSIA

ESTONIA

Gulf of Finland

Tallinn

LATVIA

Gulf of Riga

Riga

LITHUANIA

Vilnius

BELARUS

Kaliningrad (RUSSIA)

POLAND

Gdansk

Poznan

Vistula

Warsaw

Lodz

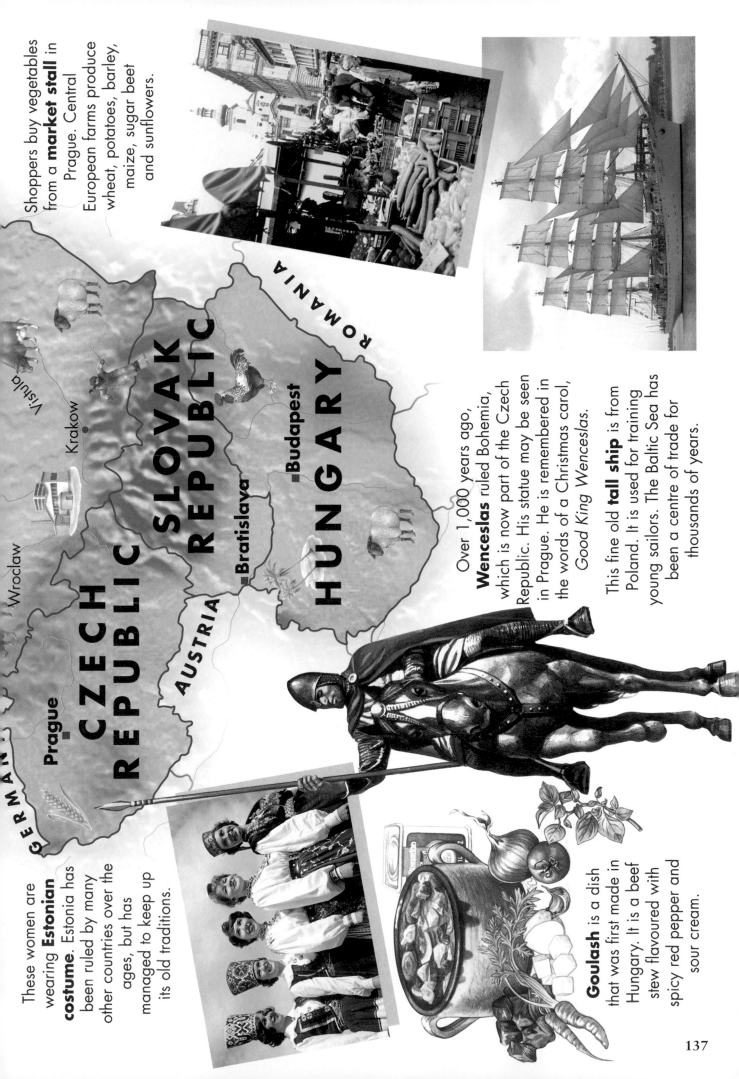

Shoppers buy vegetables from a **market stall** in Prague. Central European farms produce wheat, potatoes, barley, maize, sugar beet and sunflowers.

Over 1,000 years ago, **Wenceslas** ruled Bohemia, which is now part of the Czech Republic. His statue may be seen in Prague. He is remembered in the words of a Christmas carol, *Good King Wenceslas.*

This fine old **tall ship** is from Poland. It is used for training young sailors. The Baltic Sea has been a centre of trade for thousands of years.

These women are wearing **Estonian costume.** Estonia has been ruled by many other countries over the ages, but has managed to keep up its old traditions.

Goulash is a dish that was first made in Hungary. It is a beef stew flavoured with spicy red pepper and sour cream.

Vistula

Krakow

Wroclaw

GERMANY

Prague

CZECH REPUBLIC

AUSTRIA

SLOVAK REPUBLIC

Bratislava

Budapest

HUNGARY

ROMANIA

Europe

The son of an Albanian farmer shows off his favourite cow. **Albania** is a small, mountainous country on the Adriatic coast.

It is time to make hay on this **Romanian farm**. Everyone in the family lends a hand. The hay will be fed to the animals during the cold months of winter.

The **Parthenon** is a splendid temple, built in the days of the ancient Greeks. It still towers over Athens, the capital city of Greece.

UKRAINE

HUNGARY

Ljubljana
SLOVENIA

Zagreb
CROATIA

Drava

Kupa

Sava

Osijek

VOJVODINA

Belgrade

Smederevo

BOSNIA - HERZEGOVINA

Sarajevo

Split

DINARIC ALPS

YUGOSLAVIA

SERBIA

MONTENEGRO

Dubrovnik   Podgorica   KOSOVO
Lake Scutari

Skopje

MACEDONIA

Tiranë

ALBANIA

Corfu

Tisz

Timisoara

Cluj-Napoca

Alba Iulia

Tîrgu Mures

ROMANI

Brasov

Moldoveanu
2,543 m

TRANSYLVANIAN ALPS

Buchares

BALKAN MOUNTAINS

Kamc

Sofia

Kazanluk

BULGARIA

Stara Zagora

Plovdiv

Thessaloníki

Mt Olympus
2,917 m

GREECE

Lesbos

AEGEAN SEA

Chios

Ándros

Sán

Athens

Náx

Thíra

Cythera

SEA OF CRE

Iráklion

Crete

Romania and the Balkans

Romania lies on the Black Sea coast. It is a land of mountains and forests. A large triangle of land stretches southwards from Central Europe, ending in chains of islands. It is called the Balkan peninsula and is bordered by the Adriatic, Black and Aegean Seas. The region has rocky mountain ranges and often suffers from earthquakes. Summers are dry and hot. Winters are very cold in the north, but mild in the south. The region produces timber, wines, olives, fruit and dairy products.

Bulgaria lies in the northeast of the peninsula. It has large areas of rich farmland. The northwestern Balkan lands used to be part of one big nation called Yugoslavia, but they now make up five different countries. Greece is the southernmost country of the Balkans and includes many islands. Its ancient villages and fine beaches attract many tourists.

Roses are picked in the Kazanluk region of **Bulgaria**. Their sweet-smelling petals are used to make attar of roses, an oil used in making perfumes.

Churches, whitewashed villages and blue seas are typical of the Greek lands. This is **Thira**, a volcanic island which is also known as Santorini.

Greek meals might include salad with olives, seafood such as fish or squid, stuffed peppers, beans, a type of wine called retsina and sweet, sticky pastries such as baklava.

Zagreb, the capital of **Croatia**, is near the Slovenian border, on the Sava River. The city is on the main route from western Europe to Greece.

MOLDOVA
Galati
MOUTHS OF THE DANUBE
DOBRUJA
Constanta
Varna
BLACK SEA
Cos
Rhodes

Sunflowers are grown as a crop in many parts of the Balkans. Their seeds may be pressed to make vegetable oil or roasted for eating.

Russian Federation

The Russian Federation is the world's biggest country. It stretches across two continents, Europe and Asia. When the sun is rising in Vladivostok, on the Pacific Coast, it is already setting on the capital, Moscow. In the Arctic north there is an icy plain, the tundra. To the south of this there are huge forests, the home of brown bears. The countryside also takes in rolling farmland called steppes, deserts and high mountain ranges. Europe's longest river is the Volga, over 3,500 kilometres long, which flows into the Caspian Sea. To the east is Baikal, the deepest lake in the world.

Before 1991 all the countries on this map were part of one huge country called the Soviet Union. After 1991 many of the lands around the Soviet borders broke away to form separate countries. Over a hundred different peoples live in the region, beside the Russians themselves.

St Basil's Cathedral stands in Red Square, in Moscow.

In the days of the Soviet Union, big statues were put up showing people working hard for their country. These **farmers** are harvesting wheat. It is still an important crop today.

FINLAND
BARENT SEA
Murmansk
Archangel
St Petersburg
BELARUS
Minsk
Moscow
UKRAINE
Kiev
Nizhniy Novgorod
Kazan
Chisinau
MOLDOVA
Don
Volga
Samara
URAL MOUNTAIN
Ural
Yekaterinb
BLACK SEA
Aqm
GEORGIA
ARMENIA
AZERBAIJAN
Caspian Sea
KAZAKHSTAN
Aral Sea
TURKMENISTAN
Bishke
IRAN
Ashgabat
Tashkent
Dushant
TAJIKISTA

One-third of **Armenians** still work on the land. They produce vegetables and fruit or raise sheep and cattle.

In the Middle Ages, Russian monks made beautiful **Bibles** like this one, and painted holy pictures called icons.

Fine **silk** is produced and woven into cloth in the Imeretia region of Georgia.

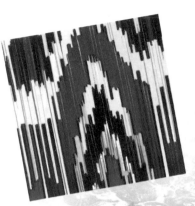

Wrangel I.

Franz Josef Land

Severnaya Zemlya

New Siberian Islands

Novaya Zemlya

KAMCHATKA PENINSULA

KARA SEA

EAST SIBERIAN UPLANDS

CENTRAL SIBERIAN PLATEAU

Lena

Yenisey

Yakutsk

SEA OF OKHOTSK

Sakhalin

RUSSIA

Ob

Angara

Khabarovsk

Sour cream

Omsk

Novosibirsk

Lake Baykal

Irkutsk

Amur

CHINA

Vladivostok

Blinis

CHINA

Beetroot

Almaty

KYRGYZSTAN

Borscht is made from beetroots and served with sour cream and blinis.

Canada and Greenland

ARCTIC OCEAN

Most Canadian towns are in the south, near the United States border, the Great Lakes or the St Lawrence River. The north is a wilderness, with frozen plains, vast forests, mountains and blue lakes. Winters are long and severe, but summers can be mild or warm. Most Canadians are English-speaking, descended from British settlers. A large number are French-speaking, especially in the province of Québec. There are also First Peoples, such as the Innu, Mohawk, Cree and Micmac. In Arctic Canada are the Inuit people, who traditionally live by hunting seals and polar bears.

Inuit people also live in Greenland, along with descendants of Danish settlers. This is the world's largest island. Its rocky land is covered in a thick sheet of Arctic ice.

Banks Island

BEAUFORT SEA

Victoria Island

ALASKA (U.S.A.)

MACKENZIE

Norman Wells

Great Bear Lake

YUKON TERRITORY

Mackenzie

Kiard

NORTHWEST TERRITORIES

Whitehorse

Great Slave Lake

R

BRITISH COLUMBIA

CAN

O

K

QUEEN CHARLOTTE ISLANDS

Y

ALBERTA

MANITOBA

Vancouver Island

Vancouver

SASKATCHEWAN

Calgary

Regina

Winnipeg

UNITED STATES OF AMERIC

Maple trees grow colourful leaves in autumn. The maple leaf is a badge of Canada and is shown on the national flag.

Totem poles are still raised outside villages by the First Peoples of British Columbia. They are carved with birds and beasts and figures from myths, legends and family history.

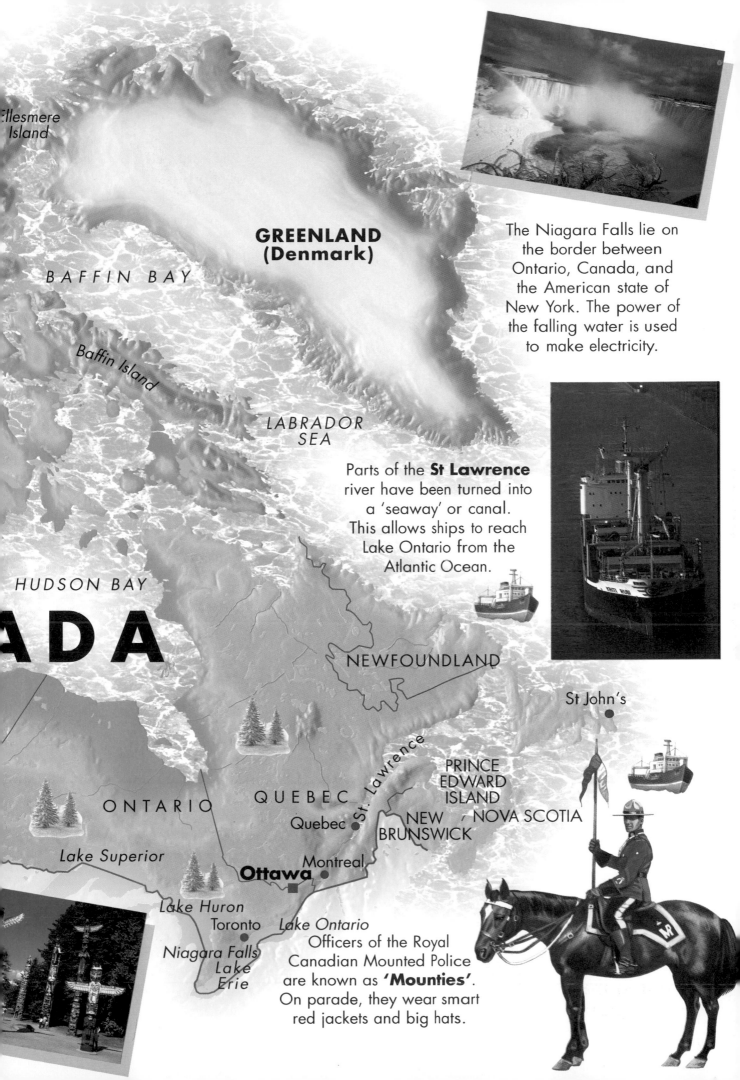

Ellesmere
Island

BAFFIN BAY

GREENLAND
(Denmark)

Baffin Island

LABRADOR
SEA

The Niagara Falls lie on the border between Ontario, Canada, and the American state of New York. The power of the falling water is used to make electricity.

Parts of the **St Lawrence** river have been turned into a 'seaway' or canal. This allows ships to reach Lake Ontario from the Atlantic Ocean.

HUDSON BAY

ADA

NEWFOUNDLAND

St John's

QUEBEC
St. Lawrence

PRINCE
EDWARD
ISLAND

ONTARIO

NEW   NOVA SCOTIA
BRUNSWICK

Quebec

Lake Superior

Montreal

Ottawa

Lake Huron
Toronto

Lake Ontario

Niagara Falls
Lake
Erie

Officers of the Royal Canadian Mounted Police are known as **'Mounties'**. On parade, they wear smart red jackets and big hats.

The United States of America

The North American **raccoon** is a furry little creature with black patches on its eyes and a ringed tail. It comes out by night.

The United States of America (USA) stretch the whole way from the Atlantic Ocean to the Pacific. There are 50 states in all. They take in woodlands, whose leaves turn red and gold each autumn, and long ranges of hills such as the Appalachians. They include the Great Lakes and the rivers Mississippi and Missouri, which flow into the steamy Gulf of Mexico. There are wide open grasslands called prairies, which are given over to farming and cattle ranching. There is the great Rocky Mountain chain. There are the burning dry deserts of the southwest and the rainy, misty forests of Oregon and Washington State. Two American states are separated from the others. They are Alaska, stretching from Canada into the frozen Arctic, and Hawaii, a group of islands and volcanoes far out in the Pacific Ocean.

CANADA

Seattle
WASHINGTON

MONTANA

IDAHO

OREGON

CASCADE RANGE

Snake

Black Hills

WYOMING

Rapid

Great Salt Lake

Rock Springs

NEVADA

Boulder

UTAH

COLORAD

San Francisco

GREAT BASIN

Grand Junction

Denver

Las Vegas

Grand Canyon

NEW MEXICO

CALIFORNIA

Colorado

Los Angeles

ARIZONA

Rio Grande

San Diego

Phoenix

Douglas

MEXICO

Rainbow Bridge is an arch of pink rock in the state of Utah. Over the ages, wind and water have worn it down into this strange shape.

144

The Roosevelt Dam stretches across the Salt River in Arizona. It was built in the early part of this century and irrigates rich farmland.

Huge heads have been carved from the rock at **Mount Rushmore**, in South Dakota. They show famous presidents of the USA.

Oranges, lemons and grapefruit are **citrus fruits**. They are grown in the far west, in California, and also in the southeastern state of Florida.

ORTH AKOTA
ismarck

Lake Superior

MINNESOTA

Marquette

Lake Huron

MAINE

VERMONT NEW HAMPSHIRE

MASSACHUSETTS
Boston
Providence
RHODE IS.
CONNECTICUT

SOUTH DAKOTA
ierre

WISCONSIN

MICHIGAN

Lake Michigan

Lake Erie

NEW YORK

NEW YORK City

IOWA

Mississippi

Chicago

OHIO

INDIANA

PENNSYLVANIA

Philadelphia

NEW JERSEY

DELAWARE

WASHINGTON D.C.

NEBRASKA

ILLINOIS

WEST VIRGINIA

MARYLAND

Richmond

 KANSA

MISSOURI

Ohio

Charleston

VIRGINIA

KENTUCKY

NORTH CAROLINA

OKLAHOMA

ARKANSAS

TENNESSEE

Chattanooga

SOUTH CAROLINA

Atlanta

MISSISSIPPI

APPALACHIAN MTS.

Columbus

T E X A S

ALABAMA

GEORGIA

LOUISIANA

Houston

New Orleans

San Antonio

Mississippi

Orlando

FLORIDA

American-style **hamburgers** and **doughnuts** are amongst the many fast foods that are now sold all over the world.

io Grande

GULF OF MEXICO

Miami

Straits of Florida

145

The USA has many big, bustling cities. In the west is San Francisco. It is a beautiful port beside the blue Pacific Ocean. Los Angeles is a huge city full of traffic. A part of it, called Hollywood, is where many famous films have been made. Chicago, on Lake Michigan, was where skyscrapers were first built, over a hundred years ago. Detroit, on Lake Erie, is where many American cars are made. And New York City, in the east, is the biggest city of them all. It is nicknamed the Big Apple. The capital of the country is Washington. This is the centre of government and is also where the US president lives, in the White House. It isn't in one of the states but in a special district called Columbia.

Many different peoples live in the USA today. Native Americans are descended from the very first people to settle in North America. They include peoples such as the Navajo, Apache and Cree. Many Americans are descended from European settlers.

ARCTIC OCEAN

BERING SEA

BROOK RANGE

CANADA

Bering Strait

ALASKA (U.S.A.)

St. Lawrence Island

Yukon

Mt McKinley 6194 m

Anchorage

GULF OF ALASKA

Juneau

ALEUTIAN ISLANDS

PACIFIC OCE

The **World Trade Centre** has two tall towers. They rise up from the water's edge on the island of Manhattan. This is right at the centre of New York City, one of the largest and busiest cities in the world.

Rattlesnakes live in the hot, dry lands of Texas and the southwest. They are very dangerous. They rattle their tails as a warning before they bite you.

Dance and song make up a **traditional welcome** to the Hawaiian islands. Hawaii's links with the USA go back 100 years.

KAUAI

NIIHAU

OAHU

Honolulu

MOLOKAI

LANAI

MAUI

KAHOOLAWE

Hilo

HAWAII

The USA has many exciting **theme parks**, where children can enjoy fun and fantasy.

The **Californian condor** is very, very rare. It has huge wings, about 3 metres across.

but other languages such as Spanish are spoken in some cities. The USA is a country with rich farmland and many mineral mines. Its factories produce computers, cars, drinks and foods, clothing and all sorts of other goods. It is also a centre of the film industry, banking and business. This has made it one of the world's richest and most powerful countries.

New settlers came from Britain and Ireland, Italy, France, Spain, Greece, Germany, Poland and the Netherlands. African Americans are the descendants of West Africans who were brought to America hundreds of years ago. Some Americans originally came from Asia, including Jews, Chinese and Vietnamese. The Hawaiians are Polynesians, one of the Pacific peoples. All these different groups are proud of their background, but they now belong to one big country, the USA. Today most Americans speak English,

A shuttle is launched into space on the back of huge rockets. It is leaving Cape Canaveral in Florida.

The bright city lights of **Las Vegas** shine out over the desert in the state of Nevada. People come here to gamble, see shows and stay in hotels.

Mexico, Central America and the Caribbean

Mexico lies between the Gulf of Mexico and the Pacific Ocean. It is a land of hot deserts, mountain ranges, forests and sandy beaches. Earthquakes are common and there are volcanoes, too. Mexico City is the country's capital. Once it was the chief city of the Aztec people and called Tenochtitlán. Many great civilizations were started in the region long ago.

To the south of Mexico are the seven small countries of Central America. Panama is crossed by a canal, which links the Atlantic and Pacific Oceans. Spanish is the main language of the region. Many of its

Guacamole

Chillies

Tortillas are cornmeal pancakes made in Central America. They may be served with beans and hot chillies.

Tortillas

Beer

Baja California

SIERRA MADRE

Rio Grande

SIERRA MADRE

Matamoros

Monterrey

Culiacán

GULF OF MEXICO

Havana

CU

Cancún

Cayman Islands (U.

Guadalajara

León

Mexico City

Veracruz

MEXICO

Coatzacoalcos

Belmopan

BELIZE

Acapulco

GUATEMALA

HONDURAS

PACIFIC OCEAN

Guatemala City

Tegucigalpa

San Salvador

NICARAGU

These Native American women from **Guatemala** wear colourful clothes they have woven by hand. Each village has its own patterns and styles.

EL SALVADOR

Managua

San José

Pana

COSTA RICA

PANA.

peoples are descended from the Spanish soldiers who invaded the Americas nearly 500 years ago. Others are descended from Native Americans. Central American crops include maize and bananas.

The Caribbean Sea lies to the east of Central America. It has thousands of islands, the largest of which is Cuba. Caribbean peoples include many whose ancestors came from West Africa. There are also some Caribbeans of Native American, Spanish, French, British, Dutch and Asian descent. The islands have a warm, tropical climate in which sugarcane and bananas grow well. Hurricanes are common in the later summer and autumn. The islands are famous for their carnivals.

Brilliantly coloured **humming birds** hover as they sip nectar from flowers. They are found in both Central America and the Caribbean.

Warm blue seas, fine beaches and watersports attract millions of tourists to the Caribbean islands each year. This is **Barbados**.

How would you like to dive off this cliff into the sea? This is one of the sights to be seen at **Acapulco**, in Mexico.

BAHAMAS

Turks & Caicos Islands (U.K.)

Virgin Is. (U.K. & U.S.)

ANTIGUA & BARBUDA

Puerto Rico (U.S.)

ST. KITTS & NEVIS

Montserrat (U.K.)
Guadeloupe (FR.)
DOMINICA
Martinique (FR.)

HAITI

DOMINICAN REPUBLIC

JAMAICA

ST. LUCIA

CARIBBEAN SEA

ST. VINCENT & THE GRENADINES

BARBADOS

GRENADA

TRINIDAD & TOBAGO

Mexico and parts of Central America have many ancient ruins and statues, like this **warrior** carved from stone. They date back to the ancient civilizations that once grew up here.

Old churches and buildings, like this one in **Costa Rica**, remind us that this region was once ruled by Spain.

149

The Northern Andes

This boat is made of reeds, by the **Aymara people**. They live around Lake Titicaca, which is on the border between Peru and Bolivia.

The green turtle lives in the sea along the coasts of Peru, Ecuador and Colombia. It breeds on lonely, sandy beaches and is becoming very rare.

South America is joined to Central America by a narrow strip of land. To the south, the Andes mountains run all the way down the continent. Their high, snowy peaks divide the hot lands along the coast from the rainforests and great rivers of the east.

Colombia is a beautiful country, which lies across three bands of the Andes range. The rocks are mined for gold and precious green stones called emeralds. Ecuador is named after the Spanish word for Equator. Bananas and sugarcane grow in the warm climate here, and coffee too on the slopes of hills. In Peru, farmers work high in the mountains, growing potatoes, maize and a grain called quinoa. Along the coast fishermen catch tuna and sardines. Bolivia has great forests and tin mines.

About 500 years ago, the Inca people ruled a huge empire into Andes. It was conquered by Spanish soldiers. Many peoples of the region are descended from Native American peoples and from the Spanish.

CARIBBEAN SEA

VENEZUELA

PANAMA

COLOMBIA

Bogota

ECUADOR

Quito

Amazon

Iquitos

maracas

Andean musicians play the rondador or pan-pipes, rattles called maracas, guitars and drums.

This peak towers above the rocks of the **Andes**. It is covered in snow, even though it is near the Equator, in Ecuador. It is called Cotopaxi and is the world's highest active volcano.

pan-pipes

Llamas live high in the Andes. They carry baggage along high, narrow mountain paths. Their wool is used for weaving into cloth.

The ancient peoples of Colombia made many beautiful things from **gold** and precious stones. They used knives like these for their religious ceremonies.

This mother and baby belong to the **Quechua people**. They live near the old Inca capital of Cuzco, in Peru. Most Quechua live in mountain villages and work as farmers. They grow potatoes and maize, and raise sheep and llamas.

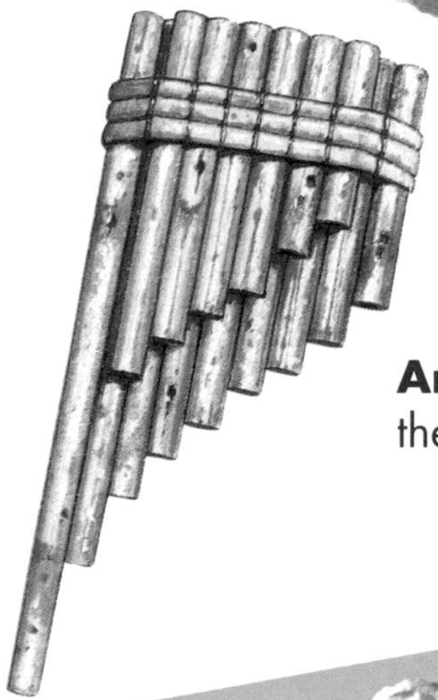

PACIFIC OCEAN

PERU

Lima

Nazca

cayali

Lake Titicaca

La Paz

BOLIVIA

Sucre

Lake Poopó

CHILE

PARAGUAY

151

Brazil and its Neighbours

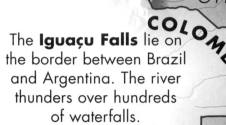

Carac

VENEZUEL

Orinoc

COLOMBIA

The **Iguaçu Falls** lie on the border between Brazil and Argentina. The river thunders over hundreds of waterfalls.

Brazil is the biggest country in South America. It is a hot country with grassland, swamps and dry bush. A large area is covered in rainforest. This is the home of monkeys, brightly coloured parrots and gigantic snakes called anacondas. One of the world's two longest rivers, the Amazon, flows through the forest to the Atlantic Ocean.

On the coast there are many big cities. Some city dwellers are rich, but many are very poor.

Venezuela is on the Caribbean coast. It is crossed by another great river called the Orinoco.

A large sea inlet called Lake Maracaibo is the centre of Venezuela's oil industry. Three other small countries, called Guyana, Surinam and French Guiana, lie on the tropical north coast. They produce sugarcane, rice, chilli peppers and fruits.

This part of South America is home to many different Native American peoples, as well as people descended from Africans and Europeans. The region was once ruled by Portugal, Spain, France, Britain and the Netherlands.

PERU

This cathedral is in **Brasília**, the capital of Brazil. This modern city was specially built inland, to the south of the great forests.

There are many different kinds of **poison-arrow frog** in South America. Their deadly poison is smeared on arrows and darts by Native American hunters.

This beautiful tropical plant is called the **bird-of-paradise flower**.

TRINIDAD & TOBAGO

Angel Falls

Georgetown

GUYANA

Paramaribo

SURINAM **Cayenne**

FRENCH GUIANA

G U I A N A

Negro

Manaus

Amazon

Santarém

BRAZIL

Teresina

Fortaleza

Salvador

Guaporé

BOLIVIA

Brasília

Belo Horizonte

Paraná

São Paulo

Rio de Janeiro

ARGENTINA

URUGUAY

Uruguay

In the southeast of **Venezuela** there are sheer, flat-topped mountains called tepuis. They rise from beautiful lakes and green tropical forests.

Many tropical trees grow in Brazil. One produces seeds called **brazil nuts**. They make delicious snacks.

The **puma** is a big, fierce cat. In North America it is called the cougar or mountain lion.

A big **statue of Jesus** looks out over the city of Rio de Janeiro, in Brazil. It is on a high mountain called the Sugarloaf.

153

Argentina and its Neighbours

Southern South America is a big triangle of land. The pointed end stretches south towards Antarctica. It breaks up into islands around Tierra del Fuego. Gales whip up huge waves around the southern tip, which is called Cape Horn. As you travel north, you come to the dry, windy valleys of Patagonia, the high Andes mountains, the rich grassland of the Pampas and the hot, damp Gran Chaco region.

Argentina is a big country, which raises beef cattle and sheep. It borders the Atlantic Ocean. Far offshore are the remote Falkland or Malvinas islands. Uruguay and Paraguay are two small countries to the north, which also raise cattle. Chile, to the west of the Andes, is a long, narrow land. It borders the Pacific Ocean. It has large areas of desert, where it hardly ever rains. It also has warm farmland, where grapes can be grown.

PARAGUAY

Concepción

Asunción

Pilcomayo

Bermejo

Formosa

Corrientes

Paraguay

Paraná

Córdoba

Rosario

GRAN CHACO

URUGUAY

Negro

Montevideo

Buenos Aires

PAMPAS

ARGENTINA

Santiago

ATACAMA DESERT

CHILE

Concepción

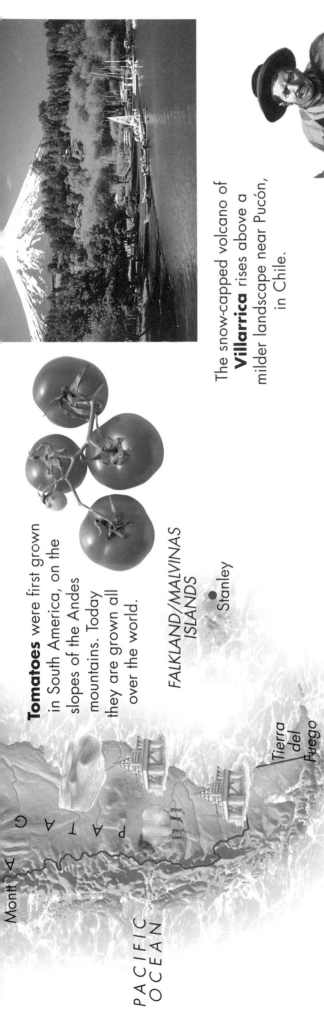

The snow-capped volcano of **Villarrica** rises above a milder landscape near Pucón, in Chile.

The **gauchos** are the cowboys of the Pampas grasslands in Argentina. They are skilled at riding horses and roping cattle. They used to be famous for their wild adventures.

Tomatoes were first grown in South America, on the slopes of the Andes mountains. Today they are grown all over the world.

FALKLAND/MALVINAS ISLANDS

• Stanley

Ushuaia is a port in **Tierra del Fuego**, in the far south of Argentina. The people who live there raise sheep and go fishing.

Tierra del Fuego

Cape Horn

PACIFIC OCEAN

Montt

PATAG

The **rhea** is a large South American bird that can grow to 1.5 m tall. It cannot fly and lives on the Pampas.

155

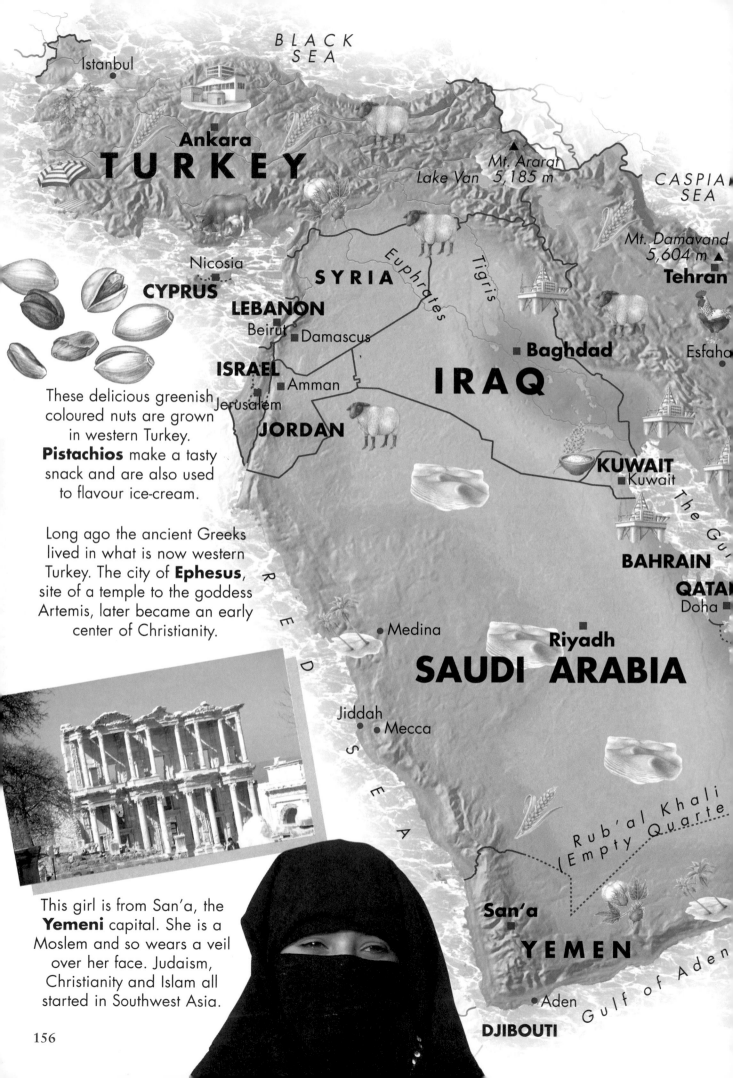

BLACK SEA

Istanbul

Ankara

TURKEY

Mt. Ararat
5,185 m
Lake Van

CASPIAN SEA

Mt. Damavand
5,604 m ▲

Tehran

Nicosia

SYRIA

CYPRUS

LEBANON

Beirut
Damascus

Euphrates

Tigris

Esfaha

Baghdad

ISRAEL

Amman

Jerusalem

IRAQ

JORDAN

These delicious greenish coloured nuts are grown in western Turkey. **Pistachios** make a tasty snack and are also used to flavour ice-cream.

KUWAIT

Kuwait

Long ago the ancient Greeks lived in what is now western Turkey. The city of **Ephesus**, site of a temple to the goddess Artemis, later became an early center of Christianity.

BAHRAIN

QATA

Doha

RED SEA

Medina

Riyadh

SAUDI ARABIA

Jiddah

Mecca

Rub' al Khali
(Empty Quarter)

This girl is from San'a, the **Yemeni** capital. She is a Moslem and so wears a veil over her face. Judaism, Christianity and Islam all started in Southwest Asia.

San'a

YEMEN

Gulf of Aden

Aden

DJIBOUTI

156

Southwest Asia

This region of Asia is often called the Near East or the Middle East. Its western parts border the Mediterranean Sea. These have a gentle, warm climate, which makes it possible to grow fruits such as oranges and lemons. The Arabian peninsula is the land surrounded by the Red Sea, the Indian Ocean and the Persian Gulf. It is occupied by Jordan, Saudi Arabia and the small countries of Yemen, Oman, United Arab Emirates (UAE), Qatar, Bahrain and Kuwait. This a land of hot, sandy deserts. Little can grow here, but it is rich in oil and natural gas.

Eastern Syria and Iraq are also desert regions, but these are crossed by the Rivers Tigris and Euphrates. It was here that the world's first farmers founded towns and cities thousands of years ago. Eastern Turkey and northern Iran include mountains, windswept plains and rolling grasslands, which are very cold in winter. Iran also has ranges of mountains and deserts.

Mashhad

IRAN

Abu Dhabi

Gulf of Oman

UNITED ARAB EMIRATES ■ Muscat

OMAN

These towers in **Kuwait** are used to take the salt out of sea water, so that it can be drunk or used on the land.

Beautiful **pearls** form in oysters in the warm seas of Southwest Asia. They are very valuable.

This camel rider is one of the **Bedouin**, a nomadic people of the region. Camels are the ideal transport for desert areas.

Socotra (YEMEN)

157

India and its Neighbours

This mass of land is so big that it is sometimes called the Indian subcontinent, or simply the subcontinent. It is separated from Central Asia by the world's biggest mountains, which are in the Himalaya and Karakoram ranges. These climb to 8,848 metres above sea level at Mount Everest. Snowy peaks stretch all the way from eastern Afghanistan, through northern Pakistan and India to Nepal and Bhutan.

To the south are the wide, dusty plains of India, crossed by the Ganges. In Bangladesh, this river splits into many channels before flowing into the Bay of Bengal. India is a country of deserts, forested hills, small villages and large bustling cities. The climate is mostly tropical and very hot, with monsoon winds bringing heavy summer rainstorms. In the far south is the tropical island nation of Sri Lanka.

The region produces wheat, tea, sugarcane, rice, jute and cotton. It includes the sites of ancient civilizations and places which are holy to Hindus, Buddhists, Sikhs and Moslems.

Mount Everest is the highest mountain on Earth. It lies on the border between Nepal and Tibet, in the Himalaya range.

Colourful, sparkling costumes are worn by these **Indian dancers.** India is famous for its richly coloured silks and cottons and its silver jewellery.

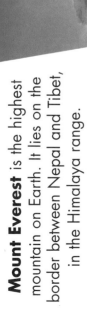

AFGHANISTAN

Kabul

Khyber Pass

Islamabad

Lahore

PAKISTAN

Indus

Karachi

HIMALAYAS

NEPAL

Delhi **New Delhi**

Agra

Coriander

Ground turmeric

Andaman & Nicobar Is. (India)

Ginger

Indian food includes delicious curries, chutneys, rice and vegetable dishes. They are cooked with different **kinds of spice.**

This **Bengal tiger** has become very rare. It is protected in special reserves in India, Bangladesh and Nepal.

Brahmaputra

Dhaka

Kanpur Varanasi
Ganges

Calcutta

INDIA

BAY OF BENGAL

Ahmadabad

Surat

Nagpur

Mumbai (Bombay)

Pune

Godavari

Hyderabad

Bangalore

Chennai (Madras)

ARABIAN SEA

INDIAN OCEAN

SRI LANKA

Colombo • Galle

MALDIVES

A woman picks **tea** in the green hills of Sri Lanka. This small island nation to the south of India is the biggest exporter of tea in the world.

Many people say that the **Taj Mahal,** a marble tomb, is the most beautiful building in the world. It was built near Agra in India by a Moslem emperor called Shah Jahan, who ruled from 1627 to 1666.

China and its Neighbours

China covers an area about the size of western Europe. It is ringed by high mountains, empty deserts and tropical seas where fierce storms called typhoons are common.

Most people live in the fertile eastern part of the country, which is crossed by great rivers such as the Huang He and the Chang Jiang. More people live in China than in any other country in the world. Chinese farmers grow rice, tea, wheat and maize. China is the center of a very ancient civilization and was famous in history for its pottery and fine silk.

The Mongols live in a northern part of China and also in the rolling grasslands and deserts of Mongolia itself. The Koreans live to the northeast, on a peninsula containing North and South Korea.

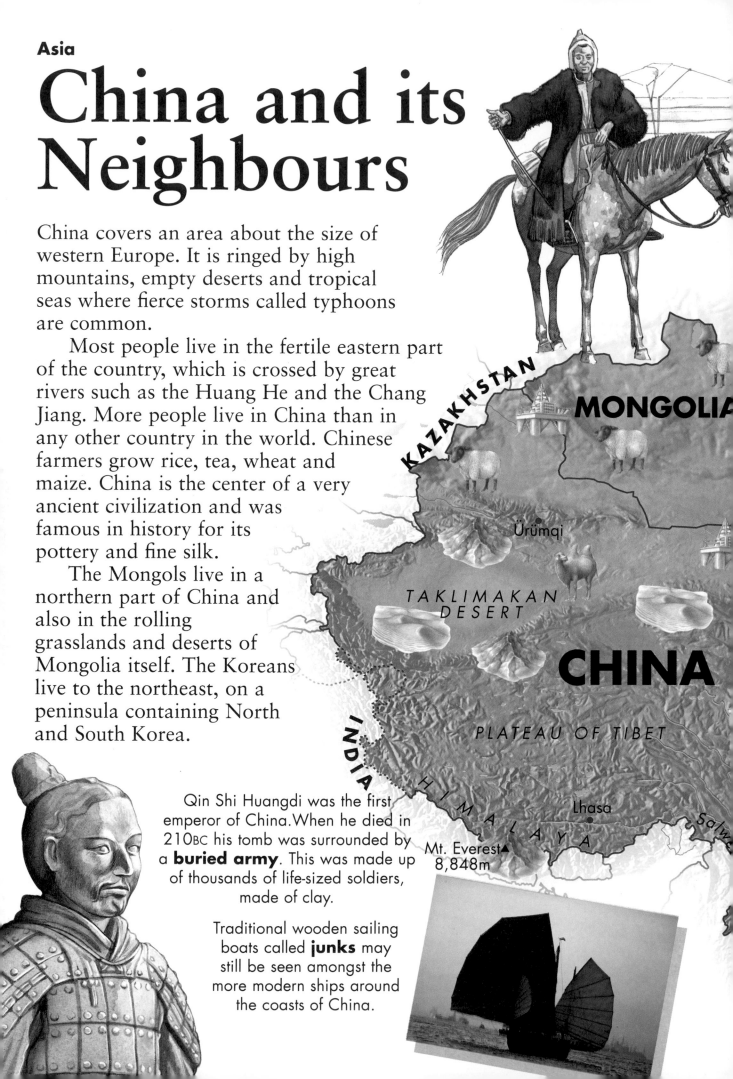

KAZAKHSTAN

MONGOLIA

Ürümqi

TAKLIMAKAN DESERT

CHINA

PLATEAU OF TIBET

INDIA

HIMALAYA

Lhasa

Salw

Mt. Everest▲ 8,848m

Qin Shi Huangdi was the first emperor of China.When he died in 210BC his tomb was surrounded by a **buried army**. This was made up of thousands of life-sized soldiers, made of clay.

Traditional wooden sailing boats called **junks** may still be seen amongst the more modern ships around the coasts of China.

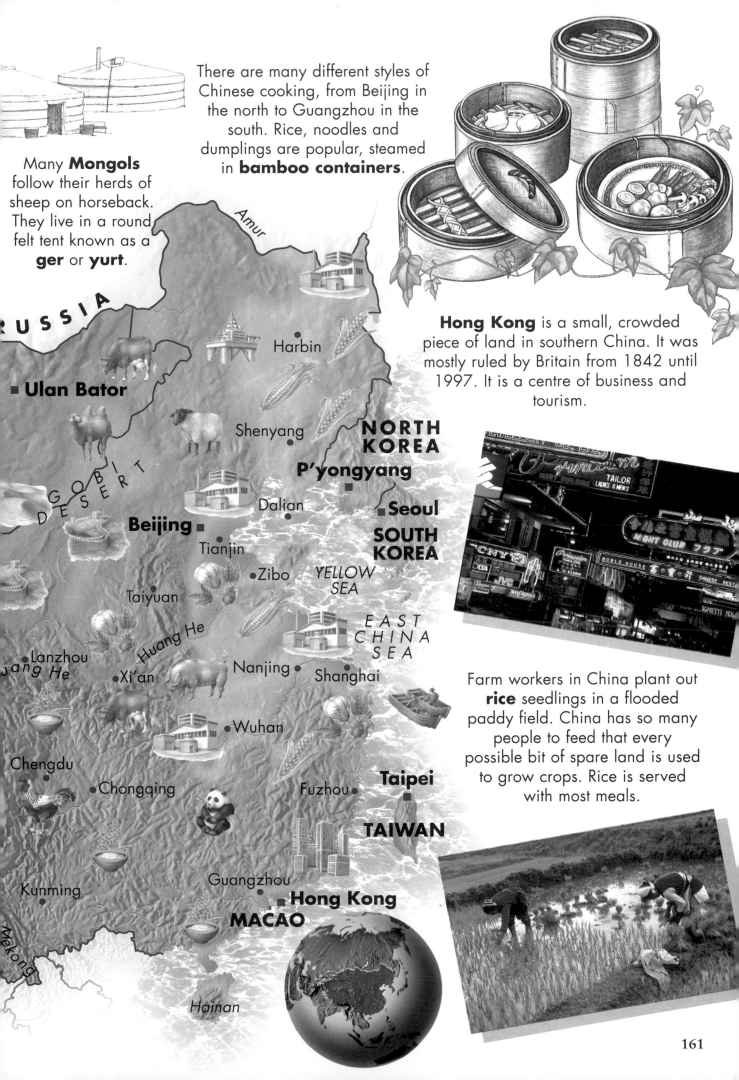

Many **Mongols** follow their herds of sheep on horseback. They live in a round felt tent known as a **ger** or **yurt**.

There are many different styles of Chinese cooking, from Beijing in the north to Guangzhou in the south. Rice, noodles and dumplings are popular, steamed in **bamboo containers**.

Hong Kong is a small, crowded piece of land in southern China. It was mostly ruled by Britain from 1842 until 1997. It is a centre of business and tourism.

Farm workers in China plant out **rice** seedlings in a flooded paddy field. China has so many people to feed that every possible bit of spare land is used to grow crops. Rice is served with most meals.

Amur

RUSSIA

Ulan Bator

GOBI DESERT

Harbin

Shenyang

NORTH KOREA

P'yongyang

Dalian

Seoul

SOUTH KOREA

Beijing

Tianjin

Zibo

YELLOW SEA

Taiyuan

EAST CHINA SEA

Lanzhou

Huang He

Xi'an

Nanjing

Shanghai

Huang He

Chengdu

Wuhan

Chongqing

Fuzhou

Taipei

TAIWAN

Kunming

Guangzhou

Hong Kong

MACAO

Mekong

Hainan

Japan

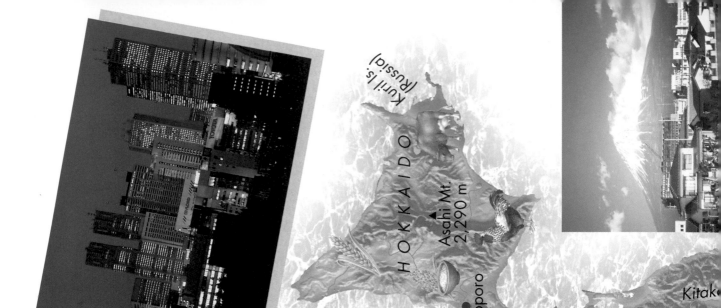

Thousands of small islands lie to the east of China on the edge of the Pacific Ocean. They make up a country called Japan. There are four main islands – Hokkaido, Honshu, Shikoku and Kyushu. These are mostly very mountainous, so the big cities have spread along the strips of flat land around the coast. This is where most of the good farmland is sited, too. Japan produces rice and tea, and has a large fishing fleet. The north of the country is cold and snowy in winter, but the south has a warm, tropical climate.

Japan has very few resources such as oil or coal. Even so, it is a very modern country which has many big businesses and produces cars and electrical goods. At the same time Japan is an ancient country, with many traditional customs and ceremonies. You can still see beautiful Buddhist temples and castles too, dating back to the Middle Ages. Japan has long been famous for its beautiful art, architecture and pottery. Japanese artists carry on these traditions in modern dance, the cinema and even in computer games.

The Japanese capital is **Tokyo**. It is a centre of business and industry and merges with another great city, the port of Yokohama. It has suffered in the past from severe earthquakes.

The high-speed **Bullet Train** has become a symbol of modern Japan. Japan's islands are linked by some of the world's longest and most modern bridges and tunnels.

Kuril Is. (Russia)

HOKKAIDO

▲ Asahi Mt 2,290 m

Sapporo

Kitak

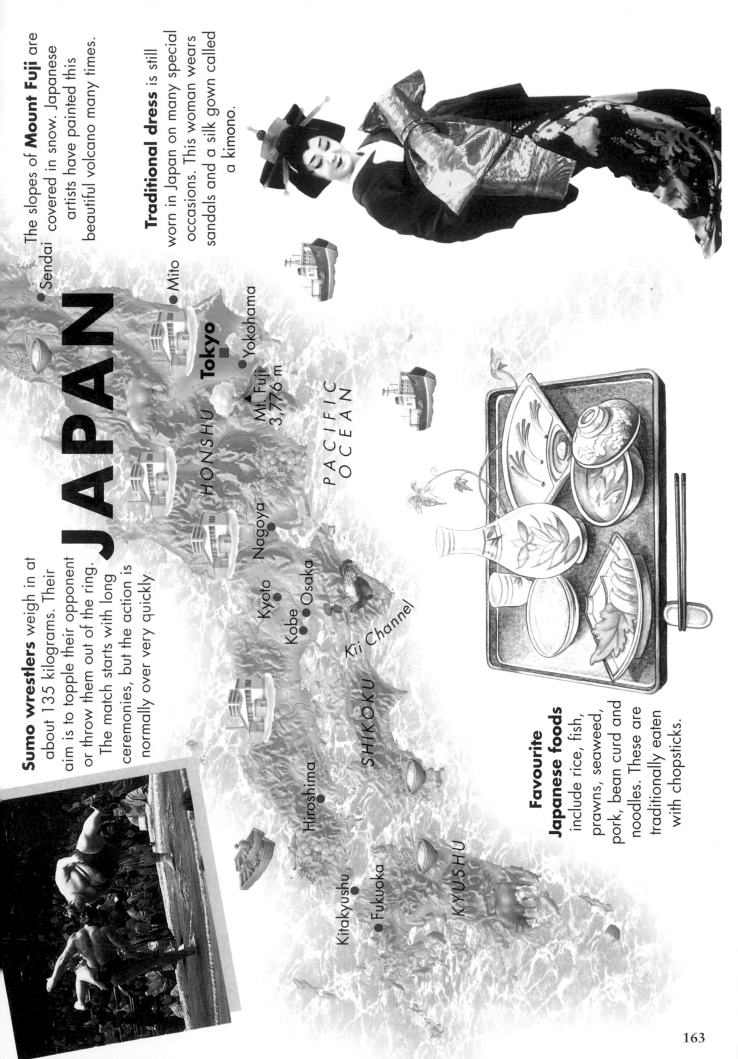

JAPAN

The slopes of **Mount Fuji** are covered in snow. Japanese artists have painted this beautiful volcano many times.

Traditional dress is still worn in Japan on many special occasions. This woman wears sandals and a silk gown called a kimono.

Sumo wrestlers weigh in at about 135 kilograms. Their aim is to topple their opponent or throw them out of the ring. The match starts with long ceremonies, but the action is normally over very quickly.

Favourite Japanese foods include rice, fish, prawns, seaweed, pork, bean curd and noodles. These are traditionally eaten with chopsticks.

Sendai

Mito

Yokohama

Tokyo

HONSHU

Mt. Fuji 3,776 m

PACIFIC OCEAN

Nagoya

Kyoto

Osaka

Kobe

Kii Channel

SHIKOKU

Hiroshima

Kitakyushu

Fukuoka

KYUSHU

Southeast Asia

The southeast of the Asian continent borders India and China. It is a land of flooded ricefields, forests, remote hill country and great rivers, such as the Irrawaddy and the Mekong. This region has beautiful Buddhist temples and ruins left behind by ancient civilizations. Sadly, it has also seen terrible wars in the last 50 years, while in some areas the traditional way of life has been completely changed by tourism or, in the cities of Singapore or Kuala Lumpur, by big business.

The mainland states include Myanmar, Thailand, Cambodia, Laos and Vietnam. Malaysia takes up part of the mainland but also most of the forested, tropical island of Borneo. The small state of Brunei is in the north of Borneo. The south of the region is occupied by the long chains of islands which make up Indonesia. In the far east, bordering the Pacific Ocean are the Philippines.

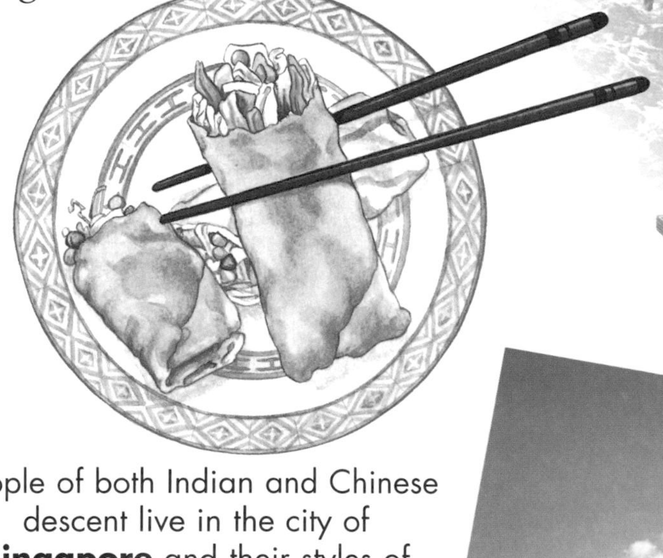

INDIA

MYANMAR (BURMA)

CHINA

Yangon (Rangoon)

Hano

LAOS

Vientiane

THAILAND

Bangkok

CAMBOD

Phnom Penh

Ho Ch Minh Ci

Gulf of Thailand

M A L

Medan

Kuala Lump

Strait of Malacca

Sumatra

SINGAPO

Jakart

People of both Indian and Chinese descent live in the city of **Singapore** and their styles of cooking have mingled – deliciously!

This ornate stone demon guards the royal palace in **Bangkok**, capital of Thailand.

The **orang-utan** lives in the rainforests of Borneo and Sumatra. Throughout Southeast Asia forests are threatened by logging, clearance and fires.

A boat is anchored by the banks of the Hue river, in northeastern **Vietnam**. Cone-shaped straw hats protect the wearer from tropical sun and monsoon rains.

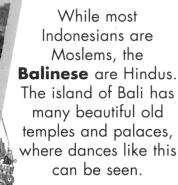

While most Indonesians are Moslems, the **Balinese** are Hindus. The island of Bali has many beautiful old temples and palaces, where dances like this can be seen.

Luzon

■ Manila

PHILIPPINES

VIETNAM

SULU SEA

Mindanao

Bandar Seri Begawan

BRUNEI

SIA

CELEBES SEA

BORNEO

Moluccas

Sulawesi

I N D O N E S I A

NEW GUINEA

AVA

SEA

BANDA SEA

FLORES SEA

va

• Surabaya

Lombok

Bali

Sumba

Timor

Singapore is a tiny independent country. Most of it is taken up by the city of Singapore, an international centre of business and trade.

Meet the **komodo dragon**, the world's biggest lizard. It lives only on Komodo and a few neighbouring islands in Indonesia.

165

North and West Africa

The Mediterranean coast has a pleasant, warm climate. To the south, beyond the Atlas mountains, is the world's largest desert, the Sahara. Its burning hot sands and rocks stretch all the way from Mauritania to Egypt. The River Nile, the world's longest river, meets the sea in Egypt after a long journey northwards across Sudan. It rises in the mountains of Central Africa and Ethiopia.

The countries bordering the southern edge of the Sahara make up the Sahel. This is a dry, dusty region where thin grass is grazed by cattle and goats. Nearer the coast, on the Gulf of Guinea, there is fertile farmland, forest and the oil-rich lands around the River Niger. West Africa produces peanuts, cocoa, palm oil and cotton.

Peoples of the north include Berbers and Arabs. The many different peoples living to the south of the Sahara are mostly Black Africans. Religions of the region include Islam, Christianity and spirit religions.

Strait of Gibralt
Madeira Casablanca Rabat
MOROCCO
CANARY
ISLANDS   ATLAS MTS
**Western
Sahara**   **ALGER**
                          S   A
Cape
Blanc
MAURITANIA   **MALI**
  Nouakchott
                          Timbuktu
Dakar   Niger
SENEGAL
Banjul **GAMBIA**   Ouagadougou Nian
Bissau   Bamako **BURKINA FAS**
GUINEA- GUINEA
BISSAU Conakry
Freetown **SIERRA IVORY**
        LEONE COAST
Monrovia Yamoussoukro Lomé La Po
LIBERIA Abidjan Accra   No

This grumpy-looking camel is looking out over the **Pyramids**, the royal burial sites of ancient Egypt. Africa's first great civilization grew up in Egypt about 5,000 years ago.

Tutankhamun died in 1327BC. He was ruler, or pharaoh, of ancient Egypt and was buried with all sorts of rich treasures.

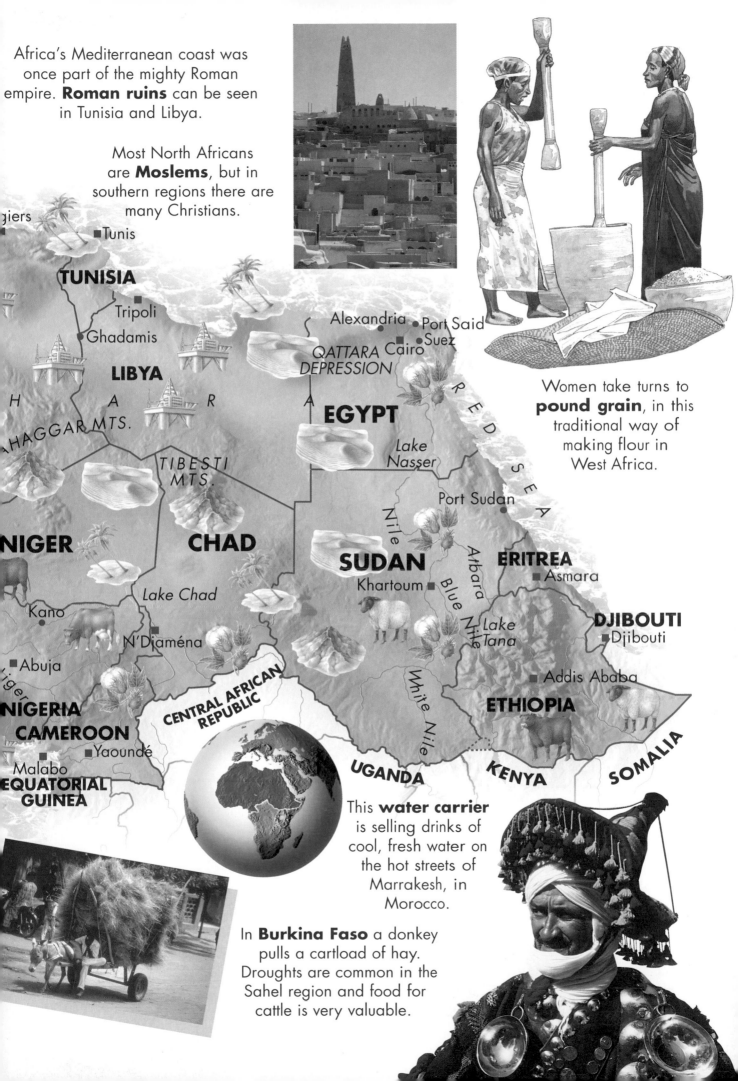

Africa's Mediterranean coast was once part of the mighty Roman empire. **Roman ruins** can be seen in Tunisia and Libya.

Most North Africans are **Moslems**, but in southern regions there are many Christians.

Women take turns to **pound grain**, in this traditional way of making flour in West Africa.

giers

Tunis

TUNISIA

Tripoli

Ghadamis

Alexandria · Port Said
Suez

QATTARA Cairo
DEPRESSION

LIBYA

EGYPT

H   A   R   A

AHAGGAR MTS.

TIBESTI MTS.

Lake Nasser

Port Sudan

R
E
D

S
E
A

NIGER

CHAD

Lake Chad

Kano

N'Djaména

Abuja

NIGERIA

CAMEROON

Yaoundé

Malabo

EQUATORIAL GUINEA

Niger

Nile

SUDAN

Khartoum

Arbara

Blue Nile

Lake Tana

ERITREA

Asmara

DJIBOUTI

Djibouti

Addis Ababa

ETHIOPIA

White Nile

CENTRAL AFRICAN REPUBLIC

UGANDA

KENYA

SOMALIA

This **water carrier** is selling drinks of cool, fresh water on the hot streets of Marrakesh, in Morocco.

In **Burkina Faso** a donkey pulls a cartload of hay. Droughts are common in the Sahel region and food for cattle is very valuable.

Central, Eastern and Southern Africa

Central Africa is a land of rainforests, crossed by the River Congo. To the south are the Kalahari and Namib deserts, and the mountains and grasslands of South Africa. The east of the continent is divided by the Great Rift Valley, a network of deep cracks in the Earth's surface. It is fringed by volcanoes and in places has filled with water to form long lakes. East Africa includes rich farmland, which produces tobacco, fruit and vegetables. There are wide grassy plains dotted with thorny trees, grazed by great herds of wild animals including zebra, giraffe and many types of antelope. The continent is bordered by the Atlantic to the west and by the Indian Ocean to the east. Madagascar is Africa's largest island.

The **Masai people** live in southern Kenya and northern Tanzania. Many of them herd cattle.

SÃO TOMÉ & PRÍNCIPE

Libreville

GABON

REP. CONG

Brazzav

Kinsha

Cabinda (ANGOLA)

Luanda

A N

Vast herds of wild animals still roam eastern and southern Africa. They include lion, antelope, **elephant** and rhinoceros.

Wind shapes the shifiting sands of the **Namib desert** in southwestern Africa. This harsh, dry region borders the Atlantic coast for 1,280 kilometres.

Windh

NAMIB DESERT

Cape T

Cape Good H

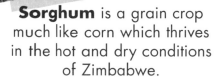

Sorghum is a grain crop much like corn which thrives in the hot and dry conditions of Zimbabwe.

The **Zulus** are the largest group of peoples living in South Africa. Many different peoples live in the region, each with their own language and traditions.

The River Zambezi forms **Victoria Falls,** a huge waterfall, between Zambia and Zimbabwe. Its local name is Mose-la-Tunya, the 'smoke that thunders'.

SOMALIA

CENTRAL AFRICAN REPUBLIC

Bangassou

ngui

Uele

ongo

UGANDA

KENYA

Mogadishu

Kampala

RWANDA

Lake Victoria

Nairobi

Kigali

EMOCRATIC REP. OF CONGO

BURUNDI

▲ Kilimanjaro 5,895 m

Dodoma

SEYCHELLES

Kananga

Lake Tanganyika

Kasai

Sankuru

TANZANIA

INDIAN OCEAN

Lake Malawi (Nyasa)

COMOROS

LA

MALAWI

Lilongwe

Moçambique

ZAMBIA

Lusaka

Zambezi

Blantyre

Harare

MOZAMBIQUE

ZIMBABWE

AMIBIA

Limpopo

Mozambique Channel

Antananarivo

BOTSWANA

Gaborone

MADAGASCAR

MAURITIUS

ALAHARI DESERT

Pretoria

Maputo

Mbabane

SWAZILAND

Maseru

LESOTHO

SOUTH AFRICA

This animal is a ring-tailed **lemur**. Lemurs are only found on the island of Madagascar. They live in forest and dry scrub land, where they eat fruit and insects.

169

Oceania
Australia

The centre of Australia is an empty wilderness of desert, rocks and scrub. It is bordered by grasslands, tropical forests and creeks. In the east are the mountains of the Great Dividing Range. The chief rivers are the Murray and the Darling, in the southeast. The remote country regions of Australia are known as the 'outback'. They are grazed by huge herds of sheep and cattle, and in places are worked by mining companies.

Most Australians live in the big cities around the coast, such as Brisbane, Sydney, Melbourne, Adelaide and Perth. Across Bass Strait is the island of Tasmania, which has a cooler climate.

Today's Australians include the first inhabitants of the land, the Aborigines, as well as the descendants of British people who seized their lands about 200 years ago. There are also many people from other European countries and from Asia.

Sydney Opera House rises from Sydney Harbour like a giant sailing ship.

A **giant clam** lies in the tropical waters of this 2,000 kilometre-long bank of coral.

GREAT SAND DESER

GIBSO DESER

WESTERN AUSTRALIA

GREAT VICTOR DESER

Perth

Archipelago of R Recherche

Through the surf **rowers** break white water during a beach contest. Australia is famous for its surf.

The **kookaburra** is a common Australian bird. It has a loud cackling call which gives it the nickname of the laughing jackass.

Surfers' Paradise is one of many resorts built along the eastern coast of Australia. Sunshine and surf attract many visitors.

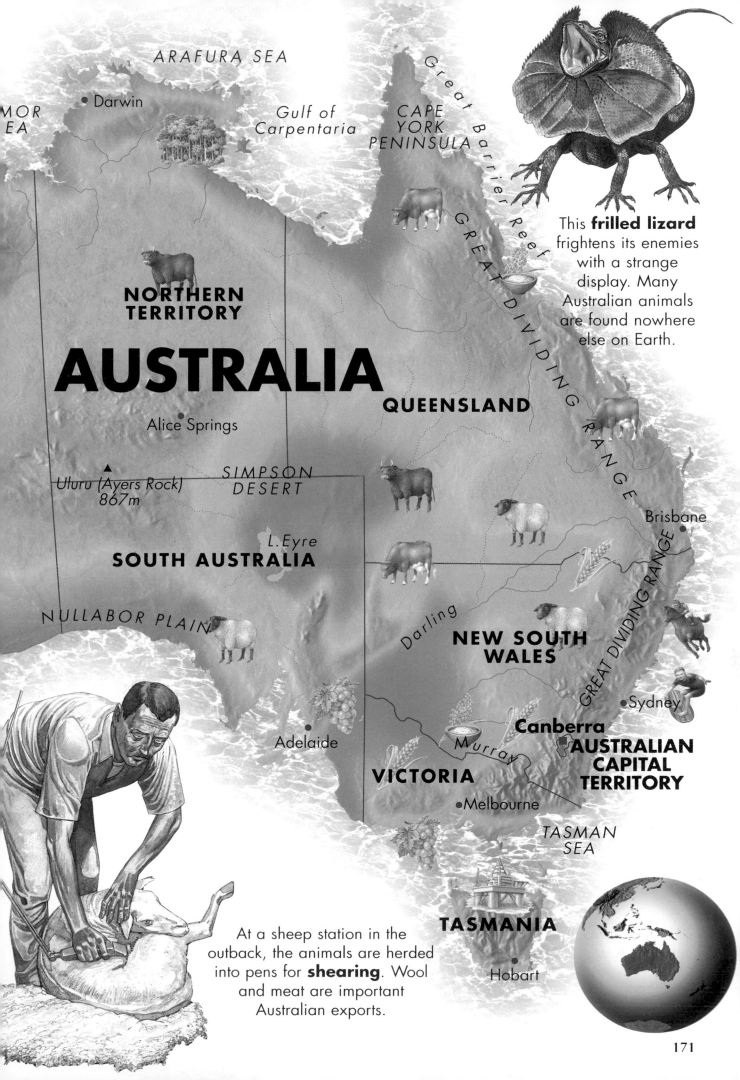

ARAFURA SEA

Darwin

MOR
EA

Gulf of
Carpentaria

CAPE
YORK
PENINSULA

Great Barrier Reef

NORTHERN
TERRITORY

AUSTRALIA

Alice Springs

QUEENSLAND

This **frilled lizard** frightens its enemies with a strange display. Many Australian animals are found nowhere else on Earth.

Uluru (Ayers Rock)
867m

*SIMPSON
DESERT*

L.Eyre

SOUTH AUSTRALIA

NULLABOR PLAIN

Darling

**NEW SOUTH
WALES**

GREAT DIVIDING RANGE

Brisbane

Sydney

Adelaide

Canberra
**AUSTRALIAN
CAPITAL
TERRITORY**

Murray

VICTORIA

Melbourne

*TASMAN
SEA*

At a sheep station in the outback, the animals are herded into pens for **shearing**. Wool and meat are important Australian exports.

TASMANIA

Hobart

171

New Zealand and the Pacific

If you sail eastwards from Australia, you reach a group of islands about 1,600 kilometres out into the Pacific Ocean. They make up a country called New Zealand. There are two main islands, North and South. They include high mountains and glaciers, hot springs, gushing spouts called geysers and grassy plains. The Maori people were the first people to settle these islands, followed after the 1800s by Europeans, especially the British. New Zealand raises sheep and exports dairy products, fruit and meat.

The Pacific is the world's biggest ocean stretching all the way to the Americas. It is dotted with small islands, and these are home to three main groups of people – the Polynesians (who include the Maoris), the Micronesians and the Melanesians. They live by fishing, growing crops such as coconuts and yams, by mining and by tourism.

Yellow Sea

East China Sea

Philippine Sea

SOUTH CHINA SEA

Northern Marian Islands (USA)

Guam

Federated States of Micronesia

Palau

Celebes Sea

Papua New Guinea

Solo Isla

Coral Sea

Papua New Guinea is made up of many islands. Some small islands are surrounded by shallow reefs.

This is a market in **Vanuatu,** a Pacific nation made up of 80 islands. They produce cocoa, dried coconut and bananas.

The **Kiwi** is a flightless bird which comes out by night to search for insects on the forest floor. It is the national emblem of New Zealand.

This **Karawari woman** from Papua New Guinea has painted her face for a traditional tribal gathering.

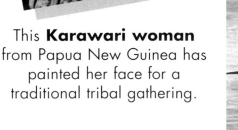

BERING SEA

*NORTH
PACIFIC
OCEAN*

Giant tortoises live on the Galapagos Islands. In fact the islands' name means 'tortoises' in Spanish. These Pacific Islands are governed by the South American country of Ecuador.

Midway
Island (USA)

Wake Island
(USA)

Hawaii (USA)

Marshall
Islands

The brown nut of the **coconut**, with its white centre, is found inside a large green fruit. Coconuts are a valuable Pacific island export.

South Island, New Zealand, has snowfields, glaciers and **high mountains**. Mount Cook reaches 3,764 metres above sea level.

Nauru   Kiribati

Tuvalu

Vanuat   Samoa   American
        Fiji   Samoa
                                        French
New   Tonga   Cook Islands   Polynesia
Caledonia   (New
(France)   Zealand)

*Galapagos
(Ecuador)*

Auckland•

Hamilton•   •Rotorua
            Waikato

        L. Taupo
        ▲
Ruapehu   Napier
2,797m   •Hastings

•Palmerston North

Huge stone heads were carved by Polynesian settlers on **Easter Island**, about 1,000 years ago.

**NEW
ZEALAND**

Kaibola canoes are the traditional means of transport of the Pacific Islands. This crew is from Papua New Guinea.

Mt.Cook
3,764m▲
            •Christchurch

SOUTHERN ALPS

Cook Strait

Wellington

This fine **wooden carving** was placed above the door of a Moari building.

Clutha •Dunedin

•Invercargill

Stewart Island

Traditionally, **Maoris** wore cloaks and tattooed their faces. Maoris today retain many customs.

173

Polar Lands

The northern part of the globe is called the Arctic. It takes in the northern parts of North America, Europe and Asia. These are lands of ice and snow and deep-frozen treeless soil, called tundra. They surround the Arctic Ocean, of which large areas are permanently capped in thick ice. At the centre of this ice cap is the northernmost point on Earth, the North Pole.

Peoples of the Arctic include the Inuit of Greenland and Canada, the Saami of Scandinavia and the many peoples from the north of the Russian Federation, such as the Chukchi, Yupigyts, Evenks and Samoyeds. Some live by hunting and fishing, some by herding reindeer and some in more recent Arctic industries, such as oil and mining. The Arctic Ocean supports fish, whales, walrus and seals.

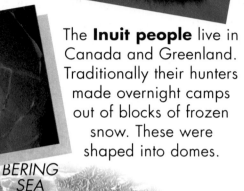

The **Inuit people** live in Canada and Greenland. Traditionally their hunters made overnight camps out of blocks of frozen snow. These were shaped into domes.

BERING SEA

ALASKA (USA)

Mackenzie

New Siberian Islands

Lena

ARCTIC OCEAN

North Magnetic Pole

CANADA

Victoria Island

Ellesmere Island

★ North Pole

Yenisei

Franz Josef Land

Novaya Zemlya

KARA SEA

Ob

GREENLAND (DENMARK)

Svalbard (Norway)

Murmansk

Archangel

ICELAND

Polar bears hunt seals on the ice.

The **Snowy owl** lives in Arctic regions.

Teams of dogs known as huskies, pull sleds across the snow in Antarctica.

The southernmost point on the globe is called the South Pole. It is surrounded by Antarctica, the coldest and windiest land on Earth. This is a land of mountains and dazzling white icefields, split by deep cracks called crevasses. Large areas of frozen sea surround the land. Massive slabs of ice break off in spring to form icebergs. No people have ever settled in Antarctica, but there are scientific bases. Some countries claim parts of Antarctica and there may be rich minerals in the rocks deep beneath the ice. However, many people think that Antarctica should be left alone, as the last real wilderness on our planet.

The southern part of the world has its winter while the northern part has summer. Polar regions stay dark for the whole day at midwinter, and stay light during the night at midsummer.

Walruses are big blubbery animals with flippers and long tusks, which they use to scrape clams off the seabed. They swim in bitterly cold Arctic waters.

Ships entering **polar waters** must be strengthened so that they can smash their way through floating ice.

The big tails of **whales** are called flukes. Many kinds of whale come to feed in polar waters.

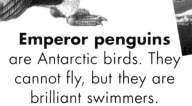

Emperor penguins are Antarctic birds. They cannot fly, but they are brilliant swimmers.

Many different kinds of **seal** breed in polar waters. They gather in large numbers on rocks, ice-floes and beaches.

Up to nine-tenths of an **iceberg** may be under water. They are a hazard to shipping.

ATLANTIC OCEAN

Permanent Extent of Sea Ice

INDIAN OCEAN

Drake Passage

WEDELL SEA

Coats Land

Maud Land

Enderby Land

Antarctic Peninsula

Ronne Ice Shelf

Cape Darnley

Vinson Massif 5,410m

South Pole

GREATER ANTARCTICA

TRANSANTARCTIC MTNS.

LESSER ANTARCTICA

Wilkes Land

Ross Ice Shelf

Erebus 3,794m

ROSS SEA

PACIFIC OCEAN

F I R

DICTIC

S   T

ONARY

How to use your dictionary

First Dictionary is a book that tells you about words. It tells you how to spell words and it tells you what words mean. It also shows you how to use words. It has been specially written for people who are just starting to learn to read and write. Most of the words are the kind that you see and use every day and we have given examples of how to use them in simple, easy-to-understand language.

To make the best use of your dictionary, you need to understand how it works. Here are some of its key features.

Alphabetical order

All the words are in the order of the **ABC** - so all words beginning with **A** are grouped together and come before the group of words beginning with **B**; and these **B** words come before words beginning with **C**... and so on all the way to **Z**. The coloured letters on the opposite page shows you the order of the alphabet.

Same but different

You will also discover that there are some words with different meanings but exactly the same spelling.

Carefully selected entries

There are more than 1,500 specially selected entries, or headwords. These are printed in **bold** type.

For example, if you want to find out more about the word **different**, first of all you go to that part of the book where all the words starting with the letter **d** begin. Then you start looking for words beginning with **di**, and then words beginning with **dif**, and so on until you find the word.

bat

1 A **bat** is an animal that looks like a mouse with wings. **Bats** hunt for food at night.

2 A **bat** is also a kind of wooden or metal stick. You use a **bat** for hitting the ball in games such as baseball or cricket.

Clear definitions

Next to the word is the definition. The definition is the part which tells us what the word means. This is written clearly and simply. So if you look up the definition of **different** you find that it means "not the same".

different

Different means not the same. *These houses are different in twelve ways. Can you see how?*

Example sentences

These show you how to use many of the words. They are written in *italic* text.

Helpful illustrations

Every page has carefully chosen illustrations and photographs that help to make the meaning of a word even clearer.

octopus *(octopuses)*
An **octopus** is a sea animal with a soft round body and eight long arms called tentacles. **Octopuses** live at the bottom of the sea. They hide in caves and eat crabs and shellfish.

Finding out about words

When looking up words in this dictionary you will discover that most words have different forms. These are shown after the **headword** and are in *italic* type.

The *plural* form is when there is more than one of something. We make a simple plural by adding an "s" or "es" to the end of certain words *(nouns)*.

The plural form of **octopus** is **octopuses**.

If you add different endings to other kinds of words *(verbs)* you can show when something is happening or has happened.

This tells us that Zoe is sewing the button on her shirt now.

By making these kinds of discoveries you will learn something about how to use words correctly. This is called *grammar*.

Extra everyday words

Last of all, at the end of your dictionary there are some useful facts and a list of words that we use all the time. We all know what these words mean but sometimes may not know how to spell them.

sew *(sews sewing sewed sewn)*
When you **sew**, you use a needle and thread to join pieces of cloth together, or to fix things to cloth. *Zoe is sewing a button on her shirt.*

We hope you will enjoy using your First Dictionary and exploring the world of words and their meanings. We also hope you will find it a useful reference book for many years to come as you find out more and more about how language works.

Aa

abroad
If you go **abroad**, you go to another country. *We went abroad for our holidays last year.*

accident
An **accident** is something bad that you did not expect to happen. *I had an accident with the pot of paint. I dropped it and it spilled everywhere.*

ache
An **ache** is a pain in a part of your body that goes on hurting for a long time. *Sam is going to the dentist because he has toothache.*

acrobat
An **acrobat** is a person who can do difficult and exciting balancing tricks. *We watched the acrobats walking along a wire high above the ground.*

act *(acts acting acted)*
If you **act** in a film or play, you play a part in it.

active
Somebody who is **active** moves about a lot and is always very busy doing things.

actor
An **actor** is a person who pretends to be somebody else in a film or play. *That film we saw on TV had really good actors in it.*

add *(adds adding added)*
1 When you **add** something, you put it with something else. *Elliott added sugar to the cake mixture.*
2 When you **add** numbers, you put them together. *If you add three and six you get nine.*

address *(addresses)*
Your **address** is the name of the house, street and town where you live. *Dan's address is 24 River Road, Oaktown OK1 2AD.*

adult
An **adult** is a grown-up person.

adventure
An **adventure** is something exciting or dangerous that happens to you. *Ali's first trip in an aeroplane was quite an adventure.*

advertisement
An **advertisement** in a newspaper or on television tells you about something and tries to make you want to buy it. **Advertisements** are also known as adverts or ads.

aeroplane
An **aeroplane** is a machine that flies. **Aeroplanes** have wings and one or more engines.

afford
If you can **afford** something, you have enough money to pay for it. *I'm going to save up my pocket money until I can afford to buy some new skates.*

afraid
If you are **afraid**, you feel something nasty will happen to you. *Our dog is afraid of thunder.*

afternoon
Afternoon is the part of the day between morning and evening. *We go home from school at 3 o'clock in the afternoon.*

age
Your **age** is the number of years you have lived.

ago
Ago means at some time in the past. *The puppies were born only a week ago, so they are still tiny.*

agree *(agrees agreeing agreed)*
If somebody **agrees** with you, they think or feel the same way as you. *My brother and I never agree about what to watch on television.*

air
Air is what we breathe. **Air** is all around us, but we cannot see it. *We went for a walk in the fresh air.*

aircraft

An **aircraft** is any machine that can fly. Aeroplanes, gliders and helicopters are all different kinds of **aircraft**.

airport

An **airport** is a place with buildings and runways. Aircraft take off and land there, and people get on and off planes.

alarm

An **alarm** is something such as a bell or a flashing light that tells us that there is danger. *When they heard the fire alarm, everybody quickly left the building.*

album

1 An **album** is an empty book in which you can put such things as photos or stamps.
2 An **album** is also several different pieces of music together on a CD or tape.

alike

If two or more things or people are **alike**, they are the same in some way. *Lauren and her twin sister look so alike.*

alive

A person, plant or an animal that is **alive** is living and is not dead. *My great-grandma is still alive, but my great-granddad died last year.*

alligator

An **alligator** is an animal with a long tail, short legs and a large mouth with sharp teeth. **Alligators** are reptiles and live in rivers in some hot countries.

allow

(allows allowing allowed)
If you **allow** somebody to do something, you let them do it. *My mum doesn't allow me to watch television before school.*

almost

Almost means nearly, but not quite. *It's almost 4 o'clock.*

alone

If you are **alone**, there is nobody else with you. *Our dog gets upset if we leave her alone.*

aloud

Aloud means so that other people can hear. *The teacher read the story aloud to the class.*

alphabet

The **alphabet** is all the letters that we use to write words in a special order. The English **alphabet** starts with A and ends with Z.

always

1 **Always** means all the time. *You should always be kind to animals.*
2 **Always** also means every time. *Our dog is always pleased to see me when I get home from school.*

amazing

Something that is **amazing** surprises you very much. *I've got an amazing story to tell you.*

ambulance

An **ambulance** is a van or car that carries people to hospital when they are ill or hurt.

amount

An **amount** of something is how much there is. *Different sizes of container hold different amounts of food.*

amphibian

Amphibians are animals that live in water when they are young, and then live on land for most of the time when they are adults. Frogs, toads and newts are all kinds of **amphibians**.

ancient

Something that is **ancient** is very, very old.

angry *(angrier angriest)*

If you are **angry**, you are very cross. *Laura was angry when I let her hamster out of its cage.*

animal

An **animal** is anything that is alive and that can move from one place to another. Horses, tigers, elephants, birds, bees, fish and frogs are all **animals**.

ankle

Your **ankle** is the part of your leg where it joins your foot. *Lucy fell and hurt her ankle.*

anniversary *(anniversaries)*

An **anniversary** is a day that you remember because something important happened on that day in a past year. My aunt and uncle's wedding **anniversary** is on the 20th May.

annoy *(annoys annoying annoyed)*

If somebody **annoys** you, they make you cross by doing something you do not like. *It annoys me when my sister leaves her clothes lying all over the floor in our bedroom.*

another

Another means one more. *Have another sandwich.*

answer *(answers answering answered)*

1 When somebody speaks to you or asks you a question, you **answer** by speaking to them. *I asked him the time but he didn't answer.*

2 An **answer** is what you say to somebody who asks you a question. *Put up your hand if you know the answer.*

ant

An **ant** is a tiny insect. **Ants** live under the ground in groups called colonies.

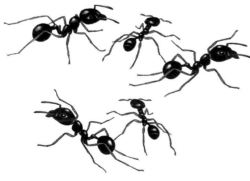

apart

1 Apart means away from each other. *Jim planted the flowers 15 centimetres apart.*

2 Apart also means in pieces. *Tom took the clock apart to see how it worked and then he put it back together again.*

ape

An **ape** is a large animal that looks like a monkey, but without a tail. Gorillas and chimpanzees are all kinds of **apes**.

apologize *(apologizes apologizing apologized)*

When you **apologize** you say you are sorry about something you have said or done. *Kevin apologized for being late.*

appear *(appears appearing appeared)*

When something **appears** you begin to see it. *Tim suddenly appeared from behind the tree.*

apple

An **apple** is a round green, red or yellow fruit. **Apples** grow on trees.

area

An **area** is a part of a place. *Which area of town do you come from?*

argue *(argues arguing argued)*

If you **argue** with somebody, you talk in an angry way because you do not agree with them.

arm

Your **arms** are the parts of your body between your shoulders and your hands.

armour

Armour is a covering made of metal that soldiers wore long ago to protect themselves in battle.

army *(armies)*

An **army** is a large group of soldiers who are trained to fight together in wars.

arrive *(arrives arriving arrived)*

When you **arrive**, you get to a place. *What time does grandma's flight arrive?*

arrow

1 An **arrow** is a long thin stick with a point at one end. You shoot arrows from a bow.

2 An **arrow** is also a sign that shows the way.

art

Art is something special such as a painting, a drawing or a statue that somebody has made.

artist

An **artist** is a person who draws or paints pictures or makes other special and beautiful things.

ash (ashes)

Ash is the grey powder that you can see after something such as wood has burned.

ask (asks asking asked)

1 If you **ask** a question, you want to find the answer to something. *"Where is the railway station, please?" she asked.*
2 If you **ask** for something, you say you would like to have it. *Tamsin asked her brother to help her clean her bike.*

asleep

When you are **asleep**, you are sleeping. *I was asleep in bed when the telephone rang in the middle of the night and woke me up.*

assembly (assemblies)

Assembly is when a large group of people meet in one place. *We have school assembly every morning.*

astronaut

An **astronaut** is a person who travels in space.

ate Look at **eat**.
The baby ate all her breakfast.

atlas (atlases)

An **atlas** is a book of maps.

attack (attacks attacking attacked)

If somebody or something **attacks** you, they try to hurt you.

attention

1 When you pay **attention**, you listen and watch carefully.
2 If somebody or something attracts your **attention**, you notice them. *Rose tried to attract my attention by waving her umbrella.*

attic

An **attic** is a room inside the roof of a house.

attract (attracts attracting attracted)

1 If something **attracts** you, you notice it and become interested in it. *I was attracted by the poster in the shop window.*
2 **Attract** also means to make something come closer. *Brightly coloured flowers attract bees. A magnet attracts some kinds of metals.*

audience

An **audience** is a group of people who have come to a place to see or listen to something such as a film, play or piece of music.

aunt

Your **aunt** is your father's sister, your mother's sister or the wife of your uncle.

author

An **author** is a person who has written a book, play or poem.

automatic

A machine that is **automatic** can work on its own without a person looking after it. *Traffic lights are usually automatic.*

autumn

Autumn is the part of the year between summer and winter, when leaves fall off the trees.

awake

If you are **awake**, you are not asleep. *Owls stay awake at night to hunt for food.*

183

Bb

ball
A **ball** is a round thing that you use to play all kinds of games. *He kicked the ball into goal.*

ballet
Ballet is a special way of dancing. *Amy goes to ballet lessons on Saturdays.*

baby *(babies)*
A **baby** is a very young child.

back
1 The **back** is the part of a person or an animal between the neck and the bottom or tail.
2 The **back** of something is behind or opposite the front. *She left her bike at the back of the library.*

backwards
If you count **backwards** from 100, you start with 100 and finish with 1.

bad *(worse worst)*
1 Things that are **bad** are not good. *Too many sweets are bad for your teeth.*
2 **Bad** also means nasty or serious. *Megan has a bad cold so she isn't going to school today.*

bag
You use a **bag** to carry things in. **Bags** are made of paper, plastic, cloth or leather.

bake *(bakes baking baked)*
When you **bake** food, you cook it in an oven. *I am baking a chocolate cake for my uncle's birthday.*

balance *(balances balancing balanced)*
When you **balance** something, you keep it in place without letting it fall over. *Tara is balancing a book on her head very carefully.*

balloon
A **balloon** is a coloured bag made of rubber or plastic which you fill with gas or air to make it float. Some large **balloons** can float high in the sky and carry people in a special basket underneath.

banana
A **banana** is a long fruit with a yellow skin. **Bananas** grow in bunches on trees in hot countries.

band
1 A **band** is a group of people who play musical instruments together. *James plays the drums in the school band.*
2 A **band** is also a thin piece of material that you put around something. *He put a rubber band around the pens to keep them together.*

bang
A **bang** is a sudden loud noise. *The door blew shut with a bang.*

bank
1 A **bank** is a place that looks after money for people.
2 A **bank** is also the land along the sides of a lake or river.

bar
1 A **bar** is a long thin piece of metal. Animal cages have **bars**.
2 A **bar** is also a thick hard piece of something, such as a **bar** of soap or a **bar** of chocolate.

bare
1 **Bare** means without any clothes or anything else covering it. *She walks around the house in her bare feet.*
2 **Bare** also means empty. *The cupboard is bare.*

bark
1 A **bark** is the sudden noise that a dog makes. *Our dog has a very loud bark.*
2 **Bark** is also the rough covering on the trunk of a tree.

barn
A **barn** is a large building on a farm for keeping animals in or for storing things such as hay.

basket
You use a **basket** for carrying things in. **Baskets** are made of straw, strips of thin wood, or wire.

bat
1 A **bat** is an animal that looks like a mouse with wings. **Bats** hunt for food at night.

2 A **bat** is also a kind of wooden or metal stick. You use a **bat** for hitting the ball in games such as baseball or cricket.

bath
A **bath** is a large container that you fill with water and sit in to wash yourself all over.

bathroom
A **bathroom** is a room where you wash yourself. It has a bath or shower and sometimes it has a toilet as well.

battery *(batteries)*
A **battery** is something that stores electricity inside it. You put **batteries** in things like torches and toys to make them work.

battle
A **battle** is a fight between two armies or groups of people.

beach *(beaches)*
A **beach** is the land next to the sea. **Beaches** are covered with sand or small smooth stones called pebbles.

bead
A **bead** is a small round piece of glass, plastic or wood with a hole in it. You can put a string through the holes of a set of **beads** to make a necklace.

beak
A **beak** is the hard pointed part of a bird's mouth. Birds use their **beaks** to pick up food.

bean
A **bean** is a vegetable with a large seed inside that can be cooked and eaten. There are many different kinds of **bean**.

bear
A **bear** is a large wild animal with thick fur and sharp claws.

beard
A **beard** is the hair that grows on a man's chin.

beat *(beats beating beat beaten)*
1 If you **beat** something, you hit it again and again. *Tom is beating the drums.*
2 If you **beat** somebody in a game, you win and they lose.

beautiful
A **beautiful** thing is nice to look at, to hear or to smell.

beaver
A **beaver** is a furry animal that lives in or near lakes or rivers. It has a flat tail for swimming, and strong front teeth for chewing through wood.

bed
A **bed** is a piece of furniture that you lie on to sleep.

bee
A **bee** is a flying insect that can sting. **Bees** make honey.

beef
Beef is meat that comes from cattle. Hamburgers are made from **beef**.

beetle
A **beetle** is an insect with hard shiny wings. A ladybird is a kind of **beetle**.

begin *(begins beginning began begun)*
If you **begin** something, you start it. *You usually begin a book on the first page.*

behave *(behaves behaving behaved)*
The way we do things is how we **behave**. *The children behaved well and did not make too much noise.*

believe *(believes believing believed)*
If you **believe** something, you think it is true or real. *I don't believe in ghosts, do you?*

bell

A **bell** is something that makes a ringing sound when you hit it. Most **bells** are made of metal.

belong (belongs belonging belonged)

1 Something that **belongs** to you is yours. *Who does this funny hat belong to?*

2 If you **belong** to something, you are a part of it. *The twins belong to the football club.*

belt

A **belt** is a long strip of cloth or leather that you put around your waist. *You can use a belt to stop your trousers falling down.*

bench (benches)

A **bench** is a long seat that two or more people can sit on. *He sat on the park bench and fed the birds.*

bend (bends bending bent)

1 If you **bend** something, it stops being straight. *Henry bent the wire into a circle.*

2 If you **bend**, you move the top of your body downwards. *Sophie is bending down to pick something up from the floor.*

berry (berries)

A **berry** is a small fruit that grows on a bush. There are lots of different kinds of **berry** that are good to eat, such as strawberries, blackberries and raspberries. There are a few kinds of **berry** that are poisonous.

bicycle

A **bicycle** is a machine that you can ride on. **Bicycles** have two wheels and pedals. Bike is a short word for **bicycle**.

big (bigger biggest)

Something that is **big** is not small. Elephants are **big**.

bike Look at **bicycle**.

bird

A **bird** is an animal with feathers, wings and a beak. Most **birds** can fly. **Birds** lay eggs.

birthday

Your **birthday** is a day that you remember each year because it is the same day as the day you were born.

biscuit

A **biscuit** is a flat thin dry kind of cake.

bite (bites biting bit bitten)

When you **bite** something, you use your teeth to cut it. *Tom bit into the apple.*

blade

A **blade** is the sharp edge of a knife that can cut.

blame (blames blaming blamed)

If you **blame** somebody for something bad that happened, you think they did it. *Grandma blamed my dog for stealing the food from her shopping bag.*

blanket

A **blanket** is a large thick cover that keeps you warm in bed.

blew Look at **blow**.

Bart blew out the candles on the birthday cake.

blind

1 A person who is **blind** cannot see at all or cannot see very well.

2 A **blind** is a piece of material you pull down to cover a window.

blink (blinks blinking blinked)

When you **blink**, you close both your eyes and then open them again very quickly.

block

1 A **block** is a piece of something hard with flat sides, such as a **block** of wood or stone.

2 A **block** of flats is a large building with lots of flats.

3 (blocks blocking blocked) When something **blocks** the way, other things or people cannot get through. *The broken-down lorry blocked the road.*

blood

Blood is the red liquid that your heart pumps round and round inside your body.

blow *(blows blowing blew blown)*
1 When you **blow**, you make air come out of your mouth. *The children are blowing up balloons.*
2 When the wind **blows**, it makes the air move.

blunt
If a knife or pencil is **blunt**, it is not sharp or pointed.

boat
A **boat** is something that carries people and things on water. There are many different kinds of **boat**, such as canoes and sailing boats.

body *(bodies)*
The **body** of a person or an animal is the whole of them. Snakes have very long **bodies**.

boil *(boils boiling boiled)*
When water **boils**, it gets very hot and you can see little bubbles and steam coming off it.

bone
Bones are the hard parts in the body of a person or an animal.

book
A **book** is made of pieces of paper fixed together between two covers. Most **books** have words and pictures inside. This dictionary is a **book**.

boot
1 A **boot** is a kind of shoe that covers your ankle and part of your leg.
2 A **boot** is also a place in a car where you can store things such as bags.

bored
If you are **bored**, you feel a bit cross or unhappy because you have nothing interesting to do.

born
When a baby is **born**, it begins life outside its mother's body. *The puppies were born last weekend.*

borrow *(borrows borrowing borrowed)*
If you **borrow** something from somebody, you take it to use for a short time before you give it back. *Can I borrow your pen for a moment, please?*

boss
The **boss** is the person who is in charge of other people.

bottle
A **bottle** is a container for liquids. **Bottles** are made of glass or plastic.

bottom
1 The **bottom** of something is the lowest part. *She got off her bike at the bottom of the hill.*
2 Your **bottom** is the part of your body that you sit on.

bought
Look at **buy**. *Lily bought some bananas.*

bounce *(bounces bouncing bounced)*
When something **bounces**, it springs back after hitting something hard. *Raj bounced the ball off the wall.*

bow
1 A **bow** is a special knot that you make with ribbon or string to decorate something. *Lisa is wearing a big blue bow in her hair.*
2 A **bow** is also a bent piece of wood with a string fixed from one end to the other. People use **bows** to shoot arrows.

bow *(bows bowing bowed)*
When you **bow**, you bend your body forward and down. *The knight bowed to the king.*

bowl
A **bowl** is a round deep dish for food or liquids.

box *(boxes)*
A **box** is a container for keeping things in. **Boxes** are made of cardboard, wood, plastic or sometimes metal.

boy
A **boy** is a male child. **Boys** grow up to be men.

brain
Your **brain** is inside your head. You use your **brain** to think and remember, and it sends messages to other parts of your body to control them.

branch *(branches)*
The **branches** of a tree grow out from its trunk like arms.

brave
If you are **brave**, you show that you are not afraid of something that is dangerous or frightening.

bread
Bread is a kind of food made from flour and baked in an oven.

break *(breaks breaking broke broken)*
If something **breaks**, it goes into pieces or stops working. *I dropped the glass and it broke. Our iron has broken - it doesn't get hot any more.*

breakfast
Breakfast is the first meal that you eat in the day. *I had an egg for breakfast this morning.*

breathe *(breathes breathing breathed)*
When you **breathe**, you take air into your body through your nose and mouth and let it out again. *You breathe faster when you run.*

brick
A **brick** is a block of clay that has been baked so it is very hard and strong. A lot of houses are built of **bricks**.

bridge
A **bridge** is built over a river, railway or road so that people can get across.

bright
1 Something that is **bright** gives out a lot of light and shines strongly. *You should never look straight at the sun because its light is so bright it will hurt your eyes.*
2 Colours that are **bright** are clear and easy to see and are not pale or light.
3 Somebody who is **bright** is clever and learns quickly.

bring *(brings bringing brought)*
Bring means to carry or take somebody or something with you. *Bring that chair over here please. Matt brought a friend to the party.*

broke, broken
Look at **break**.
Ben broke the window. Lucy has broken her leg.

broom
A **broom** is a kind of large brush with a long handle. We use **brooms** for sweeping floors and paths.

brother
Your **brother** is a boy or man who has the same mother and father as you.

brought Look at **bring**.
I have brought you a present.

brush *(brushes)*
A **brush** is a tool with a lot of stiff hairs called bristles. You use a toothbrush to clean your teeth and another kind of **brush** for sweeping the floor.

bubble
A **bubble** is a light floating ball of liquid or soap filled with air.

bucket
A **bucket** is a container with a handle. You use it for carrying things. **Buckets** are made of metal or plastic.

bud
A **bud** is a flower or leaf on a plant, just before it opens.

bug
A **bug** is an insect. Ants and bees are **bugs**.

build *(builds building built)*
When you **build** something, you make it by putting different parts together. *My baby sister is building a tower out of wooden blocks.*

building
Buildings are things like houses, factories, schools, shops and blocks of flats. All **buildings** have walls and a roof.

bulb

1 A **bulb** is the round part of some plants that grow under the ground. *Daffodils grow from bulbs.*

2 A **bulb** is also the round glass part of a lamp that gives light.

bull

A **bull** is the male of the cattle family. A cow is the female.

bulldozer

A **bulldozer** is a kind of big tractor that moves rocks, earth and other things to make the land flat, ready for building on.

bunch *(bunches)*

A **bunch** is a group of things that are fixed or tied together. *We bought a bunch of bananas, and a bunch of flowers for grandma.*

burn *(burns burning burned or burnt)*

1 Something that is **burning** is on fire.

2 If you **burn** something, you damage it with fire. *Don't touch the oven or you'll burn yourself.*

burst *(bursts bursting burst)*

If something **bursts**, it breaks apart suddenly. *The balloon burst with a loud bang.*

bury *(buries burying buried)*

If you **bury** something, you put it in the ground and cover it. *The dog buried its bone in the garden.*

bus *(buses)*

A **bus** is a large vehicle with rows of seats inside for carrying a lot of people from one place to another on short journeys.

bush *(bushes)*

A **bush** is a small low tree with a lot of branches. Roses and berries grow on **bushes**.

business *businesses*

A **business** is a group of people who work together to make or sell things.

busy *(busier busiest)*

1 If you are **busy**, you have a lot of things to do. *I've been busy all day making food for the party.*

2 If a place is **busy**, a lot of things are happening there. *The streets of the city are always crowded and very busy.*

butter

Butter is a yellow food that is made from cream. *I spread butter on my bread.*

butterfly *(butterflies)*

A **butterfly** is an insect with white or brightly coloured wings. **Butterflies** grow from caterpillars.

button

A **button** is a small round thing on clothes. Shirts and jackets have **buttons** to keep them done up.

buy *(buys buying bought)*

When you **buy** something, you give money to have it. *Mum bought me some new shoes for school when we went shopping.*

buzz *(buzzes buzzing buzzed)*

If something **buzzes**, it makes a sound like a bee.

Cc

cabbage
A **cabbage** is a round vegetable with lots of big green leaves.

cabin
1 A **cabin** is a small house. **Cabins** are often made of wood. *We stayed in a log cabin in the woods.*
2 A **cabin** is also a room on a ship, or the part of an aircraft where people sit.

cage
A **cage** is a kind of box for keeping animals in. The sides are made of metal bars. *My pet mice live in a cage.*

cake
A **cake** is a sweet food that is made from butter, eggs, sugar and flour, and baked in an oven.

calculator
A **calculator** is a small machine that can work out sums quickly. You make it work by pressing buttons.

calendar
A **calendar** shows all the days, weeks and months of a year.

calf *(calves)*
A **calf** is a young cow or bull. A young elephant or a young whale is also called a **calf**.

call *(calls calling called)*
1 If you **call** somebody, you shout to tell them to come to you. *"Dinner's ready," she called from downstairs.*
2 **Call** also means to use the telephone. *I'll call you this evening at about seven.*
3 When you are **called** something, you have that name. *The black and white kitten is called Archie.*

calm
If you are **calm**, you are not afraid or excited. *If you see a snake in the jungle, it's very important to try to stay calm.*

camel
A **camel** is a large animal with a long neck and either one or two humps on its back. **Camels** can go for a long time without water. They are used for carrying people and things in the desert.

camera
A **camera** is a thing that you use for taking photos.

camp
A **camp** is a place where people live or stay in tents.

can
A **can** is a metal container. You can buy a lot of different kinds of food and drink in **cans.**

candle
A **candle** is a stick of wax with a piece of string called a wick through the middle. As the wick burns, the **candle** gives light.

cap
1 A **cap** is a small soft hat with a stiff part called a peak at the front.
2 A **cap** is also a small lid. *Make sure you put the cap back on the toothpaste when you've finished using it.*

car
A **car** is a machine that you travel in on roads. A **car** has four wheels and an engine. It can usually carry four or five people.

card
1 **Cards** are thick pieces of paper with words or pictures on them. People send postcards to their friends when they go on holiday. On your birthday, people send you birthday **cards**.
2 You use special **cards** with numbers and pictures on them for playing games.

cardboard
Cardboard is thick strong paper. Some boxes and cartons are made of **cardboard**.

care *(cares caring cared)*

1 When you **care** for somebody or something, you look after them. *Ned cared for the injured rabbit until it was better.*

2 When you **care** about something, you think it is important. *The only thing my sister cares about is football!*

careful

If you are **careful**, you think about what you are doing and try to do it well and safely without making mistakes. *You can carry those plates but be careful you don't drop them.*

careless

A person who is **careless** makes mistakes because they are not thinking about what they are doing. *Careless drivers can easily cause accidents.*

carpet

A **carpet** is a large thick cover for a floor.

carrot

A **carrot** is a long vegetable that is orange in colour. **Carrots** grow under the ground.

carry *(carries carrying carried)*

When you **carry** something, you hold it and take it somewhere. *Charlie carried the box very carefully.*

cart

A **cart** is a wooden vehicle with two or four wheels that can be pulled along by a horse or pushed by a person.

carton

A **carton** is a box made of plastic or cardboard. You can buy many kinds of food and drink in **cartons**. *We bought a carton of orange juice.*

cartoon

1 A **cartoon** is a funny drawing in a newspaper.

2 A **cartoon** is also a short film using drawings that seem to move. *They show a lot of really good cartoons on television.*

carve *(carves carving carved)*

When somebody **carves** wood or stone, they make a shape from it by cutting it.

case

1 A **case** is a container for keeping or carrying things in. *I put my camera in its case so that it didn't get damaged.*

2 A **case** is also a bag that you carry your clothes in when you go on holiday. *Have you packed your case yet?*

cash

Cash is money in coins and notes. *Mum paid by cheque because she didn't have any cash.*

cassette

A **cassette** is a flat plastic box with tape inside that plays and records music and sometimes pictures. *a video cassette, a music cassette.*

castle

A **castle** is a big building with thick walls and high towers. **Castles** were built long ago to keep the people inside safe in times of war.

cat

A **cat** is a small furry animal with a long tail and sharp claws. Many people keep **cats** as pets. Some kinds of large **cats** such as lions and tigers are wild animals.

catch *(catches catching caught)*

1 When you **catch** something, you take hold of it as it moves towards you. *Tom threw a stick and his dog caught it.*

2 If you **catch** an illness from somebody, you get it too. *I think I've caught your cold.*

3 If you **catch** a train or bus, you get on it to go somewhere. *We must hurry up because we've got a train to catch.*

caterpillar

A **caterpillar** looks like a furry worm with lots of legs. **Caterpillars** turn into butterflies and moths.

cattle

Cattle are cows and bulls on a farm. Farmers keep **cattle** for their meat and milk.

caught
caught Look at **catch**.
I threw the ball and Emily caught it.

cause (*causes causing caused*)
If you **cause** something, you make it happen. *Her careless driving caused the accident.*

cave
A **cave** is a big hole in the side of a mountain or under the ground.

ceiling
A **ceiling** is the top part of a room, above your head. *Mum climbed up the ladder and began to paint the ceiling.*

centre

centre
The **centre** of something is the middle part of it. *The flower has yellow petals and a black centre.*

century (*centuries*)
A **century** lasts for exactly one hundred years.

cereal
A **cereal** is a kind of food that people eat for breakfast. **Cereals** are made from the seeds of plants such as rice and wheat.

chain
A **chain** is made of a line of metal rings joined together.

chair
A **chair** is a piece of furniture that one person can sit on. A **chair** has a seat and a back.

chalk
Chalk is soft, white rock. You can write with a stick of **chalk**.

champion
A **champion** is a person who has won a game or sports competition. *Callum is the school swimming champion this year.*

change (*changes changing changed*)
1 When something **changes**, it becomes different in some way. *The traffic lights changed from red to green. Caterpillars change into moths or butterflies.*

2 If you **change** your clothes, you put on something different. *I change out of my school uniform as soon as I get home.*

channel
1 A **channel** is a narrow sea between two pieces of land.
2 A television set has different **channels** that you can choose from. Each **channel** has different programmes.

charge
1 If you are in **charge** of something, it is your job to look after it. *Dad left me in charge of my little brother while he was cleaning his car.*
2 (*charges charging charged*) If somebody **charges** you for something, they are asking you to pay money for it.

chase (*chases chasing chased*)
If you **chase** somebody or something, you run after them to try to catch them. *The cat chased after the ball of wool.*

cheap
If something is **cheap**, it does not cost a lot of money.

check (*checks checking checked*)
When you **check** something, you make sure that it is right. *James checked his spelling carefully.*

cheek

Your **cheeks** are the two soft parts on each side of your face, under your eyes.

cheerful

If you are **cheerful**, you are happy and you smile a lot.

cheese

Cheese is a food made from milk. There are many different kinds of **cheese**.

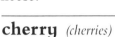

cherry *(cherries)*

A **cherry** is a small round fruit with a hard seed called a stone in the middle. **Cherries** grow on trees.

chest

1 Your **chest** is the front part of your body between your shoulders and your stomach.
2 A **chest** is also a strong heavy box with a lid. *The jewellery filled the wooden chest.*

chew *(chews chewing chewed)*

When you **chew** food, you keep biting it to make it soft. *The dog was chewing a bone.*

chick

A **chick** is a very young bird.

chicken

A **chicken** is a bird that people keep for its eggs and for its meat.

child *(children)*

A **child** is a young boy or girl. **Children** grow up to be men and women.

chimney *(chimneys)*

A **chimney** is a tall pipe above a fire inside a building. A **chimney** lets smoke escape to the outside.

chin

Your **chin** is the bottom part of your face under your mouth.

chocolate

Chocolate is a sweet brown food or drink.

choose *(chooses choosing chose chosen)*

When you **choose** something, you decide which one you want. *Mum let us choose what we wanted for dinner.*

chop *(chops chopping chopped)*

If you **chop** something, you cut it into small pieces with an axe or a knife. *Jenny chopped the carrots.*

circus *(circuses)*

A **circus** is a show with acrobats and clowns that you go to watch in a big tent. **Circuses** travel around from place to place.

city *(cities)*

A **city** is a very big town. New York and Paris are **cities**.

clap *(claps clapping clapped)*

When you **clap**, you make a noise by hitting your hands together. You **clap** to show that you have enjoyed something.

class *(classes)*

A **class** is a group of pupils who are learning together. *How many children are there in your class at school?*

claw

Claws are the sharp curved nails on the feet of birds, cats and many other animals.

clay

Clay is a special kind of mud that is used for making things such as pots and bricks. **Clay** becomes hard when it dries.

clean

1 Something that is **clean** is not dirty. *My hands are clean.*
2 *(cleans cleaning cleaned)* When you **clean** something, you take the dirt off it. *Carol cleaned the windows.*

clear

1 If something is **clear**, you can see through it easily. *Today the water is so clear I can see right to the bottom of the pond.*
2 **Clear** also means easy to understand, to see or to hear. *These instructions are very clear.*

clever

A **clever** person or animal learns and understands things quickly.

cliff

A **cliff** is a hill with one side that goes almost straight down. Most **cliffs** are by the sea.

climb *(climbs climbing climbed)*

When you **climb**, you use your hands and feet to go up or down something. *Be careful when you climb the ladder.*

clock

A **clock** is a machine that shows you what time it is.

close *(closes closing closed)*

When you **close** something, you shut it. *Please close all the windows before you go out. We closed our eyes and counted to ten.*

close

If something is **close**, it is near. *The park is close to the hospital.*

cloth

Cloth is material that clothes are made of. A lot of **cloth** is made of wool or cotton.

clothes

Clothes are the things that people wear to cover their bodies such as jeans and jumpers.

cloud

A **cloud** is a white or grey shape floating high in the sky. **Clouds** are made of millions and millions of drops of water.

clown

A **clown** is a funny person in a circus who dresses in strange clothes and makes people laugh.

clue

A **clue** is something that helps us to find the answer to a problem or puzzle. *I'll give you a clue what's in the box. It's got hands and a face, but no arms or legs. It's a clock!*

coach *(coaches)*

1 A **coach** is a bus that carries people on long journeys.
2 A **coach** is also a person who teaches people to play a game such as tennis or football.

coast

The **coast** is the land near the sea. *They live on the coast.*

coat

You wear a **coat** over your other clothes to keep you warm when you go outside. **Coats** have long sleeves and they are usually made of thick cloth.

coffee

Coffee is a drink that you make by adding hot water to a brown powder. The powder is made from the beans of the **coffee** bush.

coin

A **coin** is a piece of money made of metal. **Coins** are often round.

cold

1 **Cold** means not hot or warm. *In this country, the weather can become very cold in the winter.*
2 If you have a **cold**, you are ill and you sneeze a lot.

collar

1 A **collar** is the part of a shirt, jacket or coat that fits around your neck.
2 A **collar** is also a strip of leather or cloth that goes around the neck of a dog or cat.

collect *(collects collecting collected)*

1 When you **collect** things, you save a lot of them because you find them interesting. *Edward collects comics as a hobby.*
2 When you **collect** somebody from a place, you go there to fetch them. *Dad usually collects us from school on Mondays.*

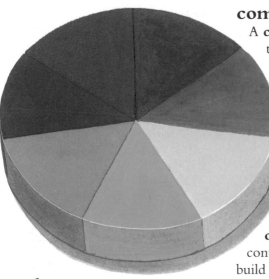

colour

Red, blue, yellow, purple and green are **colours**. *What is your favourite colour?*

comfortable

If something is **comfortable**, it is nice to be in or to wear. *This armchair is very comfortable to sleep in.*

comic

A **comic** is a kind of newspaper with cartoons and drawings that tell stories.

compact disc

A **compact disc** is a round flat silver-coloured piece of plastic with music or other sounds stored on it. It is also called a CD.

competition

A **competition** is a game or test to see who is the best at doing something. *I won first prize in the story-writing competition.*

computer

A **computer** is a machine that stores information and can work out many kinds of things very quickly. Some **computers** are used to control other machines, or to build things.

container

A **container** is something that you can put other things into. Boxes, bottles, cans and jars are all **containers**.

control *(controls controlling controlled)*

If you **control** somebody or something, you make it do what you want it to do. *You control a kite with long pieces of string.*

cook *(cooks cooking cooked)*

When you **cook** food, you make it ready to eat by using heat. You **cook** food in a cooker, or on top of it. *My dad is cooking the dinner tonight.*

cool

Something that is **cool** is quite cold. *Would you like a cool drink of lemonade or water?*

copy *(copies copying copied)*

If you **copy** something, you make it exactly the same as something else. *Darren copies everything his big brother does.*

corn

Corn is plants such as wheat that are grown for their seeds and made into flour.

corner

A **corner** is where two straight lines or edges meet. *A square has four corners.*

correct

Something that is **correct** has no mistakes. *He gave the correct answers to all the questions.*

cost *(costs costing cost)*

What something **costs** is how much money you have to pay for it. *How much does it cost to get into the zoo?*

costume

Costumes are the clothes that actors wear in plays or the clothes that people in a country wear at special times.

195

cot
A **cot** is a bed with high sides for a baby or young child.

cottage
A **cottage** is a small house. Most **cottages** are in the country.

cotton
1 **Cotton** is a light cloth made from **cotton** plants. Shirts and dresses can be made from **cotton**.
2 **Cotton** is also thread that you use for sewing.

cough (coughs coughing coughed)
When you **cough**, you make a sudden loud noise in your throat.

count (counts counting counted)
1 When you **count**, you say numbers in the right order. *Count from one to ten.*
2 **Count** also means to find how many.

country
1 A **country** is a part of the world with its own people and laws. France is a **country**.
2 The **country** is the land away from towns.

cousin
Your **cousin** is the son or daughter of your uncle or aunt.

cover (covers covering covered)
If you **cover** something, you put something else over it.

cow
A **cow** is a large farm animal that gives us milk.

crack
A **crack** is a thin line along something that has broken but that has not fallen to pieces. *Can you see the crack in this plate?*

crane
A **crane** is a machine that can move and lift very heavy things.

crash (crashes crashing crashed)
When something **crashes**, it hits or falls on to something else with a loud noise. *The bull crashed through the wooden fence.*

crawl (crawls crawling crawled)
If you **crawl**, you move along on your hands and knees. Babies often **crawl** before they can walk.

crayon
A **crayon** is a soft pencil made of coloured wax for drawing.

cream
Cream is the thick yellow part at the top of milk. *Would you like some cream on your cake?*

creature
A **creature** is any animal. *We watched a film about strange creatures from Mars.*

creep (creeps creeping crept)
When something **creeps**, it moves along slowly and quietly. *We crept upstairs so that we wouldn't wake anyone. The cat is creeping towards the bird.*

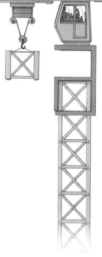

crew
A **crew** is a group of people who work together, especially on a boat, an aeroplane or a spacecraft. *The crew of the spaceship sent a message to Earth.*

cricket
1 **Cricket** is a game played with bats and a ball by two teams of eleven people.
2 A **cricket** is a jumping insect that makes a sound by rubbing its wings together.

crocodile

A **crocodile** is a large reptile with a long body. It has a huge mouth with sharp teeth. **Crocodiles** live in rivers in some hot countries.

crooked

Something that is **crooked** is bent and not straight. *A crooked branch.*

crop

Crops are plants that farmers grow as food.

cross

1 If you are **cross**, you feel a bit angry.
2 *(crosses)* A **cross** is a mark like + or X.
3 *(crosses crossing crossed)* If you **cross** something such as a road, you go from one side to the other. *We crossed the river in a boat.*

crowd

A **crowd** is a lot of people together in one place. *A large crowd of people were on the road.*

crowded

If a place is **crowded** it is full of people. *A crowded shopping centre.*

crown

A **crown** is a kind of hat made of gold or silver that kings and queens wear.

cruel *(crueller cruellest)*

People who hurt other people or animals on purpose are **cruel**.

crumb

A **crumb** is a tiny piece of bread or cake.

cry *(cries crying cried)*

When you **cry**, tears come out of your eyes. *My little sister always cries when she falls over.*

cub

A **cub** is a young bear, fox, lion, tiger or wolf.

cuddle *(cuddles cuddling cuddled)*

When you **cuddle** somebody you put your arms around them and hold them.

cup

A **cup** is a small bowl with a handle that you drink out of.

cupboard

A **cupboard** is a piece of furniture with doors and shelves for keeping things in.

curl

A **curl** is a piece of hair in a curved shape. Some people have straight hair and other people have curly hair.

curtain

Curtains are pieces of cloth that hang at the sides of a window and that you pull across to cover the window.

curve *(curves curving curved)*

When a line bends one way, it **curves**. *The road curves to the left a little way further on.*

cushion

A **cushion** is a kind of big soft bag that you put on a chair to make it more comfortable.

cut *(cuts cutting cut)*

1 When you **cut** something, you use a knife or scissors. *Kyle cut the pizza into six pieces. Harry had his hair cut.*
2 If you **cut** yourself, you hurt yourself on something sharp. *Kathy cut her finger on a very sharp piece of glass.*

Dd

damage *(damages damaging damaged)*
If you **damage** something, you break it or spoil it in some way. *The box got damaged when I dropped it on the floor.*

damp
If something is **damp**, it is a little wet. *Use a damp cloth to clean the table top.*

dance *(dances dancing danced)*
When you **dance**, you move your body about to music.

danger
Danger is something bad that might happen.

dangerous
If something is **dangerous**, it might hurt you. *It is dangerous to swim in the river.*

dark
1 When it is **dark**, there is no light. *It is dark at night.*

2 **Dark** colours are colours such as brown and black. *Elinor has very dark hair.*

darts
Darts are small arrows that you throw at a round board in a game called **darts**.

date
A **date** is the day, month and year when something happens. *What's the date today?*

daughter
A **daughter** is a girl or woman who is somebody's child.

day
1 A **day** is the 24 hours between midnight and the next midnight. There are seven **days** in a week.
2 **Day** is also the time when it is light outside. *Owls sleep when it is day and go hunting at night.*

dead
If somebody or something is **dead**, it is not alive any more.

deaf
A person who is **deaf** cannot hear well or cannot hear at all. Some **deaf** people make signs with their hands as a way of talking to one another.

dear
1 If something is **dear**, it costs a lot of money. *These rollerblades are too dear - let's look for a cheaper pair.*
2 If somebody or something is **dear** to you, you love them.
3 You put **Dear** before a person's name when you write a letter.

decide *(decides deciding decided)*
When you **decide**, you make up your mind about something. *Jade is trying to decide which dress to wear.*

decorate *(decorates decorating decorated)*
When you **decorate** something, you add things to it to make it look prettier. *Sarah is decorating the birthday cake.*

decoration
A **decoration** is a thing that has been added to make something look nicer.

deep
Something that is **deep** goes down a very long way. *We dug a deep hole to plant the tree in.*

deer
A **deer** is a wild animal that can run fast. Male **deer** have horns called antlers.

delicious
Something that is **delicious** is very good to eat or smell. *These apples are delicious.*

delighted
If you are **delighted**, you are very pleased about something. *Sue was delighted with her new bike.*

deliver *(delivers delivering delivered)*
If somebody **delivers** something to you, they bring it to you. *Dominic delivered the party invitations to his friends.*

dentist
A **dentist** is a person who looks after people's teeth.

describe *(describes describing described)*
If you **describe** something, you say or write what it is like. *Can you describe the strange bird you saw?*

desert
A **desert** is land where there is very little rain and where few plants can grow.

design
If you **design** something, you make a sketch or plan to show what it is going to look like when it is made.

desk
A **desk** is a table where you sit to read or write. Some **desks** have drawers.

dessert
Dessert is the sweet food that you eat at the end of a meal. *Billy had ice-cream for dessert and the rest of us had fruit salad.*

destroy *(destroys destroying destroyed)*
If something is **destroyed**, it is damaged or broken so badly that it cannot be used again. *The factory was destroyed by fire.*

detective
A **detective** is a person who looks for clues and tries to find out who did something such as a robbery.

diamond
A **diamond** is a shiny jewel that is clear like glass. **Diamonds** are expensive. *He bought his wife a diamond ring for her birthday.*

diary *(diaries)*
A **diary** is a book with a space for each day where you can write down important things that happen or are going to happen on that day.

dice
Dice are small blocks with a different number of dots on each side. You use **dice** for playing games.

dictionary *(dictionaries)*
A **dictionary** is a book that has a list of words from A to Z. You use a **dictionary** to check meanings and spellings.

die *(dies dying died)*
If somebody or something **dies**, they stop living. *Our dog was very old when she died.*

different
Different means not the same. *These houses are different in twelve ways. Can you see how?*

difficult
If something is **difficult**, it is not easy to do or to understand. *It's very difficult to balance for a long time on one leg.*

dig *(digs digging dug)*
When you **dig**, you move soil or sand to make a hole in the ground. *We dug a big hole on the beach.*

dinner
Dinner is the main meal of the day. Some people eat **dinner** in the middle of the day, and other people eat it in the evening.

dinosaur
A **dinosaur** is a reptile that lived millions of years ago. There were many different kinds of **dinosaurs** such as the Ultrasaurus in the picture. This **dinosaur** ate plants. Some kinds of **dinosaurs** were very strong and fierce.

dip *(dips dipping dipped)*
If you **dip** something in a liquid, you put it in quickly and take it out again. *She dipped her finger in the melted chocolate and tasted it.*

direction
A **direction** is the way you go or the way something points. *They walked in the direction of the town.*

dirt
Dirt is dust, mud or anything that makes things not clean.

dirty *(dirtier dirtiest)*
If something is **dirty**, it is covered in dirt. *Our dog always gets really dirty when we take her for a walk in the park.*

disappear
(disappears disappearing disappeared)
If somebody or something **disappears**, they go away and you cannot see them any more. *The bus disappeared over the hill.*

disappoint *(disappoints disappointing disappointed)*
If you are **disappointed**, you are sad because something you were hoping for did not happen. *Mark was disappointed because he didn't win the prize.*

disaster
A **disaster** is something very bad that happens and that may hurt a lot of people. Floods and earthquakes are **disasters**.

discover *(discovers discovering discovered)*
If you **discover** something, you find it or learn about it for the first time.

disguise
A **disguise** is something that you wear to change how you look.

dish *(dishes)*
A **dish** is a bowl for putting food in. *Our dog has her own dish.*

distance
Distance is how far two places are from one another. We can measure **distance** in miles or kilometres. *It's a short distance from our house to the school.*

disturb *(disturbs disturbing disturbed)*
If you **disturb** somebody, you stop them doing what they are doing, by making a noise or speaking to them. *Don't disturb Dad while he is on the telephone.*

dive *(dives diving dived)*
When you **dive**, you jump into water with your arms and head first.

divide *(divides dividing divided)*
1 When you **divide** something, you make it into smaller parts. *We divided the pizza into six pieces.*
2 When you **divide** numbers, you find out how many times one number goes into another number. *Ten divided by five is two.*

dizzy *(dizzier dizziest)*
When you are **dizzy**, you feel that things are spinning around you and that you are going to fall over. *I felt a bit dizzy when I got off the roundabout at the fair.*

doctor
A **doctor** is a person who helps you get better when you are ill. **Doctors** sometimes give you medicine or pills.

dog
Dogs are animals that people keep as pets or to do work. *The blind woman in our street has a dog who helps her find her way.*

doll
A **doll** is a toy that looks like a small person.

dolphin
A **dolphin** is an animal that lives in the sea. **Dolphins** are intelligent and friendly.

donkey
A **donkey** is an animal that looks like a small horse. **Donkeys** have long ears.

door
You open a **door** to go into a room or building. Things such as cars and cupboards also have **doors** that you open and close.

dot
A **dot** is a small round mark.

double
Double means twice as much or twice as many of something. *I had a double helping of ice-cream.*

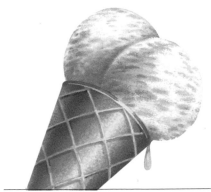

drag *(drags dragging dragged)*
If you **drag** something, you pull it along the ground slowly. *We dragged the heavy box across the floor.*

dragon

A **dragon** is a kind of monster that you can read about in stories. **Dragons** have wings and a long tail and they breathe fire.

drain

A **drain** is a pipe that takes water away. *When you have finished having a bath, you take out the plug and the water goes down the drain.*

drank Look at **drink**.
My brother drank all the orange juice.

draw *(draws drawing drew drawn)*
When you **draw**, you make a picture of something with a pencil, pen or crayon.

drawer

A **drawer** is a kind of box that slides in and out of a piece of furniture. You use a **drawer** for keeping things in.

dream

A **dream** is pictures and thoughts that go through your head when you are asleep. *Last night I had a dream that I was a famous ballet dancer.*

dress

1 *(dresses)* A **dress** is something that girls and women wear. It has a top joined to a skirt. *She wore a pink party dress.*
2 *(dresses dressing dressed)* When you **dress**, you put your clothes on your body.

drew Look at **draw**.
Look what I drew at school today.

drill

A **drill** is a tool for making holes in things such as walls and pieces of wood.

drink *(drinks drinking drank drunk)*
When you **drink**, you take liquid into your mouth and down into your stomach. *Can I have something to drink?*

drip *(drips dripping dripped)*
When liquid **drips**, it falls in drops. *The paint dripped all over the floor and made a mess.*

drive *(drives driving drove driven)*
When somebody **drives** something such as a car, bus or train, they control it and make it move along. *My uncle drives a lorry up and down the motorway.*

drop

1 A **drop** is a very small amount of a liquid.
2 *(drops dropping dropped)* If you **drop** something, you let it fall to the ground by accident. *Tom dropped the game on the floor and the pieces went everywhere.*

drown *(drowns drowning drowned)*
If somebody **drowns**, they die because they are under water where they cannot breathe.

drum

A **drum** is a musical instrument that you play by beating it with your hands or with a stick.

drunk Look at **drink**.
Somebody has drunk my milk.

dry

1 *(drier driest)* If something is **dry**, it is not wet.
2 *(dries drying dried)* If you **dry** something, you make it dry. *Jo used a hair drier to dry her hair.*

duck

A **duck** is a bird that lives near water and can swim.

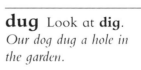

dug Look at **dig**.
Our dog dug a hole in the garden.

dungeon

A **dungeon** is an underground prison in a castle.

dust

Dust is tiny dry pieces of dirt-like powder. *The furniture in the old man's house was covered in dust.*

duvet

A **duvet** is a thick warm cover for a bed.

Ee

eagle
An **eagle** is a large bird with strong claws and a curved beak. **Eagles** catch small animals and eat other birds.

ear
Your **ears** are the two parts, one on each side of your head, that you use for hearing.

early *(earlier earliest)*
1 If you get somewhere **early**, you get there before the usual time. *We arrived at the party early to help blow up balloons.*
2 Early also means near the beginning of something. *Mum gets home from work in the early evening.*

earn *(earns earning earned)*
If you **earn** money, you get money for work that you do.

earth
1 The **Earth** is the planet that we live on. It has a round shape.
2 The ground where plants grow is called **earth**. *We dug a hole in the earth.*

earthquake
An **earthquake** happens when the ground shakes. **Earthquakes** can make buildings fall down.

east
East is the direction where the Sun rises in the morning. **East** is the opposite of west.

easy *(easier easiest)*
Something that is **easy** is not hard to do or to understand. *This machine is easy to use.*

eat *(eats eating ate eaten)*
When you **eat**, you put food in your mouth and it goes down into your stomach.

echo *(echoes)*
An **echo** is a sound that bounces back from something so that you can hear it again. *She clapped her hands in the cave and then listened for the echo.*

edge
The **edge** of something is its end or side. *Don't go too near the edge of the cliff.*

egg
Eggs are oval things with thin shells where baby birds, reptiles and fish grow until they are ready to hatch. Many people eat the **eggs** that hens lay.

elbow
Your **elbow** is the part of your arm where it bends.

electricity
Electricity is a kind of power that travels along wires. It gives us light and heat and makes many kinds of machine work.

elephant
An **elephant** is a very large animal. It has large ears, a long nose called a trunk, and two huge teeth called tusks.

emerald
An **emerald** is a green jewel. **Emeralds** cost a lot of money. *She wore an emerald necklace.*

empty (emptier emptiest)
If something is **empty**, there is nothing inside it. *His glass is empty. Can you fill it up please?*

end
1 The **end** of something is the last part of it, where it stops. *Take the end of the rope and pull.*

2 (ends ending ended) When something **ends**, it finishes. *When the film ended I went to bed.*

enemy (enemies)
An **enemy** is a person who does not like you and wants to hurt you in some way.

energy
Energy is power that makes things work. **Energy** from electricity, gas and water gives us light and heat, and makes machines work. We use our body's **energy** when we jump and run.

engine
An **engine** is a machine that uses energy to make things move. Cars and buses have **engines**.

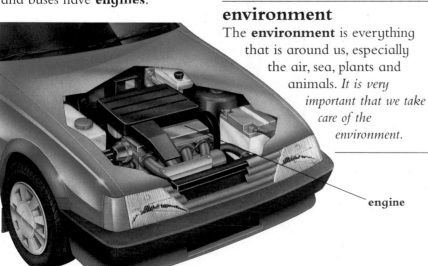

engine

enjoy (enjoys enjoying enjoyed)
If you **enjoy** something, you like doing it. *I enjoy swimming and playing the piano.*

enormous
Something that is **enormous** is very big. *Some dinosaurs that once lived on the Earth were enormous.*

enough
When you have **enough** of something, you have as much or as many as you need. *Do you have enough money to buy that book?*

enter (enters entering entered)
If you **enter** a place, you go in. *She entered the house by the back door.*

entrance
An **entrance** is the way into a building. *The entrance to the swimming baths is on the left-hand side of the building.*

envelope
An **envelope** is a paper cover for a letter. *She put her letter inside the yellow envelope and then posted it.*

environment
The **environment** is everything that is around us, especially the air, sea, plants and animals. *It is very important that we take care of the environment.*

equal
1 Things that are **equal** are the same in size, number or weight. *One metre is equal to one hundred centimetres.*
2 (equals, equalling, equalled) If one thing **equals** another, they are the same size or number. *Three plus two equals five.*

equipment
Equipment is all the things that you need to do something. *You need special equipment if you want to play tennis.*

escape (escapes escaping escaped)
When you **escape**, you get away from somebody or something. *The parrot escaped from its cage.*

especially
Especially means more than others or more than anything else. *I love all kinds of cakes, especially chocolate cake.*

even
1 Something that is **even** is smooth and flat. *Spread an even layer of icing on top of the cake.*
2 Even can mean equal. *At half time the scores were even.*
3 Even numbers are numbers that can be divided by two and leave nothing over. *Two, four, sixty and one hundred are even numbers.*

evening
Evening is the part of the day between afternoon and night, before you go to bed.

eventually

Eventually means in the end. *We got lost and then the car broke down, but we got home eventually.*

evil

A person who is **evil** is very bad or cruel. *I read a story about an evil wizard.*

evergreen

An **evergreen** tree or plant keeps its leaves all the year round. Ivy is an **evergreen** plant.

excellent

Excellent means very, very good.

except

Except means leaving out somebody or something. *Alfie has eaten everything except the cabbage.*

excited

If you are **excited**, you are so happy and interested in something that you cannot keep quiet or think about anything else. *Jamal is very excited about going to America for his holidays.*

excuse

An **excuse** is what you say to tell people why you have or have not done something. *What excuse did you give your teacher for being late again?*

exercise

1 **Exercises** are movements such as jumping, running and touching your toes that you do to make your body stronger.
2 An **exercise** is a piece of work that you do to help you learn something. *Our teacher asked us to do some exercises from our maths book.*

exit

An **exit** is the way out of a building.

expect *(expects expecting expected)*

If you **expect** something to happen, you think that it will. *I expect grandma will take us to the park at the weekend.*

expensive

Something that is **expensive** costs a lot of money. *The jewellery was very expensive.*

explain *(explains explaining explained)*

When you **explain** something to somebody, you tell them about it so that they can understand it. *Dad explained how an engine works.*

explode *(explodes exploding exploded)*

When something **explodes**, it bursts into small pieces with a loud bang. *The fireworks exploded above our heads.*

explore *(explores exploring explored)*

When you **explore**, you look around a place you have not been to before to see what it is like. *The children explored the garden of their new home.*

expression

Your **expression** is the look on your face that shows how you feel. *You should have seen his expression when he opened the birthday present!*

extinct

If a plant or an animal is **extinct**, there are no more of that kind living on the Earth. *Pterosaurs were flying reptiles that are now extinct.*

extra

Extra means more than usual or more than you need. *We took some extra food for the journey in case Sam decided to come with us.*

extremely

Extremely means very, very. Whales and elephants are **extremely** big creatures.

eye

Your **eyes** are the two parts, on each side of your face that you use for seeing.

Ff

face
Your **face** is the front part of your head, where your eyes, mouth and nose are. *The old man had a very interesting face.*

fact
A **fact** is something that is true. *We told the teacher all the facts.*

factory *(factories)*
A **factory** is a building where people work with machines to make things. *Cars and computers are made in factories.*

fair
1 Something that is **fair** seems good and right. *The teacher was fair and gave everyone a chance to speak.*
2 **Fair** hair and skin are light in colour.
3 A **fair** is a place outside where you can have fun. You can ride on big machines such as roundabouts, and play games to win prizes.

fairy *(fairies)*
A **fairy** is a very small magical person that you can read about in stories. **Fairies** have wings and can fly.

fall *(falls falling fell fallen)*
When somebody or something **falls**, they go down to the ground. *Leaves fall from the trees in autumn. Sally fell off the wall and broke her arm.*

false
If something is **false**, it is not true or real. *Theo is wearing a false nose and moustache.*

family *(families)*
A **family** is usually made up of parents and children. **Families** can also include grandparents, cousins, uncles and aunts.

famous
If somebody or something is **famous**, a lot of people know about them. *Have you ever met anybody famous?*

far *(farther farthest)*
Far means a long way away. *Sam lives farther from school than Phoebe but not as far as Jane.*

farm
A **farm** is a place where people keep animals or grow plants for food. The person who looks after a farm is called a **farmer**.

fast
Something that is **fast** can move quickly. *My mum has a fast car.*

fat
1 *(fatter fattest)* A person or an animal that is **fat** has a large round body.
2 Butter and oil that we use for cooking are also called **fat**. *Fry the vegetables in a little fat.*

father
A **father** is a man who has a child.

fault
If something bad is your **fault**, you made it happen. *It was David's fault I fell over - he pushed me.*

favourite
Your **favourite** is the one that you like best. *What's your favourite colour? Mine is blue.*

fear
Fear is what you feel when you think that something really nasty is going to happen.

feather
Feathers are the light soft things that cover a bird's body. **Feathers** help to keep a bird warm.

feed *(feeds feeding fed)*
If you **feed** a person or an animal, you give them food. *I always feed my dog in the mornings.*

feel *(feels feeling felt)*
1 If you **feel** something, you touch it or it touches you. *Feel how smooth this wood is. Can you feel rain on your face?*
2 If you **feel** ill or happy, that is the way you are. *I feel a bit hungry.*

feet Look at **foot**.

fell Look at **fall**.
Joe fell out of the tree and broke his right leg.

felt Look at **feel**.
I felt sad when my cousins went home to Australia.

female
A **female** is a person or an animal that can have babies. Women and girls are **females**, and men and boys are males.

fence
A **fence** is usually made of wood or wire. **Fences** are put around fields and gardens.

fetch *(fetches fetching fetched)*
If you **fetch** something, you go to get it and bring it back. *Mum asked the waiter to fetch her a clean knife and fork.*

few
Few means not many of something. *There are only a few chocolates left in the box.*

field
A **field** is a piece of land where farmers grow plants for food or keep animals. A **field** can also be a piece of land where you play sports such as football.

fierce
An animal that is **fierce** is frightening and dangerous. *That dog looks fierce!*

fight *(fights fighting fought)*
When people **fight**, they are angry and they are trying to hurt one another.

figure
A **figure** is one of the signs that we use for writing numbers, such as 1, 2, 3 and so on.

fill *(fills filling filled)*
If you **fill** something, you put as much into it as it can hold. *I filled the jug with water.*

film
1 A **film** is a story in moving pictures that you watch on a screen. *Last night there was a really good film on TV.*

2 A **film** is also a roll of plastic that you put inside a camera to take photos.

finally
Finally means at last or at the end. *The climbers finally reached the top of the mountain.*

find *(finds finding found)*
When you **find** something that you were looking for, you see it. *Mark looked everywhere for his glasses and then found them in a drawer.*

fine
1 **Fine** means good. *I felt ill, but I'm fine now.*
2 A **fine** day is sunny and warm.
3 A **fine** is money that you have to pay as a punishment for doing something wrong. *He had to pay a fine for parking his car in a "No Parking" area.*

finger
Your **fingers** are the parts that you can move at the end of your hand. *You have five fingers on each of your hands.*

finish *(finishes finishing finished)*
When you **finish** something, you get to the end of it. *Can I borrow that book when you've finished it?*

fire
Fire is the heat, flames and light that are made by something that is burning.

firefighter
A **firefighter** is a person who puts out fires. **Firefighters** ride in a truck called a fire engine.

fireworks
Fireworks are paper tubes filled with a special powder. When you light **fireworks**, they send out a shower of bright coloured lights. Some **fireworks** make a loud bang as well.

first
First means at the beginning or before anything else. *January is the first month of the year.*

fish
(fish or fishes)
A **fish** is an animal that lives in water. **Fish** are covered in scales, and they have parts called gills for breathing.

fist
If you close your hand tightly, you make a **fist**.

fit
1 *(fits fitting fitted)* If something **fits**, it is not too big or too small and it is the right shape. *These red shoes don't fit Laura.*
2 *(fitter fittest)* A person who is **fit** is healthy and strong. *My mum goes running every morning to keep fit.*

fix *(fixes fixing fixed)*
1 If you **fix** things together, you join them.
2 If you **fix** something that was broken, you mend it. *Helen fixed the tap to stop it dripping.*

flag
A **flag** is a piece of cloth with colours and patterns on it. **Flags** fly on poles. Every country has a **flag**.

flame
Flames are the bright moving lights that you see in a fire.

flash *(flashes)*
A **flash** is a bright light that appears and disappears again very quickly. *Before the thunder there was a flash of lightning.*

flat
1 *(flatter flattest)* If something is **flat**, it is smooth and has no parts that are higher than the rest. The top of a table is **flat**.
2 A **flat** is a set of rooms in a building for living in. **Flats** are usually on one floor. *Do you live in a flat or a house?*

flavour
The **flavour** of food is what it tastes like.

flew Look at **fly**.
The kite flew high above the trees.

float *(floats floating floated)*
If something **floats**, it stays on the top of a liquid, or it moves gently in the air. *The balloon floated over the roof. Wood floats on water.*

flood
A **flood** is a lot of water that suddenly covers an area of land that is usually dry. **Floods** sometimes happen after heavy rain or when snow melts.

floor
1 A **floor** is the part of a building that you walk on. *The puppy left mud all over the floor.*
2 A building that has more than one **floor** has rooms on top of other rooms. A block of flats usually has several **floors**.

flour
Flour is a powder made from wheat that we use for baking bread and cakes. It can be white or brown in colour.

flow *(flows flowing flowed)*
When a liquid such as water **flows**, it moves along. *The river flows into the sea.*

flower

A **flower** is the pretty coloured part of a plant, where the seeds are made.

fly

1 *(flies flying flew flown)* When something **flies**, it moves through the air. Insects, birds and aeroplanes **fly**.
2 *(flies)* A **fly** is a small insect which has wings.

foal

A **foal** is a young horse.

fog

Fog is thick grey cloud near the ground. You cannot see far in **fog**.

fold *(folds folding folded)*

If you **fold** something, you bend one part over another part. *Fold the paper carefully in half.*

follow *(follows following followed)*

If you **follow** somebody or something, you go along behind them. *My little brother follows me everywhere and copies everything I do.*

food

Food is all the things that people and animals eat to stay alive and grow.

foot *(feet)*

Your **foot** is the part at the end of your leg. You stand and walk on your **feet**.

football

Football is a game played by two teams who kick a ball and try to score goals.

forehead

Your **forehead** is the part of your face that is above your eyes and just below your hair.

forest

A **forest** is a large area of land where a lot of trees are growing. *We had a picnic in the forest.*

forget *(forgets forgetting forgot forgotten)*

If you **forget** something, you cannot remember it. *You told me your telephone number, but I've forgotten it.*

forgive *(forgives forgiving forgave forgiven)*

If you **forgive** somebody for doing something bad, you stop being angry with them. *Thomas forgave his sister when she said she was sorry for breaking his train.*

fork

A **fork** is a tool with a long handle and pointed parts called prongs at the end. You use one kind of **fork** to pick up food and put it in your mouth. You use a big **fork** for digging the ground.

forwards

Forwards means in the direction of what is in front of you.

fossil

A **fossil** is what is left of an animal or a plant that lived a long time ago. You can sometimes find **fossils** in rocks.

fought Look at **fight**.

The armies fought a long battle.

found Look at **find**.

Chris found some money in the street.

fox *(foxes)*

A **fox** is a wild animal with red-brown fur and a long thick tail. **Foxes** look a bit like dogs. They live in the countryside and in the towns.

frame

A **frame** is the wooden or metal part that fits around something such as a picture, a photograph or a window.

free

1 If something is **free**, you do not have to pay any money for it. *Children under five travel free on buses in most towns.*
2 If a person or an animal is **free**, there is nothing to stop them going where they want or doing what they like. *Animals in the wild are free.*

freeze *(freezes freezing froze frozen)*

When water **freezes**, it changes into ice. You can **freeze** food to stop it going bad.

fresh

1 Food that is **fresh** is not old or bad. *fresh fish.*
2 **Fresh** water comes from lakes and rivers and is not salty like water from the sea.
3 **Fresh** air is clean and good to breathe.

friend

A **friend** is somebody that you like and who likes you too.

friendly *(friendlier friendliest)*

A person who is **friendly** is kind and helpful.

frighten *(frightens frightening frightened)*

If something **frightens** you, it makes you afraid. *She's frightened of spiders.*

frog

A **frog** is a small animal with strong back legs for jumping. **Frogs** live near water.

front

The **front** of something is the part that you usually see first. Your face is on the **front** of your head. *There is a big oak tree in front of our house.*

frost

Frost is ice-like white powder that covers things outside when the weather is very cold.

frown

When you **frown**, you pull your eyebrows down to show that you are angry or thinking hard.

froze, frozen

Look at **freeze**.
The pond froze last night. We bought a packet of frozen peas.

fruit

Fruit is the part of a plant that has seeds in it. Apples, pineapples, lemons and oranges are all kinds of **fruit**.

fry *(fries frying fried)*

If you **fry** food, you cook it in hot fat. *The sausages were frying in the pan.*

full

If something is **full**, it cannot hold any more. *The car park is full.*

fun

If you are having **fun**, you are happy and enjoying yourself.

funny *(funnier funniest)*

1 Something that is **funny** makes you laugh. *Have you seen that film? It's really funny.*
2 **Funny** can also mean strange. *There's a funny noise coming from next door.*

fur

Fur is the thick hair that covers the body of animals such as cats, dogs and rabbits.

furniture

Beds, chairs, desks and tables are all pieces of **furniture**.

furry

An animal that is **furry** is covered in fur. Hamsters are **furry**.

future

The **future** is the time that has not happened yet. Tomorrow is in the **future**.

Gg

gallop *(gallops galloping galloped)*
When a horse **gallops**, it runs very fast.

game
A **game** is something that you play for fun. **Games** have special rules. Cricket and football are **games**, and so is chess.

gap
A **gap** is an empty space between two things. *Rosie has a gap where her tooth has fallen out.*

garage
1 A **garage** is a building where cars are kept.
2 A **garage** is also a place that sells petrol or mends cars.

garden
A **garden** is a piece of land by a house where people grow flowers and vegetables.

gas *(gases)*
Gas is something that is not solid or liquid and it has no shape. There are many different **gases**. We use one kind of **gas** to cook food and warm our homes. Air is a mixture of other **gases**.

gate
A **gate** is a door in a fence or wall. *Please shut the gate so the dog doesn't get out.*

gave Look at **give**.
Auntie Sue gave me a calculator for my birthday.

geese Look at **goose**.

gentle
A person who is **gentle** is quiet, careful and kind. *Be gentle with the younger children.*

gerbil
A **gerbil** is a small furry animal with long back legs. Some people keep **gerbils** as pets.

ghost
A **ghost** is the shape of a dead person that some people believe they have seen.

giant
A **giant** is a very big person in stories.

gift
A **gift** is a present.

giggle *(giggles giggling giggled)*
If you **giggle**, you laugh in a high voice.
The children all giggled when the clown fell over.

giraffe
A **giraffe** is a wild animal with a very long neck and long legs. **Giraffes** live in Africa.

girl
A **girl** is a female child. **Girls** grow up to be women.

give *(gives giving gave given)*
If you **give** something to somebody, you let them have it. *Ben didn't want his cake so he gave it to me.*

glad
If you are **glad** about something, you are happy about it. *I'm glad you like your present.*

glass
1 **Glass** is a hard material that you can see through. Windows are made of **glass**.
2 *(glasses)* A **glass** is something you drink from.

glasses
Some people wear **glasses** over their eyes to help them see better. **Glasses** are made of two pieces of special glass joined together in a frame.

glove
A **glove** has parts that cover each finger and thumb. People wear **gloves** to keep their hands warm or to protect them.

glue
Glue is a thick liquid that you use for sticking things together.

goal
1 A **goal** is the net between two posts that players have to kick or hit a ball into in games such as football.
2 A **goal** is also a point that you score when you hit or kick a ball into the goal in a game.

goat

A **goat** is an animal with short rough hair. Some **goats** have horns. **Goats** are sometimes kept on farms for their milk.

gold

Gold is a shiny yellow metal that is used to make things such as rings, necklaces and coins. **Gold** costs a lot of money.

good *(better best)*

1 If something is **good**, you like and enjoy it. *This is a good book.*
2 If you are **good** at something, you do it well. *My sister is really good at tennis.*
3 If a person or an animal is **good**, they do what they are told. *Mum asked us to be good while she was out.*
4 A person who is **good** is kind and helpful.

goose *(geese)*

A **goose** is a large bird with a long neck. **Geese** can swim and they live near water.

grab *(grabs grabbing grabbed)*

If you **grab** something, you take hold of it suddenly. *She grabbed the little boy's hand as he was about to step into the road.*

grandfather

Your **grandfather** is the father of your mother or father.

grandmother

Your **grandmother** is the mother of your father or of your mother.

grape

A **grape** is a small round green or purple fruit. **Grapes** grow in bunches on a bush called a grapevine.

grapefruit

A **grapefruit** is a round fruit like a big orange but with a yellow skin.

grass

Grass is a plant with thin green leaves. **Grass** grows in fields and gardens. Cows and horses and other animals eat **grass**.

great

1 Great means very good or very important. *It was a great party. She is a great actor.*
2 Great can also mean very big. *She gave me a great big kiss!*

grew Look at **grow**.
The little puppy soon grew into a huge dog.

ground

The **ground** is what we walk on when we are outside.

group

A **group** is a number of things that are in one place. *There is a group of tall trees in the park. I'll meet you there.*

grow *(grows growing grew grown)*

When somebody or something **grows**, they become bigger or taller. *The seed we planted will grow into a tall tree.*

grownup

A **grownup** is a person who is not a child any more.

guard *(guards guarding guarded)*

To **guard** means to watch somebody or something to make sure that nothing bad happens to them. *A big dog guards the chocolate factory at night.*

guess *(guesses guessing guessed)*

When you **guess**, you try to think of an answer to something without knowing if the answer is right. *Can you guess what I've bought Paul for his birthday?*

guinea-pig

A **guinea-pig** is a small furry animal with no tail. Some people keep **guinea-pigs** as pets.

guitar

A **guitar** is a musical instrument with strings that you play with your fingers. *I am learning to play the guitar.*

gym

A **gym** is a room where you can play games or do exercises to keep your body fit and strong.

Hh

habit
A **habit** is something you do so often that you do not think about it. *Brushing your teeth after meals is a good habit.*

hair
Hair is what grows on your head. *Lily has long red hair.*

half *(halves)*
A **half** is one of two parts of something that are the same size. Two **halves** make a whole.

hall
1 A **hall** is a room in a house or flat that has doors leading to the other rooms.
2 A **hall** is also a very big room. *All the children in our school meet in the hall every morning for assembly.*

hamburger
A **hamburger** is a flat round kind of food made from tiny pieces of meat. We eat **hamburgers** in bread rolls.

hammer
A **hammer** is a heavy tool that people use to hit nails into things.

hamster
A **hamster** is a small furry animal that can store food in its cheeks. Some people keep **hamsters** as pets.

hand
Your **hands** are at the end of your arms. A **hand** has four fingers and a thumb. We use our **hands** to pick things up and to hold them.

handle
A **handle** is part of something that you use for holding or moving it with your hand. Things such as cups, doors and knives have **handles**.

hang *(hangs hanging hung)*
When you **hang** something somewhere, you fix the top of it to something above it. *Emily hung her coat up on the hook.*

happy
(happier happiest)
When you are **happy**, you feel good about something and you laugh or smile a lot.

hard
1 If something is **hard**, you cannot shape or break it easily with your hands. *Nutshells are hard but stones are harder.*
2 If something is **hard** to do, it is difficult. *These sums are quite hard. Can you help me with them?*

hat
A **hat** is something you wear on your head to keep it warm or dry.

hatch *(hatches hatching hatched)*
A baby bird **hatches** when it breaks out of an egg.

hate *(hates hating hated)*
If you **hate** somebody or something, you do not like them at all.

haunted
If people say that a place is **haunted**, they mean that a ghost is supposed to live there. *I read a story about a haunted house.*

hay
Hay is dry grass that is used to feed animals such as horses and cattle in winter.

head
1 Your **head** is the part of your body above your neck. Your face and ears are part of your **head**.
2 A **head** is also the person in charge. *We have a new head teacher at our school.*

headache
If you have a **headache**, your head hurts.

heal *(heals healing healed)*
When a cut **heals**, it gets better. *He cut his finger but it soon healed.*

health
Your **health** is how well your body is. *Fresh fruit and vegetables are good for your health.*

healthy *(healthier healthiest)*
If you are **healthy**, you feel really well. *a healthy child.*

hear *(hears hearing heard)*

When you **hear** something, you take in sounds through your ears. *Did you hear the thunder?*

heart

Your **heart** is inside your chest. It sends blood around your body. You can feel the beat of your **heart** when you run.

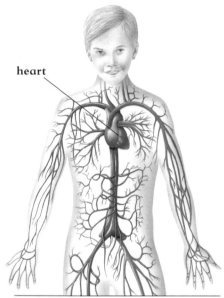

heart

heat

1 Heat is what makes things warm. *I can feel the heat of the sun.* **2** *(heats heating heated)* If you **heat** something, you make it warm. *Dad heated up the soup in a pan.*

heavy *(heavier heaviest)*

Something that is **heavy** is difficult to lift. *The large box is heavier than the suitcase.*

heel

Your **heel** is the round part at the back of your foot.

height

The **height** of something is how tall or high it is.

held Look at **hold**.
Hannah held the kitten.

helicopter

A **helicopter** is an aircraft without wings. **Helicopters** have long blades on the top that turn around very fast.

helmet

A **helmet** is a hard metal or plastic hat that protects your head. *I wear my cycle helmet when I go on bike rides.*

help *(helps helping helped)*

If you **help** somebody, you do something useful for them. *Ella helped her grandma carry her shopping.*

hen

Hens are chickens that lay eggs.

hide *(hides hiding hid hidden)*

If you **hide** something, you put it where nobody can see it. *Where have you hidden my birthday present?*

high

Something that is **high** goes up a long way. *We couldn't see over the fence because it was too high.*

hill

A **hill** is a piece of land that is higher than the land around it.

hippopotamus *(hippopotamuses)*

A **hippopotamus** is a large wild animal with short legs and a big mouth. **Hippopotamuses** live near lakes and rivers in Africa and like to take mud baths. They are often called hippos for short.

hit *(hits hitting hit)*

If you **hit** something, you touch it very hard. *Ewen hit the ball and it hit me on the head.*

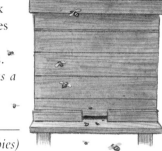

hive

A **hive** is a box for keeping bees in. Bees make honey in **hives**. *My granddad has a a beehive in his back garden.*

hobby *(hobbies)*

A **hobby** is something that people like doing when they are not working. *My brother's hobbies are collecting coins and fishing.*

hold *(holds holding held)*

1 When you **hold** something, you have it in your hand. *Jemma held her little sister's hand.*
2 To **hold** also means to have space inside for something. *How much milk does the carton hold?*

hole

A **hole** is a gap or empty space in something. *The children dug holes in the sand.*

holiday

A **holiday** is a time when you do not work or go to school.

hollow

Something that is **hollow** is empty inside.

home

Your **home** is where you live.

honey

Honey is a sweet sticky liquid that bees make. *I like honey on my bread for breakfast.*

hoof *(hooves)*

A **hoof** is the hard part of a horse's foot. Cattle, sheep and deer also have **hooves**.

hop *(hops hopping hopped)*

1 When you **hop**, you jump on one foot.
2 When an animal **hops** it moves along in small jumps.

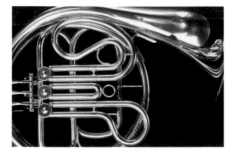

hope *(hopes hoping hoped)*

If you **hope** that something will happen, you want it to happen very much and you believe that it will. *My sister is hoping to get a new bike for her birthday.*

horn

1 A **horn** is one of the hard pointed things that grow out of the head of some animals. Cows and goats have **horns**.
2 A **horn** is also a musical instrument that you play by blowing into it.

horrible

If something is **horrible**, it is nasty or frightening. *This food tastes really horrible.*

horse

A **horse** is a large animal with hooves. Some people like to ride **horses**.

hospital

A **hospital** is a large building where doctors and nurses look after people who are ill or hurt.

hot *(hotter hottest)*

Something that is **hot** can burn you if you touch it. *Don't touch the oven - it's very hot.*

hotel

A **hotel** is a building with lots of bedrooms where people can stay when they are away from home.

hour

An **hour** has sixty minutes. There are twenty-four **hours** in a day.

house

A **house** is a building that people live in.

hug *(hugs hugging hugged)*

If you **hug** somebody, you put your arms around them and hold them tight. *Tom hugged his aunt when she left.*

huge

Something that is **huge** is very big. *That's a huge plate of chips!*

human

A **human** is a man, woman or child.

hump

A **hump** is a big round lump on the back of a camel.

hung Look at **hang**.
I hung my coat on the hook.

hungry *(hungrier hungriest)*

When you are **hungry**, you want something to eat.

hunt *(hunts hunting hunted)*

1 When animals **hunt**, they chase other animals to catch them and eat them.
2 If you **hunt** for something, you look carefully for it. *We hunted everywhere for Mum's necklace.*

hurry *(hurries hurrying hurried)*

When you **hurry**, you do something very quickly. *Unless you hurry you'll miss the bus.*

hurt *(hurts hurting hurt)*

If a part of your body **hurts**, you feel pain there. *My finger hurt when I hit it with a hammer.*

husband

A woman's **husband** is the man that she is married to.

hut

A **hut** is a very small simple house. Many **huts** are made of wood or grass.

hutch

A **hutch** is a cage for a pet rabbit or guinea pig.

Ii

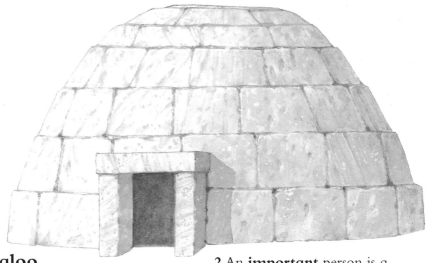

ice
Ice is water that is frozen so that it is hard. *The pond is covered with a layer of ice.*

iceberg
An **iceberg** is a huge block of ice that floats in the sea.

ice-cream
Ice-cream is a soft sweet frozen food.

ice-skating
When you go **ice-skating** you slide along the ice in special boots called ice-skates that have a thin piece of metal on the bottom.

icicle
An **icicle** is a long, pointed piece of ice that hangs down.

icing
Icing is a smooth, sweet paste made of sugar that you sometimes spread over cakes.

idea
An **idea** is something you have thought of. *I've got a good idea for a birthday present.*

igloo
An **igloo** is a round house made of blocks of snow and ice.

iguana
An **iguana** is a large lizard that lives in trees in hot countries.

ill
If you are **ill** you are not well. *Jasmine is too ill to go to school today.*

illness
An **illness** is something that makes you feel ill. *Jill is recovering from her illness.*

imagine *(imagines imagining imagined)*
If you **imagine** something, you have a picture of it in your mind. *Can you imagine what the world was like when dinosaurs were alive?*

imitate *(imitates imitating imitated)*
If you **imitate** somebody, you try to copy or do the same as them. *Sam made us laugh when he tried to imitate a dog barking.*

immediately
When you do something **immediately**, you do it now, without waiting. *Go to your room immediately!*

important
1 Something that is **important** matters a lot. *It's important to eat well if you want to stay healthy.*

2 An **important** person is a person who is powerful or special in some way.

impossible
If something is **impossible** it cannot be done. *It's impossible for a person to walk on water.*

information
Information is the facts that tell you about something. *We need some information about the times of trains to Bristol.*

initial
An **initial** is the first letter of a name or word. *Jane Adam's initials are J.A.*

injection
If a doctor or a nurse gives you an **injection**, they put medicine into your body by pushing a special needle into your skin.

injure
If you **injure** yourself, you hurt a part of your body. *Jim injured his arm when he fell off his bike.*

ink
Ink is a coloured liquid that we use for writing and printing.

215

insect

An **insect** is a small creature with six legs. Some **insects** have wings and can fly. Ants, bees, butterflies and flies are different kinds of **insects**, but spiders are not.

instead

Instead means in the place of somebody or something. *We couldn't go to the beach because it was raining, so we watched a film instead.*

instructions

Instructions are words or pictures that tell you how to do something. *The video recorder is quite easy to use if you follow the instructions properly.*

instrument

1 An **instrument** is a tool that helps you to do something. *A microscope is an instrument for looking at tiny objects.*
2 A musical **instrument** is something that you play to make music. Drums, pianos, trumpets and violins are types of musical **instruments**.

interesting

If something is **interesting**, you like it and you want to find out more about it. *That was a very interesting programme.*

interfere *(interferes interfering interfered)*

If you **interfere**, you try to do something for somebody when they do not want your help. *My little sister keeps interfering when I'm playing my computer game.*

interrupt *(interrupts interrupting interrupted)*

If you **interrupt** somebody, you stop them doing or saying something for a moment. *Kurt interrupted me when I was talking on the phone.*

interview

An **interview** is when you meet somebody to answer questions about yourself. *She watched an interview about her favourite singer.*

invent *(invents inventing invented)*

If you **invent** something, you are the first person to think of it or to make it. *I wonder who invented the first computer?*

invention

An **invention** is something new that somebody invents. *Televisions and computers are great inventions.*

inventor

An **inventor** is a person who invents things.

invisible

If something is **invisible**, it cannot be seen. Air is **invisible**. *The magician did a trick and made the rabbit invisible.*

invite *(invites inviting invited)*

If you **invite** somebody, you ask them to visit you or to do something with you. *Sophie invited her friends to a party. She wrote out invitations and then posted them to everybody.*

iron

1 Iron is a strong heavy metal.
2 An **iron** is a kind of tool with a flat metal bottom. We make an **iron** hot and use it to make clothes smooth and flat.

island

An **island** is a piece of land with water all around it.

itch *(itches itching itched)*

When a part of your body **itches**, you want to scratch it.

ivy

Ivy is a plant with shiny leaves that climbs up walls and trees. *Our old garden wall is covered in ivy.*

Jj

jacket

A **jacket** is a short coat. *Matt is wearing a blue denim jacket.*

jail

A **jail** is a place where some people have to stay when they have done something that is against the law.

jam

1 **Jam** is a sweet food made by cooking fruit and sugar together for a long time.
2 A traffic **jam** is a lot of cars so close together that they cannot move. *We were late because we got stuck in a traffic jam.*
3 (jams jamming jammed) If something **jams**, it becomes difficult to move. *The door won't open because it's jammed.*

jar

A **jar** is a wide glass container. You buy jam in a **jar**.

jealous

If you are **jealous** of somebody, you feel angry or unhappy because they have something that you would like to have.

jeans

Jeans are trousers made from strong cotton cloth called denim.

jelly *(jellies)*

Jelly is a sweet food that you can see through. **Jelly** shakes when you move it.

jet

A **jet** is an aeroplane that can fly very fast.

jewel

A **jewel** is a beautiful stone such as a diamond or an emerald. **Jewels** are worth a lot of money and they are used to make things such as rings and necklaces.

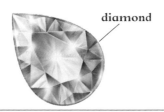

diamond

job

1 A **job** is the work that somebody does to earn money.
2 A **job** is also something that has to be done. *Why is it always my job to feed the cat?*

join *(joins joining joined)*

1 If you **join** things, you put or fix them together. *She joined the two pieces of wood with glue.*
2 If you **join** something such as a club, you become part of it.

joke

A **joke** is a kind of short story that makes people laugh.

journey

When you go on a **journey**, you travel from one place to another.

juice

Juice is the liquid that comes out of fruit when you squeeze it.

jump
(jumps jumping jumped)
When you **jump**, you push yourself up into the air with your feet off the ground.

jumper

A **jumper** is something that you wear to keep you warm. It covers your arms and the top part of your body. **Jumpers** are often made of wool.

jungle

A **jungle** is a thick forest in a hot country where it rains a lot. A lot of different animals live in the **jungles** of the world.

Kk

kangaroo

A **kangaroo** is a wild animal with strong back legs that it uses for jumping. **Kangaroos** live in Australia.

keep

(keeps keeping kept)

1 If you **keep** something, you have it and you do not give it to anybody else. *My best friend gave me this photo and I'm going to keep it for ever.*

2 If you **keep** something in a place, that is where you always put it. *Simon keeps his toy cars in a box under the bed.*

3 If you **keep** doing something, you do it again and again. *Why do you keep making that noise?*

4 Keep can also mean to stay the same way. *Please keep quiet while I'm talking.*

kettle

A **kettle** is a thing that you use for making water hot. A **kettle** has a lid and a pointed part called a spout for pouring.

key

1 A **key** is a piece of metal that you use to open or close a lock.

2 The **keys** of a piano or computer are the parts that you press with your fingers.

kick

(kicks kicking kicked)

If you **kick** something, you hit it with your foot. *Sam kicked the ball into the goal.*

kill

(kills killing killed)

To **kill** is to end the life of somebody or something. *The fox killed a chicken.*

kind

1 If you are **kind**, you are nice to people and try to help them. *It was kind of you to do the shopping.*

2 Kind also means a group of things that are the same in some way. *Apples, bananas and plums are all kinds of fruit.*

king

Some countries have a ruler who is a man called a **king**. The wife of a **king** is called a queen.

kingdom

A **kingdom** is a country where a king or queen rules.

kiss

(kisses kissing kissed)

When you **kiss** somebody, you touch them with your lips to show that you like or love them. *Billy always kisses his dad before he goes to bed.*

kit

A **kit** is a set of tools or equipment that you need to do something. *I got a puppet-making kit for my birthday.*

kitchen

A **kitchen** is a room where people cook food.

kite

A **kite** is a toy that you can fly on windy days by holding the end of a long string.

kitten

A **kitten** is a very young cat.

knee

Your **knee** is the part in the middle of your leg where it bends.

kneel

(kneels kneeling knelt)

When you **kneel**, you go down on your knees.

knife

(knives)

A **knife** is a tool with a sharp edge called a blade for cutting.

knight

A **knight** was a soldier who lived a long time ago. **Knights** rode into battle on horses, and many **knights** wore armour.

knit

(knits knitting knitted)

When people **knit**, they use wool and needles to make clothes such as jumpers.

knock

(knocks knocking knocked)

When you **knock** something, you hit it. *Who's knocking at the door?*

knot

You make a **knot** when you twist and tie pieces of string or ribbon. *Can you untie this knot in my shoelace?*

koala

A **koala** is a grey furry animal that looks like a small bear. **Koalas** live in trees in Australia.

Ll

ladder

A **ladder** is a set of steps that you climb up to reach high places. You can carry **ladders** from one place to another.

ladybird

A **ladybird** is a small beetle. It has a red or yellow body with black spots. **Ladybirds** can fly.

lain Look at **lie**.
She must have lain down and fallen fast asleep.

lake

A **lake** is a lot of water with land all around it.

lamb

A **lamb** is a young sheep. *The lambs played in the field.*

lamp

A **lamp** is something that gives light where you need it. Most **lamps** use electricity. *Freddie has a lamp on his desk to help him see what he is doing.*

land

1 **Land** is any part of the Earth that is not covered in water.
2 *(lands landing landed)* When an aeroplane or bird **lands**, it stops flying and comes down on to the ground. *The plane has just landed.*

language

A **language** is all the words that the people of one country use to speak or write to each other. *People in France speak a language that is called French.*

lap

Your **lap** is the top part of your legs when you are sitting down. *Christina is sitting on her mum's lap.*

large

Something that is **large** is big. *An elephant is a very large animal.*

last

1 If somebody or something is **last**, they are at the end or they come after all the others. *Z is the last letter of the alphabet.*
2 **Last** also means before this one. *Last week we were at school, but this week is a holiday.*
3 *(lasts lasting lasted)* To **last** means to go on for a certain amount of time. *The film lasted nearly two-and-a-half hours.*

late

If you are **late**, you get to a place after the usual time or after the time that you were supposed to. *Lucy was late for school this morning because she woke up late.*

laugh *(laughs laughing laughed)*

When people **laugh**, they make sounds to show that they think something is funny.

law

Laws are the rules made by a country. They tell people what they can and cannot do. *Stealing other people's money is against the law.*

lawn

A **lawn** is a part of a park or garden that is covered in grass. You cut a **lawn** with a machine called a lawnmower.

lay *(lays laying laid)*

1 When you **lay** something somewhere, you put it down carefully. *Liam laid the box of eggs on the table.*
2 When you **lay** a table, you put things such as knives and forks on it, ready for a meal.
3 When a bird **lays** an egg, the egg comes out of the bird's body. *Our duck laid five eggs in her nest this morning.*
4 Look at **lie**.
Jenny lay on her bed and read her favourite book.

layer

A **layer** is a flat piece of something that lies on or under something else. *The cake had a layer of icing on top and two layers of jam in the middle.*

lazy *(lazier laziest)*

A person who is **lazy** does not want to work or does not want to do very much at all. *Come on you lazy girl - time to get up!*

lead

1 *(leads leading led)* When you **lead** somebody to a place, you go in front to show them where it is. *The woman at the cinema led us to our seats.*
2 *(leads leading led)* If a road or path **leads** to a place, it goes there. *This path leads to the beach.*
3 A **lead** is a rope, chain or long piece of leather that you fix to a dog's collar so that you can control the dog when you take it for walks.

lead

Lead is a heavy grey metal that is quite soft.

leader

A **leader** is a person who is in charge of other people.

leaf *(leaves)*

A **leaf** is one of the flat thin parts that grow on the stem of a plant. Most **leaves** are green. In autumn, **leaves** change colour and fall off some trees.

lean *(leans leaning leant or leaned)*

To **lean** means to bend one way or to rest against something. *Josh leant his bike against the wall.*

learn *(learns learning learnt or learned)*

When you **learn**, you find out about something or how to do something. *My little brother is learning to read.*

leather

Leather is a material made from the skin of animals. A lot of shoes are made of **leather**.

leave *(leaves leaving left)*

1 When you **leave**, you go away from a place.
2 If you **leave** something somewhere, you do not take it with you. *I left my bike at home and walked to school.*

leaves Look at **leaf**.

The leaves fall off the trees in autumn.

led Look at **lead**.
Hassan led me to his room.

left

1 You are reading the words on this page from the **left** to the right. **Left** is the opposite of right.
2 Look at **leave**.
He left his bag on the bus.

leg

1 **Legs** are the long parts of your body that you use for walking on. People have two **legs**, and cows and dogs have four **legs**.
2 The **legs** of a chair or table are the parts that it stands on.

lemon

A **lemon** is a yellow fruit with a thick skin that tastes very sour.

length

The **length** of something is how long it is.

lesson

A **lesson** is a time when somebody is teaching you something. *Lina has ballet lessons twice a week.*

letter

1 A **letter** is one of the signs that we use for writing words, such as A, B and C. **Letters** make up the alphabet.
2 A **letter** is also a message that you write on paper and send to somebody.

lettuce

A **lettuce** is a vegetable with large green leaves that we eat raw in salads.

library *(libraries)*

A **library** is a place where books are kept for people to borrow and read at home. A lot of **libraries** also have computers where you can find information.

lick *(licks licking licked)*

When you **lick** something, you touch it with your tongue to taste it or to make it wet.

lid

A **lid** is the top part that covers a container such as a jar or box. *Put the lid back on the biscuit tin when you've finished with it.*

lie

1 A **lie** is something you say that you know is not true. *She said she was going straight home but it was a lie. She went to her best friend's house instead.*

2 *(lies lying lay lain)* When you **lie** somewhere, you put your body down flat so that you are not sitting or standing. *Lie down and go to sleep.*

life *(lives)*

Your **life** is the time when you are living on the earth.

lift

1 *(lifts lifting lifted)* When you **lift** something, you pick it up. *This box is too heavy for me to lift by myself.*

2 A **lift** is a kind of box that travels up and down inside tall buildings to carry people and things to different floors.

light

1 **Light** comes from the Sun and from lamps. Without **light** it would be dark and we would not be able to see anything.

2 Something that is **light** is easy to lift. *Feathers are light.*

3 **Light** colours are pale. *Tom's T-shirt is light green.*

4 *(lights lighting lit)* When you **light** something, you start it burning. *We lit the candles on the cake.*

lighthouse

A **lighthouse** is a tower near the sea with a bright light on top. **Lighthouses** show ships where there are dangerous rocks.

lightning

Lightning is the flash of light that you see in the sky when there is a thunderstorm.

like

1 *(likes liking liked)* If you **like** somebody or something, they make you happy. *Billy likes dancing.*

2 If something is **like** something else, it is the same in some way. *Jodie looks like her sister.*

likely

If something is **likely**, it will probably happen. *It's likely to rain this evening.*

line

1 A **line** is a long thin mark. *It's easier to draw a straight line if you use a ruler.*

2 A **line** is also a row of people or things. *Stand in a line.*

lion

A **lion** is a large wild animal of the cat family. **Lions** live in Africa. A female **lion** is a lioness.

lip

Your **lips** are the two soft pink edges of your mouth.

liquid

A **liquid** is anything wet that you can pour. Water, oil and milk are all **liquids**.

list

A **list** is a group of things that you write down one after the other. *Make a list of all the people that you would like to invite to your birthday party.*

listen *(listens listening listened)*

When you **listen**, you are trying carefully to hear something. *If you listen, you can hear the sound of the sea in the distance.*

lit Look at **light**.

It was cold so Cleo lit the fire.

litter

1 **Litter** is rubbish such as bits of paper that people have left lying around.

2 A **litter** is all the baby animals that a mother has at one time. *The pig has had a litter of piglets.*

little

1 Something that is **little** is small. *A mouse is a little animal.*

2 A **little** means not very much. *The cat only drank a little milk.*

live *(lives living lived)*

1 To **live** means to be alive and growing. *People need air, food and water to live.*

2 If you **live** somewhere, that is where your home is. *We live near the park.*

lives Look at **life**.

We have been here all our lives.

221

loaf (loaves)

A **loaf** is a large piece of bread that can be cut into slices.

lock

1 A **lock** is something that you need a key to open. You use **locks** to keep things like doors, windows and drawers shut.

2 (locks locking locked) If you **lock** something, you keep it closed with a key. *Did you remember to lock the front door?*

log

A **log** is a round piece of wood that has been cut from a tree. People sometimes burn **logs** to make heat.

lonely (lonelier loneliest)

If somebody is **lonely**, they are unhappy because they are all alone.

long

1 Something that is **long** measures a lot from one end to the other. *Giraffes are animals with very long necks.*

2 If something is **long**, it takes a lot of time. *We watched a very long, boring film.*

look (looks looking looked)

1 If you look at something, you turn your eyes towards it to see it. *Look at that huge bird in the tree.*

2 If you look for something, you try to find it. *Can you help me look for my book?*

loose

If something is **loose**, it is not held firmly in place. *Jamie's front tooth is very loose - it will probably fall out soon.*

lorry (lorries)

A **lorry** is a big machine for carrying heavy things by road.

lose (loses losing lost)

1 If you **lose** something, you do not have it any more and you cannot find it. *Larry has lost one of his shoes.*

2 If you **lose** a game, you do not win it. *Our team lost the match by one goal.*

lost

If you are **lost**, you cannot find your way home. *We took the wrong path and got lost in the forest.*

lottery (lotteries)

A **lottery** is a kind of game in which you can win prizes. You pick numbers or buy tickets with numbers on them. If your numbers are chosen, you win.

loud

Something that is **loud** is easy to hear because it makes a lot of noise. *The fireworks exploded with a loud bang.*

love (loves loving loved)

If you **love** somebody or something, you like them very very much.

lovely (lovelier loveliest)

If something is **lovely**, it is beautiful or very nice. *These flowers smell lovely.*

low

Something that is **low** is near the ground. *There's a low wall around the park.*

lower (lowers lowering lowered)

If you **lower** something you move it down. *We watched the bulldozer lowering the logs.*

lucky (luckier luckiest)

If you are **lucky**, nice things happen to you that you did not expect to happen.

luggage

Luggage is all the bags and suitcases that you take with you when you go on holiday.

lump

A **lump** is a solid piece of something, sometimes with a round shape. *Ellie is making a model from some lumps of clay.*

lunch (lunches)

Lunch is a meal that people eat in the middle of the day.

lung

Your **lungs** are the two parts inside your chest that you use for breathing. They fill with air when you breathe in and empty again when you breathe out.

Mm

machine
A **machine** is a thing with moving parts that does a job. Video recorders, computers and aeroplanes are all **machines**.

magazine
A **magazine** is a kind of thin book with pictures and stories that you can buy each week or each month.

magic
Magic is a way of making strange or impossible things seem to happen.

magician
A **magician** is a person who seems to make strange or impossible things happen.

magnet
A **magnet** is a piece of metal that can make other metal things move towards it and stick to it.

magnifying glass
A **magnifying glass** is a special piece of glass. When you look through it, it makes things seem bigger than they really are.

main
Main means the most important. *The village shop is on the main road.*

male
A **male** is a person or an animal that can be a father. Boys and men are **males**, and girls and women are females.

mammal
A **mammal** is an animal that drinks milk from its mother's body when it is young. Dogs, horses, whales and people are different kinds of **mammals**.

man *(men)*
A **man** is a grown-up male.

map
A **map** is a drawing that shows what a place looks like from above. **Maps** show you where different towns are as well as roads, rivers and mountains. People use **maps** to help them find their way about.

marble
1 **Marble** is a kind of smooth hard stone. **Marble** is used in building or for making statues.
2 **Marbles** are small glass balls used in games.

mark
A **mark** is a spot on something that spoils it. *There are dirty marks on your white shirt.*

marry *(marries marrying married)*
When a man and woman **marry**, they become husband and wife.

mask
A **mask** is something that you can wear over your face to hide or protect it. Actors in plays sometimes wear **masks**. *We saw people wearing silver masks when we were in Italy.*

match
1 *(matches)* A **match** is a small thin stick of wood that makes a flame when you rub the end on something rough. *Young children should never play with matches.*
2 *(matches)* A **match** is also a game between two teams or players, such as football or cricket or tennis.
3 *(matches matching matched)* If two things **match**, they are the same in some way. *Jenna's top matches her trousers.*

material
1 **Material** is anything that we use to make things with. Wood, glass and paper are all **materials**.
2 **Material** is also cloth that we make clothes from. *Mum bought some material to make me a dress.*

matter *(matters mattering mattered)*
If something **matters**, it is important. *It doesn't matter if we're a bit late.*

mattress *(mattresses)*
A **mattress** is the soft thick part of a bed that you lie on.

meal
A **meal** is all the food that you eat at one time. Breakfast, lunch and dinner are **meals**.

mean
1 *(means meaning meant)* If you tell somebody what something **means**, you try to explain it. *That sign means that you can't park in this street.*
2 *(means meaning meant)* If you **mean** to do something, you plan to do it. *I meant to phone you last night, but I forgot.*
3 A person who is **mean** does not like spending money or giving things to people.

measure
(measures measuring measured)
When you **measure** something, you find out its size, amount or weight. *We measured Jamie to see how tall he was.*

meat
Meat is any part of an animal that we use as food such as beef, lamb or chicken.

medal
A **medal** is a round piece of metal with writing or a picture on it. **Medals** are given to people who win in sports or who have done something brave.

medicine
Medicine is a pill or liquid that a doctor gives you when you are ill to make you better.

medium
Medium means not big or small, but in between. *a medium-sized T-shirt.*

meet *(meets meeting met)*
When you **meet** somebody, you come together in the same place at the same time. *We agreed to meet after school outside the library in town.*

melt *(melts melting melted)*
When something **melts**, it changes into a liquid as it becomes warmer. *My ice-cream melted in the sun.*

memory
Memory is being able to remember things. *Mary has a good memory - she can remember all her friends' telephone numbers.*

men Look at **man**.
Two men got out of the car.

mend *(mend mending mended)*
When you **mend** something that is broken, you make it useful again. *Luke is trying to mend his bike.*

mess
A **mess** is when things are untidy or dirty. *Please tidy up the mess in your room.*

message
A **message** is words that you send to somebody when you cannot speak to them yourself. *She was out when I phoned but I left a message with her sister.*

met Look at **meet**.
They met at midnight.

metal
Metal is a hard material that melts when it is very hot. Gold, lead and iron are all **metals**.

mice Look at **mouse**.
Our cat likes catching mice.

microscope
A **microscope** is an instrument that makes tiny things look much bigger than they really are.

microwave
A **microwave** is a kind of oven that cooks food very quickly.

midday
Midday is twelve o'clock in the middle of the day.

middle
The **middle** of something is the part that is farthest away from the outsides.

midnight
Midnight is twelve o'clock at night. *We arrived home at midnight.*

milk

Milk is a white liquid that female mammals make in their bodies to feed their babies. People drink the **milk** that comes from cows.

mind

1 Your **mind** is what makes you think, learn, feel and remember.
2 (minds minding minded) If you do not **mind** something, it does not worry or upset you. *I don't mind if you borrow my things - as long as you bring them back when you've finished with them.*
3 Mind also means to be careful. *Mind that glass door!*

minus

We use **minus** to talk about taking one number away from another number. We often write **minus** as −. *Seven minus two is five (7−2=5).*

minute

A **minute** is an amount of time. There are sixty seconds in a **minute** and there are sixty **minutes** in an hour.

mirror

A **mirror** is a piece of special glass that you look into to see yourself.

miss (misses missing missed)

1 If you **miss** something that you were trying to hit or catch, you do not hit or catch it. *We were late so we missed the train.*
2 If you **miss** somebody, you are unhappy because they are not with you. *I missed my cousins when they went to Africa.*
3 If something is **missing**, it is not there. *Joe's two front teeth are missing because they have fallen out.*

mistake

If you make a **mistake**, you do something wrong, but not on purpose. *Rosie's sums were full of mistakes so she had to do them again.*

mix (mixes mixing mixed)

When you **mix** different things, you stir or put them together in some way so that they make something new. *If you mix blue and yellow paint, you get green.*

mixture

A **mixture** is different things that you stir or put together to make something new. *We added melted chocolate to the cake mixture and stirred it.*

model

1 A **model** is a small copy of something. *Peter has just made a model aeroplane.*

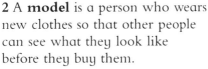

2 A **model** is a person who wears new clothes so that other people can see what they look like before they buy them.

moment

A **moment** is a very short time. *Wait here - I'll be back in a moment.*

money

Money is the coins and pieces of paper that we use to buy things.

monkey

A **monkey** is a furry wild animal with long arms and legs and a long tail that it uses to swing through trees. **Monkeys** live in hot countries.

monster

A **monster** is a large fierce animal in stories. *The hydra was a monster in ancient Greek stories which had nine snake heads.*

month

A **month** is a part of a year. There are twelve **months** in a year.

moon

The **Moon** is a planet that travels around the earth once every four weeks. You can often see the **Moon** in the sky at night.

morning

The **morning** is the beginning part of the day. The **morning** ends at twelve o'clock.

moth

A **moth** is an insect with large wings that looks like a butterfly. **Moths** fly at night.

mother

A **mother** is a woman who has a child.

motorbike

A **motorbike** is a kind of heavy bicycle with an engine.

mouse

A **mouse** is a small furry animal that has a long thin tail and sharp teeth.

mouth

Your **mouth** is the part of your face that you use for eating and speaking. Your teeth and tongue are inside your **mouth**.

move (moves moving moved)

If you **move**, you go from one place to another.

mud

Mud is wet sticky earth. *Take off your boots - they are covered in mud.*

mug

A **mug** is a big cup with straight sides and a handle. You drink things like tea and coffee from **mugs**.

multiply (multiplies multiplying multiplied)

When you **multiply**, you add a number to itself several times. *Three multiplied by two is six (3x2=6). It is the same as three plus three.*

muscle

Your **muscles** are parts of your body under your skin that get tight and loose and help you to move around.

museum

A **museum** is a building where you can go to see a lot of interesting things. *We saw the bones of a huge dinosaur in the museum.*

mushroom

A **mushroom** is a plant without leaves that is shaped a bit like an umbrella. You can eat some kinds of **mushroom**.

music

Music is the sounds made by people singing or playing musical instruments such as violins, guitars or pianos.

musical instrument

A **musical instrument** is something that you play to make music. Recorders and trumpets are **musical instuments**.

mystery (mysteries)

A **mystery** is something strange that has happened that you cannot understand or explain.

motorway

A **motorway** is a very wide road where traffic can travel fast.

mountain

A **mountain** is a very high hill. *The mountains are covered in snow.*

Nn

nail

1 Your **nails** are the hard parts at the end of your fingers and toes.

2 A **nail** is also a short piece of metal with a pointed end and flat top. You hit **nails** with a hammer to fix one thing to another.

name

The **name** of somebody or something is what they are called. *My name is Thomas.*

narrow

Something that is **narrow** does not measure very much from one side to the other. *The road was too narrow for two cars to pass.*

nasty *(nastier nastiest)*

If somebody or something is **nasty**, they are not kind or nice. *What nasty weather!*

natural

Something that is **natural** is made by nature and not by people. Wool is a **natural** material but plastic is not.

nature

1 **Nature** is everything in the world that has not been made by people or machines. Animals, plants and the sea are all part of **nature**, but buildings and cars are not.
2 A person's or an animal's **nature** is what they are like. *Ella has a kind nature.*

naughty *(naughtier naughtiest)*

A child who is **naughty** behaves badly and makes people cross.

near

Something that is **near** is not very far away. *Do you know where the nearest garage is?*

nearly

Nearly means not quite. *Ned can swim nearly as well as his brother.*

neat

Something that is **neat** is tidy and in the right place. *We put the books in neat piles.*

neck

Your **neck** is the part of your body between your head and your shoulders. *Swans and giraffes have long necks.*

necklace

A **necklace** is something pretty, such as a silver chain or beads, that you wear around your neck.

need *(needs needing needed)*

If you **need** something, you must have it. Everybody **needs** sleep to stay healthy.

needle

1 A **needle** is a long pointed piece of metal that you use for sewing. It has a hole at one end for thread to go through.
2 A **needle** is also a long plastic or metal stick that you use for knitting.
3 A **needle** is also one of the thin sharp leaves of trees such as pines.

neighbour

A **neighbour** is somebody who lives near you. *We are good friends with our next-door neighbours.*

nephew

Somebody's **nephew** is the son of their brother or sister.

nervous

If you are **nervous**, you are worried about something that might happen. *My brother was really nervous before his piano exam.*

nest

A **nest** is a home that birds and some other animals build so that their babies can be born there.

net

A **net** is made from string that has been tied together so that there are big holes in between. You can catch fish with one kind of **net**. Games like football, tennis and netball use **nets**.

never
Never means not at any time. *Peter never stops talking.*

new
Something that is **new** has just been made or bought or it has never been used before. *Mum took me shopping to buy a new coat and some new shoes.*

news
News tells you all about what is happening in the world. *We listened to the news on the car radio this morning.*

newspaper
A **newspaper** is sheets of paper folded together with stories and photographs of things that have happened in the world. *Joe is reading today's newspaper.*

next
1 **Next** means the one that comes after this one. *Next week we go back to school.*
2 **Next** to means by the side of. *Harry sat next to his uncle.*

nibble *(nibbles nibbling nibbled)*
If you **nibble** something, you eat it by taking tiny bites of it. *The rabbit nibbled the carrot.*

nice
If somebody or something is **nice**, you like them.

niece
Somebody's **niece** is the daughter of their brother or sister.

night
Night is the time when it is dark outside.

nightmare
A **nightmare** is a frightening dream. *I had a nightmare that I was being chased by a hairy monster.*

nod *(nods nodding nodded)*
If you **nod**, you move your head up and down quickly as a way of saying "yes".

noise
A **noise** is a sound that somebody or something makes.

noisy *(noisier noisiest)*
If somebody or something is **noisy**, they make a lot of noise.

noon
Noon is twelve o'clock in the middle of the day. *We met outside the restaurant at noon.*

normal
Something that is **normal** is usual and ordinary. *Cold weather is normal in winter in this country.*

north
North is a direction. If you face the Sun as it rises in the morning, **north** is on your left.

nose
Your **nose** is the part of your face above your mouth and below your eyes. You use your **nose** for breathing and for smelling things.

note
1 A **note** is a short letter. *Billy left a note to say he was going to Jack's house.*
2 A **note** is also one sound in music.

notice
1 *(notices noticing noticed)* If you **notice** something, you see it, hear it or smell it and think about it. *Lola noticed a smell of burning.*
2 A **notice** is a sign with writing on it that tells you something. *The notice on the fence said "Keep out".*

nuisance
A **nuisance** is a person or a thing that keeps annoying you. *We had a nice picnic in the park, but the wasps were a real nuisance.*

number
We use **numbers** when we count. **Numbers** tell us how many things there are.

nurse
A **nurse** is a person who looks after people who are ill or hurt.

nursery
A **nursery** is a place where young children can go in the day to be looked after when they are too young to go to school.

nut
A **nut** is a hard shell with a seed or fruit inside that you can eat. **Nuts** come from trees or plants.

Oo

oar
An **oar** is a long pole with a flat end. You use **oars** for moving a boat through water.

oasis *(oases)*
An **oasis** is a place in a desert where there is water and where plants can grow.

obey *(obeys obeying obeyed)*
When you **obey** somebody, you do what they tell you to do. *We have trained our dog to obey us when we tell her to sit.*

object
An **object** is anything that you can see or touch that is not living. Books, chairs, cups and desks are all **objects**.

obstacle
An **obstacle** is something that gets in your way and stops you doing what you want to do. *There were fallen trees and other obstacles in the road after the storm.*

ocean
An **ocean** is a very very big sea. The Pacific and the Atlantic are both **oceans**.

o'clock
We use **o'clock** to say what time it is. *We go to bed at nine o'clock and get up at half-past seven.*

octopus
(octopuses)
An **octopus** is a sea animal with a soft round body and eight long arms called tentacles. **Octopuses** live at the bottom of the sea. They hide in caves and eat crabs and shellfish.

odd
1 An **odd** number is a number that cannot be divided by 2 without leaving something over. *1, 3, 5, 7 and 9 are odd numbers.*
2 Something that is **odd** is strange. *The computer is making an odd noise.*
3 Odd things do not belong in a pair or a group. *Which thing is the odd one out?*

offer *(offers offering offered)*
If you **offer** to do something or give something, you are ready to do it or give it without being asked. *I offered to take the old lady's dog for a walk.*

office
An **office** is a place where people work. **Offices** have desks, telephones and computers.

officer
An **officer** is an important person in the army or the police who tells people what to do. *Dan's mother is a police officer.*

often
If something happens **often**, it happens many times. *We often go to the park after school if the weather is warm.*

oil
1 Oil is a thick liquid that people burn to make heat and to make engines work. **Oil** comes from the ground or from under the sea.
2 Another kind of **oil** comes from animals and the seeds of plants. We use it for cooking.

old
1 A person who is **old** has lived for many years. *My grandparents are quite old.*
2 Something that is **old** was made a long time ago.
3 Old can also mean the one that you had before. *I like my new coat better than my old one.*

onion
An **onion** is a round vegetable that grows in the ground. **Onions** have a strong taste and smell.

only

Only means no more than. *We only have ten minutes to get ready for the party.*

open

If something is **open**, people or things can go into it or through it. *The gate was open so the sheep got out of the field.*

operation

If somebody has an **operation**, a doctor mends a part of that person's body to make it well.

opinion

Your **opinion** is what you think about somebody or something.

opposite

1 Opposite means different in every way. Young is the **opposite** of old, and good is the **opposite** of bad.

2 Opposite also means on the other side, looking straight at somebody or something. *I sat opposite Sam.*

orange

1 An **orange** is a round sweet fruit with a thick skin.

2 Orange is also a colour. You can make it by mixing red and yellow paint.

orchestra

An **orchestra** is a large group of people who play different musical instruments together.

order

1 Order is the way that things are put, one after the other. *The letters of the alphabet are always in the same order.*

2 *(orders ordering ordered)* If somebody **orders** you to do something, they say you must do it. *She ordered us to clear up the mess we had made.*

3 *(orders ordering ordered)* If you **order** something in a restaurant, you say what you want to eat. *My sister and I both ordered cheese and tomato pizzas.*

orang-utan

An **orang-utan** is a large kind of ape with long brown fur.

ordinary

Something that is **ordinary** is not special, different or unusual. *He wore his ordinary clothes to his brother's party.*

organ

1 An **organ** is a large musical instrument like a piano. It has long metal pipes which make different sounds when air passes through them.

2 An **organ** is a part of your body that does a special job. Your heart, your liver and your stomach are **organs**.

ostrich *(ostriches)*

An **ostrich** is a very large bird that lives in Africa. **Ostriches** cannot fly but they run very fast.

otter

An **otter** is an animal with brown fur and a long tail. **Otters** live near water and catch fish to eat.

oval

Something that is **oval** is shaped like an egg.

oven

An **oven** is the part like a box inside a cooker, where you bake food. *Bake the cake in a hot oven.*

owe *(owes owing owed)*

If you **owe** money to somebody, you have not yet paid them but you must. *I owe you the £5 that you lent me last week.*

owl

An **owl** is a bird with large eyes that help it to see in the dark. **Owls** hunt small animals, such as mice, at night.

own *(owns owning owned)*

If you **own** something, it is yours. *Do you know who owns that bike?*

Pp

pack (packs packing packed)

When you **pack** a bag or box, you put a lot of things inside it. *Jenni packed her bag the night before she went on a school trip.*

package

A **package** is something that you wrap in paper or put in a box or envelope and send.

paddle (paddles paddling paddled)

When you **paddle**, you walk in water at the edge of the sea or in a shallow stream or river. *We took off our shoes and went paddling.*

page

A **page** is one side of a piece of paper. Books and newspapers have **pages**.

pain

Pain is what you feel when a part of your body hurts. *I've got a pain in my leg.*

paint

1 Paint is a coloured liquid that we use to put colour on things such as walls or to make pictures.

2 (paints painting painted) When you **paint** something, you use **paint** to put colour on it or to make a picture. *Jane painted her bedroom green and yellow. Connor has painted a picture of his dog.*

painting

A **painting** is a picture that somebody has painted.

pair

1 A **pair** is two things, people or animals that go together. *a pair of shoes.*
2 You can also talk about a **pair** of something, like scissors or trousers, where two parts that are the same have been joined together.

palace

A **palace** is a very big important house. People such as kings, queens and presidents live in palaces. The British Queen lives in Buckingham **Palace**.

pale

Something, such as skin, that is **pale** is almost white. *Her face is very pale - is she feeling all right?*

palm

1 Your **palm** is the inside part of your hand between your wrist and your fingers.
2 A **palm** is also a tree with no branches and big leaves that grow from the top of the trunk. **Palm** trees grow in hot countries.

pan

A **pan** is a metal dish with a long handle. You use **pans** for cooking. *Put some oil in the pan and fry the onion until it is brown.*

pancake

A **pancake** is a kind of very flat round cake. **Pancakes** are made from flour, eggs and milk and cooked in a pan in hot oil.

panda

Pandas are large furry black and white animals that look a bit like bears. **Pandas** live in China but they are now very rare animals.

panic

Panic is sudden fear that you cannot control. *There was panic when the fire alarm went off.*

pant (pants panting panted)

When you **pant**, you breathe quickly with your mouth open. *Penny was panting because she had been running.*

pantomime

A **pantomime** is a kind of play that tells a fairy tale. The actors wear colourful costumes and **pantomimes** have a lot of singing, dancing and jokes.

paper
Paper is a material that we use for writing on and wrapping things in. Books and envelopes are made of **paper**.

parcel
A **parcel** is something wrapped in paper that you can send through the post.

parent
A **parent** is a mother or father.

park
1 A **park** is a place with trees and grass where people can go to enjoy themselves.
2 (parks parking parked) When somebody **parks** a car, they leave it somewhere for a time.
Mum parked her car outside the house.

parrot
A **parrot** is a bird with a curved beak and brightly coloured feathers. Some **parrots** can learn to say a few words.

part
A **part** is one piece of something bigger. *Your fingers are parts of your hand.*

party *(parties)*
A **party** is a time when a group of people meet to have fun together. *Claire is having a party for her birthday.*

pass *(passes passing passed)*
1 If you **pass** somebody or something, you go by them. *Mum usually passes our school on her way to work so she gives us a lift.*
2 If you **pass** something to somebody, you give it to them. *Please pass me the milk.*
3 If you **pass** a test, you do well. *Becky passed all her exams.*

passenger
A **passenger** is a person who is travelling in a car, bus, train, boat or an aeroplane.

past
1 The **past** is time that has already happened. *In the past people did not have computers.*
2 **Past** means after. *Come on - it's past your bedtime.*

paste
Paste is thick wet stuff that you use for sticking things together.

pastry
Pastry is made from flour, fat and water mixed together and rolled flat. You use it to make things such as pies which are baked in the oven.

path
A **path** is a narrow piece of land that you can walk along. *If you follow the path through the woods you won't get lost.*

patient
1 A **patient** is a person who is ill and who is being looked after by a doctor or nurse.
2 A person who is **patient** does not mind waiting a long time for something to happen.

pattern
A **pattern** is the way the shapes and colours are on something. *Harriet's scarf has a pattern of red and yellow spots.*

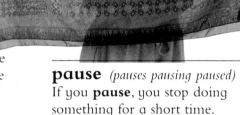

pause *(pauses pausing paused)*
If you **pause**, you stop doing something for a short time.

pavement
A **pavement** is a path at the side of a road where people can walk.

paw
A **paw** is an animal's foot. Cats, dogs and rabbits have **paws**.

pay *(pays paying paid)*
When you **pay** for something, you give money to somebody so that you can have it. *How much did you pay for your lunch?*

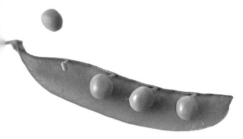

pea

A **pea** is a small round green vegetable that grows in a long covering called a pod.

peace

Peace is a time when everything is quiet and people are not fighting or arguing.

peach *(peaches)*

A **peach** is a soft round fruit. **Peaches** have a yellow and red skin, juicy yellow flesh and a big stone in the middle.

peanut

A **peanut** is a nut that grows under the ground in a thin shell.

pear

A **pear** is a green or yellow fruit that is narrow at the top and big and round at the bottom.

pebble

A **pebble** is a small smooth stone. *The beach was covered with pebbles.*

pedal

A **pedal** is a part of a machine that you push with your foot to make the machine work. You press the **pedals** of a bike to make the wheels go round.

peel

1 Peel is the skin of some fruit and vegetables. *My little sister will only eat apples if we take off the peel.*
2 *(peels peeling peeled)* If you **peel** a piece of fruit or a vegetable, you take the skin off it. *Ross peeled an orange for me.*

pen

A **pen** is a tool that you use for writing. **Pens** are filled with ink.

pencil

A **pencil** is a thin wooden stick that you use for writing or for drawing pictures.

penguin

A **penguin** is a large black and white bird that can swim but cannot fly. **Penguins** live near oceans in parts of the world where it is very cold.

people

Men, women and children are called **people**.

pepper

1 Pepper is a hot-tasting powder that you can put on food. *Pepper can make you sneeze!*
2 A **pepper** is a red, green, yellow or orange vegetable.

person

A **person** is any man, woman or child.

pet

A **pet** is a small animal that you keep in your home. People keep animals such as dogs, cats, rabbits and fish as **pets**. *Do you have any pets? I've got a hamster.*

petal

A **petal** is one of the soft coloured parts of a flower. *Daisies have white petals and a yellow centre.*

petrol

Petrol is a liquid that is made from oil. We use it in cars and lorries to make them go.

phone

Phone is a short word for telephone. *Who's on the phone?*

photograph

A **photograph** is a picture that you take with a camera. We often say photo for short.

piano

A **piano** is a musical instrument with black and white keys that you press with your fingers to make sounds.

pick *(picks picking picked)*

1 When you **pick** something, you choose it because it is the one you want. *Mum helped me pick a nice card for Gran's birthday.*
2 If you **pick** flowers or fruit, you take them with your fingers from where they are growing.
3 If you **pick** something up, you lift it. *Please could you pick up that box for me?*

picnic

A **picnic** is a meal that you take with you to eat outside somewhere nice. *We had a picnic on the beach.*

picture

A **picture** is something that you draw or paint or that you take with a camera.

pie

A **pie** is pastry filled with meat, vegetables or fruit and baked in an oven.

piece

A **piece** is one part of something. *Can I have a small piece of your chocolate cake please?*

pierce *(pierces piercing pierced)*

When a sharp thing **pierces** something, it makes a hole in it. *Sam had her ears pierced.*

pig

A **pig** is a farm animal that has a fat body, a curly tail and a flat nose called a snout.

pile

A **pile** is a lot of things on top of one another. *Fold your clothes and put them in a neat pile.*

pill

A **pill** is a small round piece of medicine that you swallow.

pillow

A **pillow** is a bag filled with soft material that you put under your head when you are in bed.

pilot

A **pilot** is a person who flies and controls an aeroplane.

pin

A **pin** is a small thin piece of metal with a sharp point. People use **pins** to hold things such as cloth or paper together.

pipe

A **pipe** is a long hollow tube that carries liquids or gas from one place to another.

pirate

A **pirate** is a person who attacks and robs ships at sea. *Jim dressed up as a pirate for the school play.*

pizza

A **pizza** is a flat round kind of bread baked in an oven with things such as tomatoes, cheese, meat and vegetables on top.

place

A **place** is where something is or where something happens.

plain

Something that is **plain** is just one colour with no pattern on it. *a plain blue shirt.*

plan *(plans planning planned)*

If you **plan** something, you think carefully about what you are going to do and how you are going to do it. *We are planning our summer holiday.*

plane

Plane is a short word for aeroplane.

planet

A **planet** is a big round thing in space that moves around a star. Earth is a **planet** that moves around the Sun.

plant

1 A **plant** is a living thing that grows in earth.
2 *(plants planting planted)* When you **plant** flowers, you put them in earth to grow.

plastic

Plastic is a material made in factories. It is used to make a lot of different things such as bottles, bags and toys.

plate
A **plate** is a flat round thing for putting food on.

pocket
A **pocket** is a small bag sewn into your clothes that you can keep things in.
Matt put the ticket in his pocket so that he would not lose it.

pointed
Something that is **pointed** has an end with a sharp point.
She has long pointed fingernails.

poisonous
If you eat something **poisonous**, you become ill or may even die. *Some berries are poisonous and so are some snakes.*

pole
A **pole** is a long thin piece of wood or metal. Flags fly on the end of **poles**.

police
The **police** are a group of people who make sure that we obey the law and that everybody is safe.

play
1 *(plays playing played)* When you **play**, you do something for fun. *The children had a good time playing in the snow.*
2 *(plays playing played)* When you **play** a musical instrument, you make music with it. *My brother can play the piano better than I can.*
3 A **play** is a story with people acting in it that you watch in a theatre or on television, or listen to on the radio.

playground
A **playground** is a place where children can play outside.

please
Please is a word that you say when you ask for something. *Please may I have a drink?*

plenty
If there is **plenty** of something, there is more than enough of it. *There is plenty of time before the train goes - let's go and have a cup of coffee.*

plus
We use **plus** to talk about adding one number to another number. We often write **plus** as **+**. *Five plus four is nine (5+4=9).*

poem
A **poem** is a piece of writing that uses words in a special way. The words at the ends of the short lines sometimes rhyme.

poet
A **poet** is a person who writes poems. *William Wordsworth was a famous English poet.*

point
1 A **point** is the sharp end of something. Things such as nails and pins have **points**.
2 A **point** in a game is a score of one.
3 *(points pointing pointed)* When you **point** at something, you lift a finger towards it to show where it is. *Sally pointed out the monkey when she was at the zoo.*

polite
If you are **polite**, you behave well. It is **polite** to say "please" and "thank you"

pond
A **pond** is a small lake. *We fed the ducks on the pond.*

pony *(ponies)*
A **pony** is a kind of small horse.

pool
A **pool** is a place filled with water for swimming in. *Our school has an indoor pool.*

poor
1 A person who is **poor** does not have much money.
2 You sometimes say **poor** when you feel sorry for somebody. *Poor Emily has broken her wrist.*

possible

If something is **possible**, it can be done or it can happen. *It is now possible to travel to the Moon.*

post

1 The **post** is all the letters and parcels that are sent and delivered.
2 A **post** is a strong pole fixed into the ground.
3 *(posts posting posted)* When you **post** a letter or a parcel, you send it to somebody.

pot

A **pot** is a deep round container. Some **pots** are used for cooking, and some for keeping food in. Another kind of **pot** is used for growing plants in.

potato *(potatoes)*

A **potato** is a vegetable that grows under the ground. **Potatatoes** have to be cooked before you can eat them.

pour *(pours pouring poured)*

When you **pour** a liquid, you make it flow from one thing into another. *Sally poured the juice from the jug into a glass.*

powder

Powder is dry stuff that is made up of a lot of very tiny pieces. Flour is a kind of **powder**.

power

Power is the strength to do work or to make something happen. The energy from electricity is one kind of **power**.

practise *(practises practising practised)*

When you **practise** something, you do it again and again until you can do it very well. *We practised throwing the ball very high and catching it.*

prepare *(prepares preparing prepared)*

If you **prepare** something, you get it ready. *We prepared the room for Gran's visit.*

present

1 A **present** is something that you give to somebody. *I got loads of nice presents for my birthday.*
2 The **present** is now. *Mr Smith is not here at present.*

president

A **president** is a person who has been chosen to rule a country that does not have a king or queen.

press *(presses pressing pressed)*

If you **press** something, you push down on it. *You press the keys of a computer to make it work.*

pretend *(pretends pretending pretended)*

When you **pretend**, you try to make people believe something that is not true. *Pretend you're a baby and I'll be your mum.*

pretty *(prettier prettiest)*

A **pretty** person or thing is nice to look at. *What pretty decorations!*

price

The **price** of something is how much money you must pay for it.

prickle

A **prickle** is a sharp point on the skin of some animals and plants. A cactus is covered in **prickles**, and so is a hedgehog.

prime minister

A **prime minister** is a person who has been chosen by the people of a country to lead that country.

prince

A **prince** is the son of a king or queen or of another royal person.

princess *(princesses)*

A **princess** is the daughter of a king, queen or other royal person, or the wife of a prince.

print *(prints printing printed)*

To **print** means to put words and pictures on paper using a machine. *Newspapers, books and magazines are printed.*

prison

A **prison** is a place where some people have to stay when they have done something that is against the law.

prize

A **prize** is something that you win for doing a thing very well. *Jack won first prize for his poem.*

problem

A **problem** is something that is difficult to answer, decide or understand. *My sister has a problem deciding what to wear.*

programme

A **programme** is something that you watch on television or listen to on the radio. *We watched an interesting programme about dinosaurs last night.*

project

If you do a **project** at school, you try to find out all you can about something and then write about it. *Last term we did a project about animals in danger.*

promise *(promises promising promised)*

If you **promise**, you say that you really will or will not do something. *I promise I won't tell anybody your secret.*

protect *(protects protecting protected)*

If you **protect** somebody or something, you keep them safe. *A helmet protects your head when you ride a bike.*

proud

If you are **proud**, you feel really happy about what you or somebody else has done well. *Nancy's mum was very proud of her when she won first prize.*

prove *(proves proving proved)*

When you **prove** something, you show that it is true. *The police cannot prove that he is the thief.*

pudding

Pudding is something sweet that you eat at the end of a meal. *There was apple pie for pudding.*

puddle

A **puddle** is a small pool of water lying on the ground.

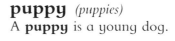

pull *(pulls pulling pulled)*

When you **pull** something, you hold it and move it towards you.

puncture

A **puncture** is a small hole in a tyre that lets the air out. *Our car has got a puncture.*

punish *(punishes punishing punished)*

To **punish** somebody means to do something to them that they do not like because they have done something wrong. *Pete's dad punished him for being naughty by not letting him watch his favourite programme on television.*

pupil

A **pupil** is somebody who is learning at school. *How many pupils are there in your class?*

puppet

A **puppet** is a doll that can be made to move. Some **puppets** have strings that you pull. Others are moved by putting your hand inside and moving your fingers.

puppy *(puppies)*

A **puppy** is a young dog.

pure

Something that is **pure** is not mixed with anything else. *This is pure apple juice.*

push *(pushes pushing pushed)*

When you **push** something, you move it away from you using your hands.

puzzle

A **puzzle** is a game or question that is fun to try to work out. *Clara is doing a jigsaw puzzle.*

pyjamas

Pyjamas are trousers and a shirt that you can wear in bed.

Qq

quack
A **quack** is the loud sound that a duck makes.

quality
Quality is how good or bad something is.

quantity
A **quantity** is how much there is, or how many there are of something. *a huge quantity of food.*

quarrel *(quarrels quarrelling quarrelled)*
When people **quarrel**, they talk in an angry way to one another because they do not agree about something. *Ben and his brother are always quarrelling.*

quarry
A quarry is a place where people dig stone out of the ground to use for building and other things.

quarter
A **quarter** is one of four equal parts of something. *We divided the pizza into quarters because there were four of us.*

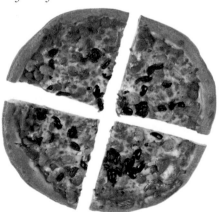

quay
A **quay** is a place in a harbour where boats can be tied up.

queen
A **queen** is a woman who is the ruler of a country or who is the wife of a king. *Some playing cards have pictures of a queen on them.*

question
When you ask a **question**, you want to find out about something.

question mark
A **question mark** is the sign ? that you write at the end of a sentence to show that somebody has asked a question.

queue
A **queue** is a line of people waiting for something. *There are long queues at the post office every Friday morning.*

quiche
A **quiche** is a kind of pie without a pastry top and filled with things made from eggs, cheese, onion, ham and tomatoes.

quick
1 If somebody or something is **quick**, they move fast. *Be quick or you'll be late.*
2 Something that is **quick** is done in a short time. *I just need to make a quick phone call.*

quiet
If somebody or something is **quiet**, they make only a little noise or no noise at all. *Ssh, please be quiet. The baby is asleep.*

quilt
A **quilt** is a thick soft cover on a bed to keep you warm. Some quilts are filled with feathers. *Lucy is hiding under her quilt.*

quit *(quits quitting quit or quitted)*
If you **quit** you leave or stop doing something. *Don't forget to quit the program before you turn off the computer.*

quite
1 **Quite** means more than a little bit. *It's quite a good film but not as good as the book.*
2 **Quite** can also mean really. *I'm not quite sure how to spell the word. I'll look in the dictionary.*

quiz *(quizzes)*
A **quiz** is a test or game in which people show how much they know by trying to answer a lot of questions about something.

quote
If you **quote** something, you say words that were said or written by somebody else before. *David quoted a line from the film he had seen.*

Rr

rabbit
A **rabbit** is a small furry animal with long ears. **Rabbits** live in holes under the ground.

race
A **race** is a way of finding out who or what can go the fastest. *Which horse won the race?*

radio
You can listen to music, the news or other programmes on a **radio**. **Radios** are machines that bring sounds through the air.

raft
A **raft** is a kind of flat boat. Some **rafts** are made from pieces of wood joined together.

rail
1 **Rails** are the long metal bars that trains travel along.
2 A **rail** is also a long metal bar that you can hold on to.

railway
A **railway** is a kind of path made of rails that trains travel along.

rain
1 **Rain** is the drops of water that fall from clouds.
2 *(rains raining rained)* When it **rains**, drops of water fall from the clouds. *It rained everyday last week.*

rainbow
A **rainbow** is a curved shape of different colours that you sometimes see in the sky after it has rained. It is made by the sun shining through rain.

raise *(raises raising raised)*
If you **raise** something, you lift it up. *Katie raised her hand.*

rake
A **rake** is a tool with a long handle and a row of sharp points at one end. You use a **rake** in the garden for collecting leaves and grass together or for making the earth smooth.

ran Look at **run**.
Tom ran out into the garden.

rang Look at **ring**.
Who rang the bell?

rare
Something that is **rare** is not seen or found very often, or it does not happen very often. *Black pandas are rare animals.*

rat
A **rat** is an animal with sharp teeth that looks like a big mouse.

raw
Raw food is not cooked. You eat **raw** lettuce in salads.

reach *(reaches reaching reached)*
1 If you **reach** for something, you stretch out your hand to touch it or hold it.
2 When you **reach** a place, you arrive there. *We reached the island by boat.*

read *(reads reading read)*
When you **read**, you look at words and know what they mean. *You are reading these words.*

ready
If somebody is **ready**, they can do something straight away.

real
Something that is **real** is true or it is not a copy. *Is that a real frog or a toy one?*

realize *(realizes realizing realized)*
If you **realize** something, you suddenly understand or know it. *When I got closer I realized the man was my next-door neighbour.*

really
1 **Really** means that something is true. *Is she really asleep or is she just pretending?*
2 **Really** also means very. *It was a really good party.*

reason

A **reason** for something tells us why it happened. *She had a good reason for being late - she had to go to the doctor's.*

record

1 A **record** is the fastest or the best that has ever been done. *He broke the world record for the high jump in the Olympic Games.*

2 A **record** is also a flat round piece of plastic with music or other sounds on it. You put **records** on a record-player to listen to them. *Put on another record.*

reflection

A **reflection** is what you see when you look into shiny things such as mirrors.

refrigerator

A **refrigerator** is a metal box with a machine inside it that keeps food and drink cold and fresh. It is often called a fridge for short. *Put the milk in the refrigerator.*

refuse *(refuses refusing refused)*

If you **refuse**, you say you will not do something that somebody has asked you to do. *Charlie refused to take the dog for a walk.*

register

A **register** is a book with a list of the names of all the pupils in a class. *The teacher opened the register.*

remember *(remembers remembering remembered)*

If you **remember** something, you bring it back into your mind. *Can you remember when Tom's birthday is?*

remind *(reminds reminding reminded)*

If you **remind** somebody of something, you help them to remember it. *Remind me to buy a birthday card tomorrow.*

repair *(repairs repairing repaired)*

If you **repair** something that is broken, you mend it.

repeat *(repeats repeating repeated)*

If you **repeat** something, you say it or do it again. *Could you please repeat what you just said?*

reply *(replies replying replied)*

When you **reply**, you give an answer. *He replied to my letter.*

reptile

A **reptile** is an animal with cold blood. Most **reptiles** have skin covered in scales.
Reptiles lay eggs. Crocodiles, lizards, snakes and tortoises are all **reptiles**.

rescue *(rescues rescuing rescued)*

If you **rescue** somebody, you help them escape from danger. *We helped to rescue a cat which was stuck up a tree.*

rest

1 *(rests resting rested)* When you **rest**, you stop what you are doing and sit or lie down quietly for a time. *She's resting because she's tired.*

2 The **rest** is what is left after everything or everybody else has gone. *She ate some of her dinner and gave the rest to the dog!*

restaurant

A **restaurant** is a place where you can go to buy and eat meals.

result

1 A **result** is something that happens because of something else. *The road was flooded as a result of all the rain.*

2 A **result** is also the goals or points at the end of a game. *We listen to the football results on the radio on Saturday evenings.*

return *(returns returning returned)*

1 When you **return**, you go back. *We had a new teacher when we returned to school after the holidays.*

2 If you **return** something that you have borrowed, you give it back. *I have to return these books to the library tomorrow.*

reward

A **reward** is something nice that somebody gives you because of something good you have done. *We were taken to see a film as a reward for helping Mum tidy the cupboards.*

rhinoceros *(rhinoceroses)*

A **rhinoceros** is a very big wild animal with thick skin. It has one or two horns on its nose.
Rhinoceroses live in Africa and Asia. They are often called rhinos for short.

rhyme *(rhymes rhyming rhymed)*
Words that **rhyme** have the same sound at the end. *The word "rice" rhymes with "mice", and "cat" rhymes with "hat".*

ribbon
A **ribbon** is a long thin piece of coloured cloth. *Jessie wore pink ribbons in her hair.*

rice
Rice is a food that comes from the small white seeds of a plant.

rich
People who are **rich** have a lot of money and expensive things.

riddle
A **riddle** is a question or puzzle that is hard to work out and that has a clever answer, such as: *"What has hands but no arms?" Answer: "A clock".*

ride
1 *(rides riding rode ridden)* When you **ride** a bike or horse, you sit on it as it goes along.

2 A **ride** is a journey in something like a car or bus.

right
1 If something is **right**, there are no mistakes. *That was the right answer.*
2 **Right** is the opposite of left. *When you read a line of writing, you start on the left-hand side and finish on the right.*

ring
1 A **ring** is a circle of metal that you wear on your finger.
2 A **ring** is also a circle. *She drew a ring in chalk on the ground and jumped into it.*
3 *(rings ringing rang rung)* If something **rings**, it makes a sound like a bell. *Did somebody ring the doorbell?*

ripe
When fruit is **ripe**, it is ready to eat. *Let's go and pick the strawberries now they are ripe.*

rise *(rises rising rose risen)*
When something **rises**, it goes up. *The Sun rises in the sky in the East every morning.*

river
A **river** is a lot of moving water that flows through a country. **Rivers** flow into the sea or into a lake. *The River Ganges is in India.*

road
A **road** is a wide path that cars, bicycles, buses and lorries travel along between one town, city or village and another.

roar *(roars roaring roared)*
To **roar** is to make a loud noise like the sound that wild animals such as lions and tigers make. *A motorbike roared past.*

rob *(robs robbing robbed)*
To **rob** means to take things that do not belong to you. *The two men who robbed the supermarket have been caught by the police and have been sent to prison.*

robin
A **robin** is a small bird with red feathers on its chest.

robot
A **robot** is a machine that can do some of the jobs that people do. Some factories use **robots** to make things such as cars.

rock
1 **Rock** is the hard stuff that mountains are made of.
2 *(rocks rocking rocked)* If something **rocks**, it moves from side to side very gently.

rocket
A **rocket** is a big machine like a metal tube that is used to send spacecraft into space. *The film began with a big rocket lifting-off into space.*

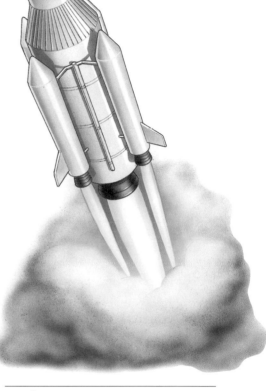

rode Look at **ride**.
I rode on Sam's new bike.

roll
1 *(rolls rolling rolled)* When something **rolls**, it moves by turning over and over. *The ball rolled under the table.*
2 A **roll** is a long piece of something that has been wrapped around itself many times. *a roll of tape.*
3 A **roll** is also a small round piece of bread made for one person.

roller skate

Roller skates are boots with wheels on the bottom for skating over smooth hard ground.

roof

A **roof** is the part that covers the top of a building or a vehicle such as a car.

room

A **room** is one of the spaces inside a building. **Rooms** have walls, a ceiling and a door. *The room you sleep in is called a bedroom and the room where you prepare food is called a kitchen.*

root

A **root** is the part of a plant that grows under the ground. Plants and trees get food and water through their **roots**.

root

rope

Rope is strong thick string for lifting and pulling things. *We tied a rope to the boat and pulled it up onto the river bank.*

rose

1 A **rose** is a flower with a nice smell. Some **roses** have sharp pointed parts called thorns on their stems.
2 Look at **rise**. *The Sun rose above the mountains.*

rotten

Something that is **rotten** has gone bad or is spoilt. *You cannot eat that apple because it is rotten.*

rough

1 Something that feels **rough** is not smooth. The bark of a tree feels **rough**.

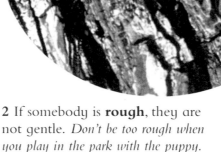

2 If somebody is **rough**, they are not gentle. *Don't be too rough when you play in the park with the puppy.*

round

Something that is **round** has no corners and has the same shape as a circle or a ball.

roundabout

1 A **roundabout** is a kind of island where different roads meet. Traffic has to go around a **roundabout** in a circle.

2 A **roundabout** is also a large machine at a fair that children can have a ride on as it goes round and round.

rounders

Rounders is a game for two teams that is played outdoors with a bat and ball. *We played rounders in the park.*

row

1 A **row** is a line of people or things. *Jennifer planted a row of flowers in the front garden.*
2 (rows rowing rowed) When you **row** a boat, you move it along by using oars. *Dad said he will take us rowing on Sunday.*

royal

Royal means belonging to a king and queen or their family. *a royal palace.*

rub *(rubs rubbing rubbed)*

If you **rub** things together, you move them against each other. *Megan rubbed her hands together to warm them up.*

rubber

1 Rubber is a strong material that stretches and bends easily and bounces. Tyres, balls and gloves can all be made from **rubber**. *Mum wears yellow rubber gloves for washing-up.*

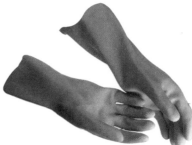

2 A **rubber** is something made from a small piece of **rubber** that can make pencil marks disappear.

rubbish

Rubbish is anything that you do not want and that you throw away, such as old paper and empty cans. *Our rubbish gets collected every Wednesday.*

ruby *(rubies)*

A **ruby** is a red jewel. **Rubies** cost a lot of money. *My aunt has a very expensive ruby ring.*

rudder

A **rudder** is a flat piece of wood or metal at the back of a ship or aircraft that makes the ship or aircraft move to the left or right.

rude

A person who is **rude** behaves in a bad way and does not think about other people's feelings.

rug

A **rug** is a thick piece of cloth that you put on the floor. It is like a small carpet.

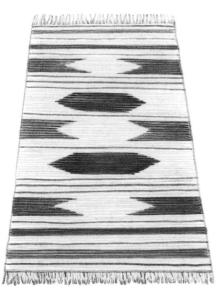

rugby

Rugby is a game played by two teams using an oval-shaped ball.

ruin

A **ruin** is what is left of a building when most of it has fallen down and been destroyed.

rule

1 **Rules** tell you what you must do and what you must not do. Games have **rules**.
2 *(rules ruling ruled)* To **rule** means to lead and control a country and all the people who live there. *Queen Victoria ruled for many years.*

ruler

1 A **ruler** is a long piece of wood, plastic or metal that you use to help you draw straight lines or for measuring how long something is.
2 A **ruler** is also a person who rules a country.

rumble *(rumbles rumbling rumbled)*

To **rumble** is to make a long low sound like thunder. *The traffic rumbled past all night.*

run *(runs running ran run)*

When you **run**, you move your legs very quickly to get somewhere. *Nick ran in the race but he came last!*

runny

If something is **runny**, it flows like a liquid. *The honey you gave me is very runny.*

rung   Look at **ring**.

I've rung the bell twice but there's nobody at home.

runway

A **runway** is a long piece of flat ground where aircraft can take off and land.

rush *(rushes rushing rushed)*

If you **rush**, you go somewhere or do something very quickly. *Tyrone rushed home to tell his dad the good news.*

rustle *(rustles rustling rustled)*

When something **rustles**, it makes the soft sound of dry leaves moving about in the wind.

rusty

If something is **rusty**, it is covered in brown stuff that spreads on some metals when they get wet.

rye

Rye is a plant that grows on farms. It can be used to make flour.

Ss

sad *(sadder saddest)*
When you are **sad**, you feel unhappy. *Harry felt sad when his hamster died.*

safe
If you are **safe**, you are not in any danger.

sail
A **sail** is a large piece of cloth on a boat. When the wind blows against the **sail**, the boat moves along. *The boat has a red-striped sail.*

sailor
A **sailor** is a person who works on a boat.

salad
A **salad** is a mixture of cold vegetables and other things.

salt
Salt is a white powder that people put on their food to give it more taste. **Salt** is found in the earth and in sea water.

same
If two things are the **same,** they are like each other in every way. *Lauren and her sister sound the same on the phone.*

sand
Sand is a kind of powder made of tiny pieces of rock. **Sand** covers deserts and some beaches. *I love playing in the sand.*

sandwich
A **sandwich** is two pieces of bread with cheese, meat or some other food in between.

sang Look at **sing**.
He sang on his own in front of the whole school.

sank Look at **sink**.
The ship sank all the way to the bottom of the ocean.

sat Look at **sit**.
We sat down to eat our dinner at eight o' clock last night.

satellite
1 A **satellite** is an object that moves around a planet in space.
2 A **satellite** is also a machine that moves around in space and sends information back to earth about things like the weather.

saucepan
A **saucepan** is a metal pot with a long handle and a lid. You use a **saucepan** for cooking.

saucer
A **saucer** is a small plate that you put a cup on.

save *(saves saving saved)*
1 If you **save** somebody, you take them away from danger. *She saved the boy from falling into the river.*
2 If you **save** money, you do not spend it but keep it somewhere for another time. *Millie is saving all her money to buy a new pair of roller-skates.*

saw
1 A **saw** is a tool for cutting hard materials such as wood. It has a metal blade with sharp points called teeth on one edge.
2 Look at **see**.
I saw that film before my friend did.

say *(says saying said)*
When you **say** something, you make words with your mouth. *I can't hear what you're saying because it's too noisy in here.*

scale
A **scale** is one of the small thin shiny pieces that cover the skin of fish and reptiles. *The fishes' scales were shining in the sunlight.*

scales
Scales are a machine that we use to find out how heavy somebody or something is. *Step on the scales and I'll weigh you.*

scare *(scares scaring scared)*
If something **scares** you, it makes you feel frightened.

scarf *(scarves)*
A **scarf** is a long piece of cloth that you wear around your neck.

school
A **school** is a place where children go to learn all sorts of different things from teachers.

science
Science is something that we learn about at school. **Science** teaches us about things like plants and animals, the Earth and the planets, and how things work.

scissors
A pair of **scissors** is a tool for cutting. It has two blades joined together in the middle.

score
1 The **score** is the number of points each side has in a game. *The score at half time was 3-2.*
2 *(scores scoring scored)* To **score** is to get a point or goal in a game. *Our team scored just before the end of the match.*

scratch *(scratches scratching scratched)*
1 When you **scratch** something, you rub something sharp against it. *Jamie scratched his head.*
2 To **scratch** also means to damage a thing with something sharp. *Our cat is always scratching the furniture with his claws.*

scream *(screams screaming screamed)*
If you **scream**, you shout in a very loud high voice. People **scream** when they are afraid, angry or hurt.

screen
A **screen** is a flat surface on which you see films and television programmes. Computers also have **screens**.

sea
A **sea** is a large area of salt water. **Seas** cover large parts of the Earth.

seal
A **seal** is a furry animal that lives in the sea and on land. Many **seals** live in icy waters.

search *(searches searching searched)*
When you **search** for something, you try to find it by looking very carefully. *We've searched everywhere for your keys.*

seaside
The **seaside** is the land next to the sea. *We went to the seaside for our holidays.*

season
A **season** is one of the four parts of a year. The **seasons** are spring, summer, autumn and winter.

seat
A **seat** is anything that you can sit on. *There are plenty of seats on the train.*

second
1 A **second** is a very short amount of time. There are sixty **seconds** in a minute.
2 **Second** also means next after the first. *I was the second person to arrive at the party.*

secret
A **secret** is something that you do not want anybody to know about. *I can't tell you where they have gone - it's a secret.*

see *(sees seeing saw seen)*
When you **see** something, you find out about it with your eyes.

seed
A **seed** is a tiny part of a plant. You put **seeds** into the ground, and new plants grow from them.

seem *(seems seeming seemed)*
To **seem** means to look or feel like something. *The puppies seem to be happy in their new homes.*

seen Look at **see**.
Have you ever seen a ghost?

shape

The **shape** of something is the way that its outside edges make a pattern. A circle is a round **shape**.

seesaw

A **seesaw** is a kind of toy for two people to play on. It has a long flat part that they sit on, one at each end, to go up and down.

selfish

Selfish people only think about themselves and do not care about other people.

sell *(sells selling sold)*

If somebody **sells** you something, they give it to you and you give them money for it. *My dad sold his car to a friend.*

send *(sends sending sent)*

When you **send** something somewhere, you make it go there. *I sent a birthday card and present in the post to my aunt.*

sensible

If you are **sensible**, you think carefully about what you are going to do and you do not do anything silly. *We can go to the fair as long as we are sensible, Mum said.*

sentence

A **sentence** is a group of words. A **sentence** starts with a capital letter (such as A, F or T) and ends with a full stop.

set

A **set** is a group of things that belong together. *We gave granddad a set of gardening tools as a present.*

settee

A **settee** is a long soft chair for two or more people to sit on. *Our settee at home is dark blue.*

sew *(sews sewing sewed sewn)*

When you **sew**, you use a needle and thread to join pieces of cloth together, or to fix things to cloth. *Zoe is sewing a button on her shirt.*

shadow

A **shadow** is a dark shape that a person or thing makes when they are blocking out the light. *It was too hot for us to sit in the sun so we sat in the shadow of the big oak tree.*

shake *(shakes shaking shook shaken)*

When you **shake** something, you move it quickly up and down or from side to side. *Shake the medicine before you open the bottle.*

shallow

Water that is **shallow** is not very deep. *We can paddle here - the river is quite shallow.*

share *(shares sharing shared)*

When you **share** something, you give a part of it to another person. *She shared her sandwiches with her friend.*

shark

A **shark** is large sea fish with sharp teeth. Some **sharks** are very fierce.

sharp

Something that is **sharp** has a point or thin edge that can cut things easily. *Be careful with that knife - it's really sharp.*

shave *(shaves shaving shaved)*

When a man **shaves**, he cuts the hair that grows on his face with a sharp tool called a razor.

shed

A **shed** is a small wooden building. *Ben keeps his bike in the shed at the end of the garden.*

sheep *(sheep)*

A **sheep** is a farm animal. We get wool and meat from **sheep**. *There are a lot of sheep in that field.*

sheet

1 A **sheet** is a large piece of thin cloth that you put on a bed.
2 A **sheet** is also a thin flat piece of something such as plastic, paper or glass.

shelf *(shelves)*

A **shelf** is a long flat piece of wood or metal fixed to a wall. You put things on **shelves** to keep them tidy or so that people can see them.

shell

A **shell** is the hard outside covering of things such as eggs, nuts and some animals. Snails and tortoises have **shells**. You can sometimes find the **shells** of some sea animals on the beach.

shine *(shines shining shone)*

Something that **shines** gives out light, or it is smooth and bright like gold or silver. *We polished the silver cup until it shone.*

shiny *(shinier shiniest)*

If something is **shiny**, it shines. *She had a shiny new car.*

ship

A **ship** is a big boat that goes on the sea.

shirt

A **shirt** is something that you wear on the top part of your body. **Shirts** have sleeves, buttons, and usually a collar.

shiver *(shivers shivering shivered)*

If you **shiver**, you shake because you are cold or afraid. *Jake was shivering when he got out of the pool.*

shoe

Shoes are what you wear on your feet to keep them warm and dry.

shone Look at **shine**.
The sun shone brightly all day.

shook Look at **shake**.
He shook his head.

shoot *(shoots shooting shot)*

To **shoot** means to send something out very fast from a gun or a bow. You **shoot** arrows from a bow, and you **shoot** bullets from a gun. *I was upset at the end of the film when he got shot.*

shop

A **shop** is a place where you can buy things. *A really good shop has just opened in town.*

shore

The **shore** is the land along the edge of the sea or a very large lake. *We collected shells at the seashore.*

short

1 A **short** time or distance is not very long. *It's only a short journey from my house to Bob's.*
2 Somebody or something that is **short** is not tall or long. *My little sister is much too short to reach the top drawer of the chest of drawers.*

shot Look at **shoot**.
He shot the arrow at the tree.

shoulder

Your **shoulder** is the top part of your body between your neck and the top part of your arm. *The little boy sat on his dad's shoulders.*

shout *(shouts shouting shouted)*

If you **shout**, you speak in a very loud voice. *She shouted to me across the room.*

show

1 *(shows showing showed)* When you **show** something, you let people see it. *Alice showed me the painting that she did at school today.*
2 *(shows showing showed)* If you **show** somebody how to do something, you teach them how to do it. *Jane showed me what to do.*
3 A **show** is something with singing or dancing that you can watch in the theatre or on the television. *Did you enjoy the show?*

shower

1 A **shower** is something that you stand under to wash yourself with a spray of water.
2 A **shower** is also rain or snow that falls for a short time. *The rain has stopped now - it was only a quick shower.*

shrink *(shrinks shrinking shrank shrunk)*

If something **shrinks**, it gets smaller. *The shirt shrank when I washed it.*

shut *(shuts shutting shut)*

When you **shut** something such as a box or a door, you move it so that it is not open. *Please shut all the doors and windows before you go out. You shut your eyes before you go to sleep.*

shy

If you are **shy**, you do not like meeting and talking to people that you do not know.

side

1 The **side** of something is the left or the right of it.
2 The **sides** of something such as a box are its flat surfaces. *Dice have six sides.*
3 The **sides** of something are also its edges. *A triangle has three sides.*
4 The **sides** in a game are the groups or teams that are playing against each other.

sight

Sight is being able to see. *My granddad wears glasses because his sight is not very good.*

sign

1 A **sign** is a notice with words or drawings that tells people something. *The arrow on the sign says: Turn right.*

2 *(signs signing signed)* When you **sign** something, you write your name on it.

silence

Silence is when there is no sound at all.

silk

Silk is a smooth shiny material. It is made from threads that are spun by insects called silkworms.

silly *(sillier silliest)*

1 If somebody or something is **silly**, they are funny and make us laugh. *He wore a silly hat.*
2 **Silly** can also mean not sensible. *It was a bit silly of you to go out in the rain with no shoes on.*

silver

Silver is a shiny grey metal that is used for making things such as rings and necklaces.

sing *(sings singing sang sung)*

When you **sing**, you use your voice to make music.

sink

1 A **sink** is the place in a kitchen where you wash dishes.
2 *(sinks sinking sank sunk)* When something **sinks**, it goes down under water. *The pebble sank to the bottom of the pond.*

sip *(sips sipping sipped)*

If you **sip** something, you drink a tiny amount at a time.

sister

Your **sister** is a girl or woman who has the same mother and father as you.

sit *(sits sitting sat)*

When you **sit**, you put your bottom on something. *We sat on the bench in the park.*

size

The **size** of something is how big it is. *What size shoes do you take?*

skate

1 Ice **skates** are special boots with blades underneath that you wear for sliding on ice.
2 Roller **skates** are special boots with little wheels underneath for moving on flat ground.

skateboard

A **skateboard** is a board with wheels on the bottom. You ride it by standing on it with one foot and pushing the ground with the other foot.

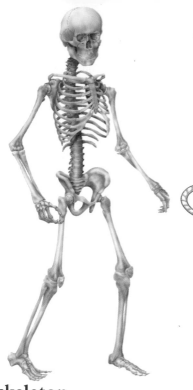

skeleton

A **skeleton** is all the bones that are inside the body of a person or an animal.

ski

Skis are long pieces of metal, plastic or wood that you wear on your feet with special boots to move quickly on snow.

skin

Skin is what covers the bodies of people and animals. Fruit and vegetables also have **skin**.

skip *(skips skipping skipped)*

When you **skip**, you move along by jumping from one foot to the other. You can also **skip** with a skipping rope.

skirt

A **skirt** is something that girls and women wear. It hangs down from the waist and covers the bottom part of the body.

sky *(skies)*

The **sky** is all the space above the Earth. You can see the Moon and stars in the **sky**.

skyscraper

A **skyscraper** is a building that is so tall that it looks as if it is touching the sky.

sledge

A **sledge** is something that you sit on to ride over snow. It has two long pieces of wood on the bottom to help it slide along.

sleep *(sleeps sleeping slept)*

When you **sleep**, you close your eyes and your body rests. *John slept well because he was very tired after his long journey.*

sleeve

A **sleeve** is the part of something such as a shirt or jacket that covers your arm.

slice

A **slice** is a thin piece that has been cut from something. *Can I have a slice of cake, please?*

slide

1 *(slides sliding slid)* When something **slides**, it moves smoothly over a surface. *Ella fell and slid on her bottom across the floor.*
2 A **slide** is something that you play on. It has steps on one side that you climb up and a long piece of slippery metal on the other side that you **slide** down.

slip *(slips slipping slipped)*

When you **slip**, you slide and fall down. *Thomas nearly slipped on the wet floor.*

slipper

Slippers are soft shoes that you wear indoors.

slippery

When something is **slippery**, it is so smooth or wet that you cannot hold it or walk on it easily. *Be careful - the step is a bit slippery after the rain.*

slow

Something that is **slow** does not move very quickly.

small

Something that is **small** is not large. *Mice are small creatures.*

smash *(smashes smashing smashed)*

If you **smash** something by hitting or dropping it, it breaks into lots of small pieces. *He threw the ball too hard and it smashed a window.*

smell *(smells smelling smelt or smelled)*

1 When you **smell** something, you notice it with your nose. *Dogs can smell things from a long way away.*
2 When something **smells**, you can find out about it using your nose. *That cake smells lovely.*

smile *(smiles smiling smiled)*

When you **smile**, the corners of your mouth turn up. People **smile** when they are happy.

smoke

Smoke is the grey or black cloud that goes up into the air when something is on fire.

smooth

If something is **smooth**, you cannot feel any rough parts on it when you touch it. *The top of the table is shiny and smooth.*

snail

A **snail** is a small creature with a soft body that lives inside a shell. **Snails** move very slowly.

snake

A **snake** is a reptile with a long thin body and no legs. **Snakes** move along the ground by sliding. Some **snakes** bite and are dangerous.

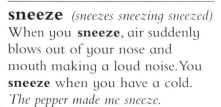

sneeze *(sneezes sneezing sneezed)* When you **sneeze**, air suddenly blows out of your nose and mouth making a loud noise. You **sneeze** when you have a cold. *The pepper made me sneeze.*

snow

Snow is soft pieces of white frozen water that falls from the sky when it is very cold.

soap

Soap is something that we use with water for washing.

sock

Socks are soft coverings that you wear on your feet inside your shoes.

soft

If something is **soft**, it is not hard.

soil

Soil is the brown stuff that plants grow in. *I filled the pot with soil and planted some seeds in it.*

sold Look at **sell**. *The shop sold all kinds of toys.*

soldier

A **soldier** is a person who is in an army and who is trained to fight in a war.

solid

1 Something that is **solid** is hard and does not change its shape. *Water is liquid and ice is solid.*
2 A **solid** object is not hollow. *That table is made of solid wood.*

son

A **son** is a boy or man who is somebody's child.

song

A **song** is a piece of music with words that you sing.

soon

If something is going to happen **soon**, it will happen in a very short time from now. *We'll soon be home.*

sore

If a part of your body feels **sore**, it hurts a little. *I've got a sore throat.*

sorry

If you are **sorry**, you feel sad because you wish that something had not happened. *I'm really sorry I shouted at you. I didn't mean to upset you.*

sort

1 A **sort** is a kind. *What sort of music do you like?*
2 *(sorts sorting sorted)* When you **sort** things, you put them into groups. *Emily is sorting the bricks into different colours.*

sound

A **sound** is anything that you can hear. *He heard the sound of somebody coming up the stairs.*

soup

Soup is a hot liquid food that you eat with a spoon. **Soup** is made from things like vegetables and meat.

sour

Something that is **sour** has a taste that is not sweet, like the kind of taste that a lemon has.

south

South is a direction. If you face the Sun as it rises in the morning, **south** is on your right.

space

1 **Space** is a place that is empty. *Can you find a space to park?*
2 **Space** is also everything far above the Earth where the planets and stars are.

spaceship

A **spaceship** is a vehicle that travels in space.

spade

A **spade** is a tool with a long handle and a wider flat part at the end that you use for digging.

speak *(speaks speaking spoke spoken)*

When you **speak**, you say words.

special

1 Something that is **special** is not ordinary but is important and better than the usual kind. *Birthdays are special days.*

2 **Special** also means made to do a job. *You need a special tool for cutting glass - you can't use a knife!*

speed

Speed is how fast something moves or happens. *Some aircrafts like Concorde travel faster than the speed of sound.*

spell

1 *(spells spelling spelt or spelled)*
When you **spell** a word, you put letters in the right order. *"How do you spell 'rough'?" "R-O-U-G-H."*
2 A **spell** is a magic rhyme or trick in fairy stories that makes something happen. *The wicked witch put a spell on the girl and turned her into a frog.*

spend *(spends spending spent)*

1 When you **spend** money, you use it to pay for something. *How much money have you spent?*
2 When you **spend** time doing something, you use your time to do it. *We spent the whole day playing in the garden.*

spider

A **spider** is a small creature with eight legs and no wings. **Spiders** spin webs in which they catch insects to eat.

spill *(spills spilling spilt or spilled)*

If you **spill** something, you make it flow out by mistake. *Ian spilt his orange juice on the kitchen floor.*

spin *(spins spinning spun)*

1 When something **spins**, it goes round and round. *The Earth spins as it travels around the Sun.*
2 To **spin** also means to pull and twist something such as cotton or wool into long threads.

spine

Your **spine** is the long line of bones down the centre of your back.

splash *(splashes splashing splashed)*

When you **splash** a liquid, you make drops of it fly around to make things wet. *I took a shower and the water splashed on the floor.*

spoil *(spoils spoiling spoilt or spoiled)*

If you **spoil** something, you make it less good than it was before. *The rain spoiled our picnic.*

spoke, spoken Look at **speak**.

He spoke very clearly. I have never spoken to her before.

spooky (spookier spookiest)
If something is **spooky**, it is strange and frightening. *The old house felt really spooky.*

spoon
A **spoon** is something that you use for picking up food with. It has a handle at one end and a round part at the other end.

sport
A **sport** is a game or something else that you do to keep your body fit. Many **sports** are played outside. Swimming, tennis and football are all **sports**.

spot
1 A **spot** is a small round mark on something. *The teapot has lots of white spots.*

2 A **spot** is also a small red mark on your skin.

spray
A **spray** is a lot of very small drops of liquid that shoot out of something.

spread (spreads spreading spread)
1 When you **spread** something, you make it cover a surface. *She spread jam on the bread.*
2 When a bird **spreads** its wings, it opens them out as far as possible. *The eagle spread its wings and flew away.*

spring
1 Spring is the part of the year between winter and summer, when trees begin to grow leaves again.
2 A **spring** is a curly piece of metal that goes back into the same shape after you have pressed or stretched it.
3 (springs springing sprang sprung) To **spring** means to jump. *The fox sprang over the fence.*

spun Look at **spin**.
The spider has spun a web.

square
A **square** is a shape with four corners and four sides that are all the same length.

squash (squashes squashing squashed)
If you **squash** something you press it hard so that it becomes flat. *She sat down on the cake and squashed it.*

squeak (squeaks squeaking squeaked)
If something **squeaks** it makes a short high sound, something like the sound that a mouse makes. *The brakes on my bike squeak.*

squeeze (squeezes squeezing squeezed)
If you **squeeze** something, you hold and press it hard on the sides. *She squeezed my hand so hard that it hurt.*

squirrel
A **squirrel** is a small furry animal with a thick tail. **Squirrels** usually live in trees, and they eat nuts.

stable
A **stable** is a building where horses are kept.

stairs
Stairs are a set of steps inside a building. *We walked up the stairs to the third floor.*

stamp
A **stamp** is a small piece of paper that you stick on a letter to show that you have paid to post it.

stand (stands standing stood)
When you **stand** somewhere, you are on your feet without moving.

star
1 A **star** is one of the bright lights that you see at night when the sky is clear. **Stars** are millions and millions of kilometres away from us.
2 A **star** is also a shape with five or six points.

stare (stares staring stared)
When you **stare** at somebody or something, you look at them for a long time without moving your eyes. *Tim was staring at the woman because he was trying hard to remember her name.*

start (starts starting started)
When you **start** to do something, you do the first part of it. *I started to read you a story but you fell asleep before I had finished.*

station

1 A **station** is a place where trains and buses stop to let people on and off.

2 A **station** is also a building for the police or firefighters.

statue

A **statue** is something made of stone or metal that looks like a person or an animal.

steady *(steadier steadiest)*

If something is **steady**, it is not moving or shaking. *Mike held the ladder steady.*

steal *(steals stealing stole stolen)*

To **steal** means to take and keep something that does not belong to you. *The robbers stole millions of pounds worth of diamonds.*

steam

Steam is a cloud made of a lot of tiny drops that come from a liquid that is boiling. Some trains are powered by **steam**.

steep

A hill that is **steep** is hard to climb because it goes up quickly.

steel

Steel is a very hard strong metal that is used for making things such as tools, machines and cars.

stem

The **stem** of a plant is the long thin part that grows above the ground. Leaves and flowers grow on the **stem**.

step

1 You take a **step** every time you move your foot and put it in a different place.

2 A **step** is also one of the places where you put your foot when you go up or down stairs or a ladder. *The ladder has fifteen steps.*

stick

1 A **stick** is a long thin piece of wood.

2 *(sticks sticking stuck)* When you **stick** things together, you fix one thing to another using glue or tape. *Tara stuck a stamp on the envelope and posted her letter.*

3 *(sticks sticking stuck)* To **stick** also means to push something pointed into something else. *When Henry stuck a pin into the balloon it burst.*

still

1 If you are **still**, you do not move at all. *Please stand still.*

2 If something is **still** happening, it has not stopped. *I am still doing my homework.*

sting *(stings stinging stung)*

If an insect or a plant **stings** you, a sharp point goes into your skin and hurts you. *Ouch! That wasp just stung me!*

stir *(stirs stirring stirred)*

If you **stir** something, you move it around with something such as a spoon or a stick. *We helped Dad stir the cake mixture.*

stole, stolen Look at **steal**.

The dog stole my tennis ball. Somebody has stolen Laura's bike.

stomach

Your **stomach** is the part inside your body where food goes when you eat it.

stone

1 A **stone** is a small piece of rock.

2 A **stone** is also the hard seed in the middle of fruits such as cherries and peaches.

stood Look at **stand**.

She stood in the queue to buy tickets for the show.

stool

A **stool** is a small seat with no back or arms.

stop *(stops stopping stopped)*

1 If you **stop** doing something, you do not do it any more. *Maggie stopped reading and turned out the light.*

2 If something that was moving **stops**, it stands still. *The bus stops here. She stopped the car.*

store *(stores storing stored)*
If you **store** something, you put it somewhere so that you can use it later. *Squirrels collect nuts in autumn and store them for winter.*

storm
A **storm** is very bad weather with strong winds and a lot of rain or snow. Some **storms** also have thunder and lightning.

story *(stories)*
Some **stories** tell you about real things that have happened and others are made up. *Do you like ghost stories?*

straight
Something that is **straight** does not bend. *You should use a ruler to draw a straight line.*

strange
1 Something that is **strange** is different and surprising. *She was wearing very strange clothes.*
2 A **strange** place is somewhere you have not been before. *He was alone in a strange town.*

straw
1 **Straw** is the dry stems of plants such as wheat. *The pony sleeps on a bed of straw.*
2 A **straw** is a long tube made of paper or plastic for drinking through.

stream
A **stream** is a small river.

street
A **street** is a road in a town with buildings along both sides.

strength
Strength is how strong something is. *the strength of a lion.*

stretch *(stretches stretching stretched)*
If you **stretch** something, you pull it to make it longer or wider.

strict
If somebody is **strict**, they make sure everybody does what they say. *Our teacher is quite strict.*

string
1 **String** is thin rope. *We tied up the parcel with string.*
2 Some musical instruments such as guitars and violins have **strings** that you touch to play different notes.

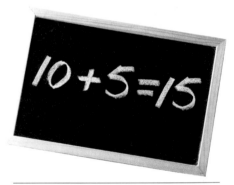

strip
A **strip** is a long narrow piece of something. *Tear the paper into strips.*

stripe
A **stripe** is a line of colour on something. *Zebras have black and white stripes on their bodies.*

strong
1 If somebody is **strong**, they have a lot of power and can carry heavy things.
2 If something is **strong**, it is not easy to break.
3 If something has a **strong** taste or smell, you notice it easily. *Onions have a strong smell.*

stuck Look at **stick**.
I stuck a pin in the balloon and it burst with a bang.

stung Look at **sting**.
Jamie was stung by a bee.

submarine
A **submarine** is a special kind of boat that can travel deep under the sea.

suck *(sucks sucking sucked)*
If you **suck** something such as a sweet, you move it around and around in your mouth.

sudden
Something that is **sudden** happens quickly when you are not expecting it. *There was a sudden flash of lightning.*

sugar
Sugar is what you put in food or drinks to make them taste sweet.

suit
A **suit** is a jacket and a pair of trousers, or a jacket and a skirt, made from the same cloth.

suitcase
A **suitcase** is a kind of box with a handle that you carry your clothes in when you travel.

sum
When you do a **sum**, you work something out with numbers.

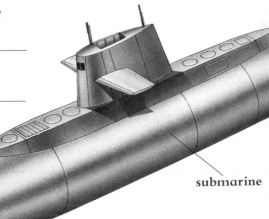

summer
Summer is the part of the year between spring and autumn. **Summer** is the hottest time of the year.

submarine

254

sun

The **Sun** is the bright star that shines and gives us heat and light during the day.

sunflower

A **sunflower** is a plant that can grow to be very tall. It has a very large flower with yellow petals.

sung Look at **sing**.
Have you sung this song before?

sunk Look at **sink**.
The boat has sunk to the bottom of the lake.

sunrise

Sunrise is the time in the early morning when the Sun comes up.

sunset

Sunset is the time in the evening when the Sun goes down. *We took a photo of the beautiful sunset.*

supermarket

A **supermarket** is a big shop that sells food and other things that people use in their homes.

supper

Supper is a meal that people eat in the evening. *I wonder what we're having for supper tonight?*

sure

If you are **sure** about something, you know that it is right or true. *Are you quite sure you closed the window?*

surface

The **surface** is the outside part of something. *The surface of the road is wet and slippery.*

surprise

A **surprise** is something that you did not expect to happen. *Don't tell Will about the party - it's going to be a surprise.*

swallow *(swallows swallowing swallowed)*

When you **swallow** food or drink, you let it go down your throat into your stomach.

swam Look at **swim**.
Kathy swam across the pool.

swan

A **swan** is a large white bird with a long neck. **Swans** live on water.

sweater

A **sweater** is something that you wear to keep you warm. It covers your arms and the top part of your body. **Sweaters** are often made of wool.

sweep *(sweeps sweeping swept)*

When you **sweep** a floor, you use a broom to clean it.
Dan swept up the leaves from the path.

sweet

1 Sweet food and drink has the taste of sugar.
2 A **sweet** is a small piece of very **sweet** food.

swim *(swims swimming swam swum)*

When you **swim**, you move through water using your arms and legs.

swing

1 *(swings swinging swung)* When something **swings**, it moves from side to side or backwards and forwards through the air. *The monkey swung from a branch.*
2 A **swing** is a seat hanging from two ropes or chains that you sit on and move backwards and forwards through the air.

switch *(switches)*

A **switch** is something that you press or turn to start or stop something working. *If you press that switch all the lights will go out and we'll be in the dark!*

sword

A **sword** is a kind of long pointed knife that people in the past used for fighting.

swum Look at **swim**.
How many lengths of the pool have you swum today?

syrup

Syrup is a sweet sticky liquid made from sugar, water and sometimes fruit juices.

table

A **table** is a piece of furniture with legs and a flat top for putting things on.

table tennis

Table tennis is a game in which players use bats to hit a small ball over a net across a large table.

tadpole

A **tadpole** is a tiny creature with a long tail that lives in water. **Tadpoles** turn into frogs and toads. They have round black heads.

eggs   tadpole

tail

A **tail** is the part of an animal's body that grows out of the back. The back of an aeroplane is also called a **tail**.

tale

A **tale** is a story. *I have a book of fairy tales.*

talk *(talks talking talked)*

When you **talk**, you say words.

tall

A **tall** person or thing goes up a long way from the ground. *What is the tallest building in the world?*

tambourine

A **tambourine** is a musical instument a bit like a drum. You can hit or shake it to make the small metal pieces around its sides ring and play a tune.

tame

A **tame** animal is not wild so it is not dangerous or afraid of people. Pets are **tame** animals. Lions and tigers are not usually **tame**.

tap

A **tap** is something that you turn to make water flow out. Sinks and baths have **taps**.

tape

1 Tape is a strip of plastic with sticky stuff on one side that you use for sticking pieces of paper together.
2 A **tape** is also a strip of plastic in a plastic case that records sounds or pictures.

taste

1 A **taste** is what food or drink is like when it is in your mouth. *Honey has a sweet taste.*
2 *(tastes tasting tasted)* When you **taste** food or drink, you put a little of it in your mouth to see what it is like. *Can you taste this soup for me to see if there is enough salt in it?*

frog

taxi

A **taxi** is a car that you have to pay to travel in. You ask the driver to take you where you want to go. *We took a taxi to the station.*

tea

Tea is a drink that you make by adding hot water to the dried leaves of tea plants. *Mum asked me to make her a cup of tea.*

teach *(teaches teaching taught)*

To **teach** means to help somebody to learn something or to show them how to do something. *My uncle taught me to ride a bike. I am teaching my sister how to swim.*

teacher

A **teacher** is a person who teaches something.

team

A **team** is a group of people who play a game together on the same side. There are eleven players in a hockey **team**.

tear

Tears are drops of liquid that come from your eyes when you cry. *Tears ran down his face.*

tear *(tears tearing tore torn)*

When you **tear** something such as paper or cloth, you pull it apart. *Tim has torn his shirt on a rusty old nail.*

tease *(teases teasing teased)*

If you **tease** somebody, you annoy them and make jokes about them.

teeth Look at **tooth**.

Sharks have very sharp teeth.

telephone

You use a **telephone** for talking to people who are far away.

telescope

You use a **telescope** for looking at things that are far away, such as stars. **Telescopes** make things look bigger and closer.

television

A **television** is a machine that shows moving pictures with sound. A **television** looks like a box with a glass screen at the front. It is often called a TV or telly for short.

tell (tells telling told)

If you **tell** somebody something, you say it to them. *Tell me that story again.*

temperature

The **temperature** of something is how hot or cold it is.

tennis

Tennis is a game for two or four people. The players hit a ball backwards and forwards to each other over a net with a thing called a racket.

tent

A **tent** is a place to sleep in that is made of cloth. **Tents** are held up by poles and ropes.

term

A **term** is the time between holidays when schools are open.

terrible

If something is **terrible**, it is very bad. *a terrible storm.*

test

A **test** is a way of finding out how much somebody knows about something, or how well they can do something. *My aunt has just passed her driving test.*

thank (thanks thanking thanked)

When you **thank** somebody you say that you are pleased with something nice they have done for you.

theatre

A **theatre** is a building where people go to see plays.

thermometer

A **thermometer** is an instrument that shows how hot something is.

thick

1 Something that is **thick** measures a lot from one side to the other. *There is a thick wall around the building.*
2 If a liquid is **thick**, it does not flow easily. Yoghurt is thick.

thief (thieves)

A **thief** is a person who steals things. *The thieves stole several bikes from the shop.*

thin (thinner thinnest)

1 If something is **thin**, it does not measure very much from one side to the other. *It's dangerous to skate on thin ice.*
2 A **thin** person or animal does not weigh much.

think (thinks thinking thought)

When you **think**, you have ideas in your mind to work out or to decide things. *I'm thinking about what to give Mum for her birthday.*

thirsty (thirstier thirstiest)

When you are **thirsty**, you need something to drink.

thistle

A **thistle** is a plant with prickly leaves and a purple flower.

thorn

A **thorn** is a sharp point that grows on the stems of some plants such as roses.

thread

Thread is a long thin piece of something such as cotton or wool. *I need a needle and thread to sew on this button.*

throat

Your **throat** is the part at the back of your mouth, where food and air go down into your body.

throw *(throws throwing threw thrown)*

If you **throw** something, you make it leave your hand and fly through the air. *Robert threw a stick for his dog to fetch.*

thumb

Your **thumb** is the short thick finger at the side of your hand.

thunder

Thunder is a loud noise from the sky that comes after a flash of lightning when there is a storm.

ticket

A **ticket** is a small piece of paper that shows that you have paid for something. *We bought tickets to go and see the film.*

tickle *(tickles tickling tickled)*

If you **tickle** somebody, you keep touching their skin very gently to make them laugh.

tie

1 *(ties tying tied)* When you **tie** something such as string, you make a knot or bow in it.
2 A **tie** is a long strip of cloth that you tie around the collar of a shirt so it hangs down the front.

tiger

A **tiger** is a large wild animal of the cat family that lives in Asia. **Tigers** have orange-coloured fur with black stripes.

tight

1 If clothes are **tight**, they fit very closely to your body. *These shoes are so tight they hurt.*
2 If something is **tight**, it is done up so that it will not move easily. *Put the lid on tight so the paint doesn't spill.*

tile

A **tile** is a flat piece of hard material that is used to cover floors and walls. *The bathroom is covered in green and white tiles.*

time

Time is what we measure in seconds, minutes, hours, days, weeks, months and years. **Time** tells us when something happens or how long it happens for.

tin

1 **Tin** is a metal that is silver in colour. *a tin box.*
2 A **tin** is a metal container for food. *a tin of beans.*

tiny *(tinier tiniest)*

Something that is **tiny** is very very small. Sand is made up of **tiny** pieces of rock.

tip

1 The **tip** of something long and thin is the end of it. *Touch it with the tip of your finger.*
2 A **tip** is also a place where you can take rubbish.

tiptoe *(tiptoes tiptoeing tiptoed)*

If you **tiptoe**, you walk on your toes very quietly. *She tiptoed out of the baby's room.*

tired

When you are **tired**, you feel that you need to rest or to sleep.

tissue

A **tissue** is a piece of thin soft paper for blowing your nose on.

toad

A **toad** is an animal that looks like a big frog. **Toads** live mostly on land but they lay their eggs in water. They have rough dry skin.

toast

Toast is a slice of bread that has been cooked on both sides so that it is brown.

toboggan

A **toboggan** is a kind of small sledge. It has a seat fixed to two long pieces of wood or metal that slide easily over snow.

toe

Your **toes** are the parts that you can move at the end of your feet. You have five **toes** on each foot.

told Look at **tell**.

Gran told us stories about when she was a little girl.

tomato *(tomatoes)*

A **tomato** is a soft round red fruit that we eat in salads.

tongue

Your **tongue** is the long pink part that moves around inside your mouth. Your **tongue** helps you to taste food and to talk.

tool

A **tool** is something that helps us to do work. *A saw is a tool for cutting wood.*

tooth *(teeth)*

1 A **tooth** is one of the hard white parts inside your mouth. We use our **teeth** to bite and chew food into pieces.

2 Teeth are also the sharp points on a comb or a saw.

toothbrush

A **toothbrush** is a small brush with a long handle for cleaning your teeth.

top

1 The **top** of something is the highest part of it. *We tied a big bow on the top of the box.*

2 A **top** is also the part that covers something such as a bottle or jar. *Don't forget to put the top back on your pen.*

torch *(torches)*

A **torch** is a small lamp that you can carry around to give light where you need it. **Torches** need batteries to make them work.

tore, torn Look at **tear**.

I tore the paper into tiny pieces. She has torn her jeans.

tornado *(tornadoes)*

A **tornado** is a storm with very strong winds that travel in circles and do a lot of damage to buildings and trees.

tortoise

A **tortoise** is an animal with a shell on its back. **Tortoises** move very slowly. **Tortoises** are reptiles.

total

A **total** is an amount that you get when you add two numbers together.

touch *(touches touching touched)*

1 If you **touch** something, you put your hand on it. *Millie tried to guess who it was by touching his face.*

2 If things are **touching**, there is no space between them. *We stood so close together that our shoulders were touching.*

tourist

A **tourist** is a person who is on holiday travelling and visiting interesting places. *Our town is busy in the summer because there are so many tourists.*

towel

A **towel** is a large piece of cloth that you use to dry yourself with.

tower

A **tower** is a tall thin building, or a tall thin part of a building.

town

A **town** is a place with streets, shops, houses and other buildings where people live and work.

toy

Toys are things you can play with. Dolls and kites are kinds of **toys**.

tractor

A **tractor** is a big strong vehicle that farmers use for pulling things.

traffic

Traffic is all the cars, buses, lorries and motorbikes moving along the road. *It took ages to get home because there was a lot of traffic.*

train

1 A **train** is a long vehicle that carries a lot of people from one place to another. **Trains** are pulled by engines and they run along railway lines.

2 *(trains training trained)* If you **train** a person or an animal to do something, you teach them how to do it. *We have trained our dog to sit when we tell her to.*

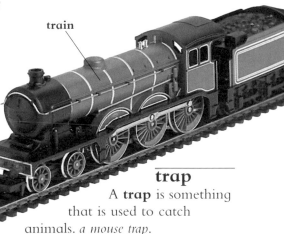

train

trap

A **trap** is something that is used to catch animals. *a mouse trap.*

travel *(travels travelling travelled)*

When you **travel**, you go from one place to another. *We travelled to Spain by boat and car.*

tray

A **tray** is a flat piece of wood or metal that you use for carrying food and drink on.

tread *(treads treading trod trodden)*

When you tread on something, you put your foot down on it.

treasure

Treasure is a big pile of gold, silver, jewels and other valuable things. *This map shows where the pirate's treasure is buried.*

tree

A **tree** is a big plant with branches and leaves growing from a thick stem called a trunk that is made of wood.

trick

1 A **trick** is something clever and amazing that you can do. *The magician's best trick was when he made a bird come out of his hat.*

2 A **trick** is also a thing that somebody does to make you believe something that is not true. *My brother played a trick on me - he put a toy spider in my drink.*

trip

1 A **trip** is a short journey. *Yesterday we went on a school trip to London.*

2 *(trips tripping tripped)* If you **trip**, you knock your foot against something and you fall over. *I tripped on the step.*

trod, trodden Look at **tread**.

I trod on a snail. You should not have trodden on the grass.

trousers

Trousers are something that you wear. **Trousers** cover the lower part of your body and each leg.

truck

A **truck** is a lorry. People use **trucks** to carry heavy things from place to place by road.

true

1 If something is **true**, it is right. *Is it true that ice is frozen water?*

2 If something is **true**, it really happened. *That's a true story.*

trumpet

A **trumpet** is a musical instrument made of metal. You blow into it to make sounds.

trunk

1 A **trunk** is the thick stem of a tree. A **trunk** is made of wood.

2 A **trunk** is also an elephant's long nose. The elephant uses its **trunk** to lift things and to carry food and water to its mouth.

3 A **trunk** is also a large box for keeping things in or for carrying things on a long journey.

trust *(trusts trusting trusted)*

If you **trust** somebody, you believe that they will do what they promise and will not do anything to hurt you. *Can I trust you to behave yourself while I'm out?*

truth

When you tell the **truth**, you are saying what is true. *You didn't break the glass? Is that the truth?*

tube

1 A **tube** is something that is long, thin and hollow such as a metal or plastic pipe.

2 A **tube** is also a long container for holding soft stuff such as toothpaste.

tunnel

A **tunnel** is a long hole under the ground or through a hill. *We saw the steam train come through the tunnel.*

turn

1 *(turns turning turned)* When something **turns**, it moves round. When a car moves, its wheels **turn**. *Jane turned her trousers inside out to sew them up.*

2 *(turns turning turned)* When something **turns** into something else, it changes. Water **turns** into steam when you boil it. *The farmer turned the milk into cheese.*

3 If it is your **turn** to do something, it is time for you to do it. *It's Maria's turn to take the dog for a walk today.*

twig

A **twig** is a very small branch of a tree or bush. *Collect some twigs so we can light a fire.*

twin

Twins are two children who have the same mother and who were born at the same time.

twist *(twists twisting twisted)*

When you **twist** two pieces of thread or wire together, you wrap them around each other many times. *She twisted the strings together.*

tyre

A **tyre** is the rubber cover around the outside of a wheel filled with air. *My bike has a flat tyre.*

ugly *(uglier ugliest)*
If something is **ugly**, it is not nice to look at.

umbrella
You hold an **umbrella** over your head to keep you dry when it rains. It has a piece of cloth stretched over wires and joined to a long handle.

uncle
Your **uncle** is your father's brother, your mother's brother or the husband of your aunt.

underneath
If something is **underneath** something else, it is below it. *The cat was asleep underneath the blanket.*

underground
Underground means below the ground. *Rabbits live underground in holes called burrows.*

understand *(understands understanding understood)*
If you **understand** something, you know what it means or how it works. *I couldn't understand what she said because she didn't speak very good English.*

undress *(undresses undressing undressed)*
When you **undress**, you take off your clothes.

unhappy
If you are **unhappy**, you are sad.

uniform
A **uniform** is a set of special clothes that show that people belong to a group. Nurses and soldiers wear **uniforms**.

universe
The **universe** is the Earth, the Sun, the Moon, the stars and everything in space.

university
A **university** is a place where people can go to study after they have left school.

untidy
If things are **untidy**, they are not in the right place. *Your room is very untidy - there are books and clothes all over the floor.*

unusual
If something is **unusual**, it is not ordinary or what we usually expect. *It is unusual for it to rain in the desert.*

upset
If you are **upset**, you feel unhappy. *Natasha was upset when her friend forgot her birthday.*

upside down
If something is **upside down**, the bottom is at the top and the top is at the bottom. *Bats always hang upside down.*

upstairs
Upstairs means in a higher part of a building. *There are four bedrooms upstairs.*

urgent
If something is **urgent**, it must be done straight away. *Please call an ambulance. It's urgent.*

useful
Something that is **useful** helps you to do something. *Keep that box - it will be useful for putting your toys in.*

usual
If something is **usual**, it happens most of the time. *We went to the swimming pool on Saturday as usual.*

usually
Usually means nearly always. *I usually watch television for a little while after school.*

Vv

vacuum cleaner
A **vacuum cleaner** is an electric machine that picks up dust and dirt from carpets.

valley
A **valley** is the low land between hills or mountains.

valuable
If something is **valuable**, it is worth a lot of money. *This gold watch is very valuable.*

van
A **van** is a small covered lorry for carrying things by road.

vegetable
A **vegetable** is a part of a plant that you can eat. Cabbages, potatoes, carrots, peas and beans are **vegetables**.

vehicle
A **vehicle** is a machine for carrying things or people from one place to another on land. Buses, cars, lorries and bicycles are all **vehicles**.

vet
A **vet** is a kind of doctor who looks after animals that are ill or hurt. *Ian wants to be a vet and look after wild animals in Africa.*

video
1 A **video** is a tape that records pictures and sounds so that you can play them on a television set.
2 A **video** is also a machine for recording and playing pictures and sounds.

view
A **view** is everything that you can see from one place. *You get a good view of the town from the bridge.*

village
A **village** is a small group of houses and other buildings in the country.

vine
A **vine** is a climbing plant that grapes grow on.

vinegar
Vinegar is a liquid with a sour taste that you put on food such as chips.

violent
A **violent** person is very strong and very rough.

violet
A **violet** is a small plant with purple or white flowers.

violin
A **violin** is a musical instrument made of wood. It has four strings. You play a **violin** by moving a long stick called a bow backwards and forwards across the strings.

visit *(visits visiting visited)*
When you **visit** somebody, you go to see them. *We visit our granddad every Saturday.*

voice
Your **voice** is the sound that you make when you talk or sing.

volcano *(volcanoes)*
A **volcano** is a mountain with a hole called a crater in the top. Sometimes hot liquid rock and gases shoot out of the crater. *The village was destroyed by the liquid rock from the volcano.*

vote *(votes voting voted)*
If you **vote** for somebody or something, you choose them by putting a mark on a piece of paper next to their name, or by putting up your hand.

voyage
A **voyage** is a long journey. *They went on a voyage into space.*

vulture
A **vulture** is a large bird that lives in hot countries and feeds on dead animals.

Ww

wait *(waits waiting waited)*
When you **wait**, you stay in one place because you are expecting something to happen. *Wait here until I get back.*

wake *(wakes waking woke woken)*
When you **wake** up, you stop sleeping. *What time do you usually wake up in the morning?*

walk *(walks walking walked)*
When you **walk**, you move along by putting one of your feet in front of the other.

wall
1 A **wall** is one of the sides of a room or building.
2 A **wall** is also something made of stone or brick that is put around a field or garden.

wallet
A **wallet** is a flat container for paper money that you can carry in a pocket or a handbag. *Always keep your wallet safe.*

walrus *(walruses)*
A **walrus** is a large sea mammal with long curved tusks and whiskers.

wand
A **wand** is a kind of short stick that fairies and magicians use to help them do magic.

want *(wants wanting wanted)*
When you **want** something, you would like to have it. *Do you want anything to eat?*

war
A **war** is when the armies of different countries are fighting one another.

ward
A **ward** is a large room in a hospital with beds in it.

wardrobe
A **wardrobe** is a place for keeping clothes in.

warm
Warm means a little hot but not too hot. *This sweater will keep you warm in cold weather.*

warn *(warns warning warned)*
If you **warn** somebody, you tell them that something bad or dangerous is going to happen. *He warned us not to go out in the boat because there was going to be a storm.*

wash *(washes washing washed)*
When you **wash** something, you make it clean with soap and water. *We washed our feet.*

wasp
A **wasp** is a flying insect with black and yellow stripes. **Wasps** can sting.

waste *(wastes wasting wasted)*
If you **waste** something, you use more of it than you need to. *Don't waste all those sheets of paper - you can draw on the other side.*

watch
1 *(watches watching watched)* If you **watch** something, you look at it for a time. *We watched a film on television.*
2 *(watches)* A **watch** is a small clock that you wear on your wrist.

water
1 **Water** is a clear liquid. It fills lakes, rivers and seas. It falls from the sky as rain. All living things need **water** to live.
2 *(waters watering watered)* If you **water** plants you pour **water** onto them.

waterfall
A **waterfall** is a place on a river where the water falls down over high rocks.

wave
1 A **wave** is a moving curved line on a sea or lake.
2 *(waves waving waved)* If you **wave**, you move your hand up and down or from side to side. *Zoe waved goodbye to her friends.*

wax
Wax is something that is used to make candles and polish. **Wax** melts when it gets warm.

weak

Somebody or something that is **weak** does not have much strength. *The pony was so weak that it could not stand up.*

wear *(wears wearing wore worn)*

1 When you **wear** clothes, you have them on your body. *Have you worn that hat before?*
2 When something **wears** out, it becomes weak and it cannot be used any more, because you have used it so much. *He wore out six pairs of boots when he walked from London to Scotland.*

weather

The **weather** is what it is like outside. For example, if it is rainy, sunny or snowing.

web

A **web** is a thin net of threads that a spider makes to catch insects to eat.

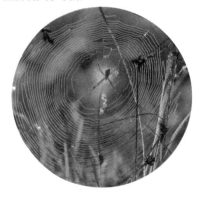

wedding

A **wedding** is a special time when a man and woman get married to each other.

week

A **week** is an amount of time. There are seven days in a **week.**

weigh *(weighs weighing weighed)*

You **weigh** something to find out how heavy it is. *Tina is standing on the scales to see how much she weighs.*

weight

The **weight** of something is how heavy it is. *Can you guess the weight of the parcel?*

well

1 *(better best)* If you are **well**, you feel good and healthy. *I don't feel well.*
2 *(better best)* If you do something **well**, you are good at it. *John plays the trumpet very well.*
3 A **well** is a deep hole that people dig in the ground to get water or oil.

west

West is the direction where the Sun goes down in the evening. **West** is the opposite of east.

wet *(wetter wettest)*

If something is **wet**, it is covered in water or full of water. *My doll got wet when it fell in the pond.*

whale

A **whale** is a very big animal that lives in the sea. **Whales** are mammals but they look more like big fish.

wheat

Wheat is a plant that farmers grow. Its seeds are used to make flour for bread.

wheel

A **wheel** is a round thing that turns. Bikes and roller-skates have **wheels** to help them move along the ground.

wheelchair

A **wheelchair** is a chair with wheels. People use **wheelchairs** when they cannot walk very well.

whisker

Whiskers are the long hairs that animals such as dogs and cats have on their faces.

whisper *(whispers whispering whispered)*

When you **whisper**, you speak in a very quiet voice. *Julie whispered something in my ear.*

whistle

1 *(whistles whistling whistled)* When you **whistle**, you blow through your lips to make a high musical sound. *The dog came back when Mia whistled.*
2 A **whistle** is a small instrument that you blow through to make a high sound.

whole

The **whole** of something is all of it. *We spent the whole morning at the pool and didn't go home until after lunch-time.*

wide

Something that is **wide** measures a lot from one side to the other. *Motorways are much wider than ordinary roads.*

wife

A man's **wife** is the woman that he is married to.

wild

Animals that are **wild** do not live with people. They find their own food. Foxes and deer are **wild** animals. **Wild** plants are not grown by people. *The field was full of beautiful wild flowers.*

win *(wins winning won)*

When you **win**, you do better than everybody else in a game or race.

wind

Wind is air that is moving fast. *The wind blew the leaves everywhere.*

windmill

A **windmill** is a tall building with sails on the front that the wind turns as it blows. As the sails move, they work machines that can turn wheat into flour or that can make electricity.

window

A **window** is a hole in a wall filled with glass. **Windows** let in light from outside.

wing

Wings are the parts that animals such as birds and insects use for flying. Aeroplanes also have **wings** to help them to stay up in the air.

winter

Winter is the part of the year between autumn and spring. **Winter** is usually the coldest time of the year.

wipe *(wipes wiping wiped)*

If you **wipe** something, you clean or dry it by rubbing it with a cloth. *Please wipe up after you.*

wire

Wire is a long thin piece of metal that is easy to bend. **Wire** is used to make fences. Electricity moves along **wires**.

wish

1 *(wishes wishing wished)*
If you **wish** for something, you want it to happen very much. *I wish I had skates like yours.*
2 A **wish** is something you would like very much to happen. *Close your eyes and make a wish.*

witch *(witches)*

A **witch** is a woman in fairy stories who can do magic things.

wives Look at **wife**.
King Henry the Eighth had six wives.

wizard

A **wizard** is a man in fairy stories who can do magic things.

woke, woken Look at **wake**.
I woke up in the middle of the night. You must have woken the baby up when you came in.

wolf *(wolves)*

A **wolf** is a wild animal that looks like a dog.

woman *(women)*

A **woman** is a grown-up female. Girls grow up to be **women**.

won Look at **win**.
Michael won the race.

wonderful
Something that is **wonderful** is very good or amazing. *We had a wonderful holiday.*

wood
1 Wood is what trees are made of. We use **wood** to make furniture like tables and chairs.
2 A **wood** is a lot of trees growing together. *We went for a walk in the woods.*

wool
Wool is the soft thick hair that grows on sheep. We spin **wool** and use it to make things such as jumpers and scarves. *a ball of wool.*

word
We use **words** when we speak or write. Each **word** is a sound or a group of letters of the alphabet that means something. *"Dog" and "today" are words.*

wore Look at **wear**.
Joe wore a yellow jacket.

work
1 Work is what somebody does to earn money, or something that they have to do. *Do you enjoy going to work everyday?*
2 *(works working worked)* When you **work**, you do or make something, often as a job. *Hilary works in a car factory.*
3 *(works working worked)* If a machine **works**, it goes as it should do. *Do you know how to make this video work?*

world
The **world** is the planet that we live on.

worm
A **worm** is a small long thin creature with no legs. **Worms** live in the ground.

worn
Look at **wear**.
This is the first time this year that I have worn this shirt.

worry
(worries worrying worried)
When you **worry**, you cannot stop thinking about problems or things that may happen. *Dad always worries when I get home late.*

worth
The amount something is worth is how much you must pay to have it. *This painting is worth a lot of money.*

wrap
(wraps wrapping wrapped)
When you **wrap** something, you cover it with something else such as paper or cloth. *Rachel is wrapping a present.*

wrinkle
A **wrinkle** is a line on somebody's face. *My gran's face is full of wrinkles.*

wrist
Your **wrist** is the part of your arm where it joins your hand. *You can wear a watch on your wrist for telling the time.*

write
(writes writing wrote written)
When you **write**, you put words on paper so that people can read them. *Mel is writing a letter to her cousin in Australia.*

wrong
Something that is **wrong** is not right. *I think that it is always wrong to tell lies.*

Xx

X-ray
An **X-ray** is a special kind of photograph that shows the inside of your body. *The doctor took an X-ray of his head to see if he had broken any bones.*

xylophone
A **xylophone** is a musical instrument with flat wooden or metal bars that you hit with small hammers to make music.

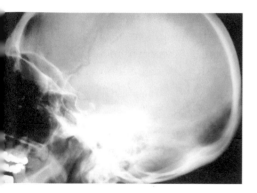

yacht
A **yacht** is a large boat with sails or an engine. Some **yachts** are very fast and are used for racing.

yawn *(yawns yawning yawned)*
When you **yawn**, you open your mouth wide and breathe in. People usually **yawn** when they are tired.

year
A **year** is an amount of time. There are twelve months in a **year**. *Hassan will be seven years old on his next birthday.*

yell *(yells yelling yelled)*
If you **yell**, you shout something very loudly. *"Come here!" she yelled across the street.*

yoghurt
Yoghurt is a food made from milk. You sometimes eat **yoghurt** mixed with fruit. *My favourite yoghurt is raspberry.*

yolk
A **yolk** is the yellow part in the middle of an egg. *Ben likes a soft yolk in his egg.*

young
A person or animal that is **young** was born not very long ago. **Young** people are children. **Young** dogs are called puppies, and **young** cats are called kittens. *What is a young sheep called?*

Zz

zebra
A **zebra** is an animal that looks like a horse with black and white stripes. **Zebras** live in Africa.

zero
Zero is the number 0.

zigzag
A **zigzag** is a line that bends sharply one way and then the other.

zip
A **zip** is made of two long pieces of metal or plastic with parts that fit together to hold two edges of cloth together. Some trousers and bags have **zips**.

zoo
A **zoo** is a place where a lot of different wild animals are kept so that people can go there to look at them.

Encyclopedia Index

(Pages 8-115)

Atlas Index
(Pages 118-175)

Acknowledgements

The publishers wish to thank the artists who have contributed to this book:
Martin Camm, John James, Gill Platt, Terry Riley, Peter Sarson, Roger Smith, Mike White, Alison Winfield

All photographs used in the First Atlas are from MKP Archives